From Controversy to Co-Existence

Evangelicals in the Church of England 1914–1980

FROM CONTROVERSY TO CO-EXISTENCE

*Evangelicals in the Church of England
1914–1980*

RANDLE MANWARING

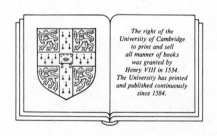

The right of the
University of Cambridge
to print and sell
all manner of books
was granted by
Henry VIII in 1534.
The University has printed
and published continuously
since 1584.

CAMBRIDGE UNIVERSITY PRESS

Cambridge
London   New York   New Rochelle
Melbourne   Sydney

Published by the Press Syndicate of the University of Cambridge
The Pitt Building, Trumpington Street, Cambridge CB2 1RP
32 East 57th Street, New York, NY 10022, USA
10 Stamford Road, Oakleigh, Melbourne 3166, Australia

First published 1985

Printed in Great Britain at
the University Press, Cambridge

Library of Congress catalogue card number: 85–4099

British Library cataloguing in publication data
Manwaring, Randle
From controversy to co-existence: evangelicals
in the Church of England 1914–1980.
1. Church of England – History. 2. Evangelistic work
I. Title
269'.2   BV3770
ISBN 0 521 30380 X

WD

In
gratitude
to
John Briggs

(from whom I learned some, at least,
of the perspectives of history)

Contents

Acknowledgements

This book started life as a thesis in a University History Department but over the last two years has undergone many changes in the course of preparation for publication.

I am particularly indebted to Dr Robert Williams of the Cambridge University Press for his patient encouragement and sympathetic guidance in dealing with the advice given by his readers and I am quite sure that, as a result, the book has become better balanced and more readable.

I am also grateful to the Rev. John Baker, a leading theologian in my diocese and to the Rev. Rex Lloyd, a winsome and knowledgeable historian, for their advice and informative contributions during the final stages of development.

My gratitude is expressed to the librarians and their assistants of The British Library, the Evangelical Library and Dr Williams' Library. All concerned with my detailed enquiries have been most helpful and the range of books available to anyone carrying out researches of the kind I have been engaged in, particularly, if I may say so, at Dr Williams' Library, has made a vital contribution.

Finally, I express my grateful thanks to Audrey Field who carried out the initial typing of the manuscript and in particular to Wendy Mallinson who managed the typescript through its succeeding revisionary processes.

Preface

I N AN AGE of class and privilege the Anglican clergyman of
1914 was a bastion of the establishment. Locally, he enjoyed
very considerable respect and even engendered a certain
amount of awe. He ranked with the family doctor as being gentle-
manly, useful in an emergency and reasonably well-known to the
community at large. All this was equally true of the evangelical
parson, noted for his emphasis on preaching the gospel and
teaching the Bible, rather than administering the sacraments
which, however, he did not neglect, but above all, he preached
for conversion, whereby he not only looked for the salvation of
the individual but also for the equipping of the church with a
workforce for its further extension.

However, our evangelical incumbent of between fifty and
seventy years ago was not a popular man outside his parish or
outside the parameters of a clearly defined Evangelicalism,
whose influence was also present in all the Free Churches.
Generally speaking, Evangelicals at that time had little or no
interest in the arts, politics, social life and feeding the hungry.
Very much in command of his local church, the evangelical
parson was head and shoulders above most members of his congregation – better educated, probably at one of the ancient universities, he only occasionally allowed a curate to preach the
Word. There thus developed in Evangelical Anglicanism something of a 'siege mentality' and, due to their isolationism, its
clergy were virtually 'black-listed' by their own Church. So, they
'dug in' and, in 1927/28, magnificently led by two very distinguished laymen, although outvoted in the counsels of the
church, they succeeded in defeating the attempt to secure the
State's authorisation of a new Prayer Book. Ironically, just over
fifty years later the reception, eventually, of the Alternative
Service Book showed how much confrontation had given way to
accommodation, at least in liturgy.

Splendid in missionary endeavour overseas, with a deep
personal devotion, the Evangelical Anglican between the wars

showed up best in parish life. He was not at his strongest in the counsels of Church or State but instead, when he moved out of parochial life, it was into his own safe brand of ecumenism, represented by the interdenominational societies and conventions. Evangelical Anglicanism (perhaps like western society as a whole) 'bottomed out' between the wars but, in the late thirties, seeds were being sown in the fields of both scholarship and academic life which were soon to yield a rich harvest of evangelical witness. Itself definitely interdenominational, the Inter Varsity Fellowship (later to become the Universities and Colleges Christian Fellowship) took strategic soundings of the whole of the educational process, both religious and secular, with a view to Evangelicals gaining influential positions wherever possible, with the result that, in due course, they occupied posts of considerable importance, thus developing their own abilities in scholarship, biblical exegesis and even in debate. Just before the outbreak of the Second World War, very negative and severely critical attitudes to fellow Anglicans gave way to a more informed, reasoned and gracious disposition.

Whilst Evangelical Anglicans of the twenties had seen themselves as fighting something of a 'last ditch' stand for Protestant integrity, their successors in the middle of the century had the backing of scholarship and literature with which to combat the indifference of a central churchmanship and the hostility to the Bible of the radicals. And this they did without compromise. The anti-intellectualism and the reductionist emphasis ('the fewer we are together, the happier and holier we shall be') had been forced out of court in favour of a truly Bible-inspired redemptionist theology, embracing both church and society, with responsibility fully felt in both spheres.

In the fifties another turning point was reached when Evangelism became front-page news in the person of Dr Billy Graham. Unable to unite under the lead into Evangelism given by Bishop Chavasse of Rochester, regarded as the leader of the Evangelicals at that time, they nonetheless closed ranks under the Graham banner and found themselves on the same platform as fellow Anglicans of all shades and churchmanship – or nearly all. Leadership in this upsurge of Evangelism was not held solely by two or three bishops, as might have been the case in earlier times, but to a large degree by the products of the evangelistic work of the Children's Special Service Mission and Crusader camps who were later caught up, at university, in the work of the

I.V.F. Evangelical Anglicans had not known such leadership (which included that of some bishops coming up through the new system), since the days of Bishop Knox of Manchester or even since Bishop Ryle of Liverpool.

No longer suspicious of bringing the Christian mind to bear on theological matters and intellectual problems, eager to work wherever possible in unison with other believers in the One Lord, the new Evangelical Anglican then found himself, in 1967 and again in 1977, at two inspiring national congresses – Keele and Nottingham – which demonstrated the overall strength of the movement and, inevitably, its diversity of vision. However, there remained the remnant of those who were suspicious of the new alignments and therefore unwilling to go along with post-Keele Evangelicals.

But the tension – perhaps the right degree in so comprehensive a church – continues. Evangelical Anglicans still stand for what they regard as historic Anglicanism with their emphasis upon the intrinsic veracity of Scripture as the sole authority for faith and life, the substitutionary death of Jesus Christ, the Son of God, and salvation by faith in the grace of God mediated thereby. Evangelicals do not nowadays see themselves as a party of eccentrics seeking toleration, as they may perhaps have been persuaded to see themselves but rather as providing the whole blood stream of Anglicanism with the life-giving strength of biblical truth. But equally they see other traditions as fully part of the Anglican Church, as indeed they must do, if they are to aspire to office within their Church; the evangelical bishop must be willing to minister to all his clergy, the evangelical chaplain to all his flock. There would seem to be no doubt that, for all its associations with other Churches, the future for Evangelical Anglicanism today lies within the Church of England.

1
Into Battle

THE EIGHTEENTH-CENTURY Evangelical Revival had run its course, the French Revolution, threatening Britain, had come and gone and England had settled down to enduring a succession of ludicrous nineteenth-century monarchs. By 1811, George III had been pronounced permanently insane, his son George IV was noted for his dissipation, his extravagance and his heartless treatment of his wife, Caroline of Brunswick, from whom he separated after a year, and in 1830 he was succeeded by William IV of the same disastrous royal house. 'Silly Billy', as he was called, had ten illegitimate children by an Irish actress before he married a German princess.

By way of sharp contrast, it was in these thirty dark years, when the throne was shamed, that Evangelicalism reached a high pitch, a fact recorded with great candour by the famous High-Churchman and Tractarian, Edward Bouverie Pusey:

The great doctrines which alone make 'repentance towards God and faith toward our Lord Jesus Christ' seriously possible were its constant theme. The world to come, with its boundless issues of life and death, the infinite value of the one Atonement, the regenerating, purifying, guiding action of God the Holy Spirit in respect of the Christian soul, were preached to our grandfathers with a force and earnestness which are beyond controversy. The deepest and most fervid religion in England during the first three decades of this century was that of the Evangelicals and, to the last day of his life, Pusey retained that 'love of the Evangelicals' to which he often adverted and which was roused by their efforts to make religion a living power in a cold and gloomy age.[1]

However, Mrs Battiscombe, in her biography of Shaftesbury, claims of the heyday of evangelical influence that:

Episcopal bricks had to be made without straw. Had there been one Evangelical of the calibre of the Broad Churchman Tait or the High Churchman Wilberforce (Samuel, a son of William) to be appointed Archbishop, or had there been a fair sprinkling of able men to fill lesser sees and to exercise some influence in the Church, the era of the 'Shaftesbury Bishops' might have marked the opening of a golden age of Evangelicalism. Nothing of the

1

sort occurred; instead, Evangelicalism continued to decline, as Shaftesbury himself saw all too clearly. 'The Evangelical body, once so powerful, is in fact, disappearing' he wrote on 16 April 1865.[2]

The first evangelical bishop had been appointed in 1815 – Henry Ryder to Gloucester – and in 1826 Charles Sumner was installed at Llandaff, with his brother made Bishop of Chester two years later. Apart from the outstanding J. C. Ryle of Liverpool (1880–1900), the only evangelical bishops of note in the second half of the century were Edward Bickersteth of Exeter (1885–1901) and Anthony Thorold of Rochester (1877–91). But, in spite of Shaftesbury's gloomy prediction, in terms of parochial clergy: 'The closing years of the nineteenth century found the Evangelicals stronger than at any previous period. Thirty years earlier Ryle had calculated that they included about one fifth of the clergy. Now fully a quarter of the parishes in England were in their hands.'[3]

Did Evangelicalism, in terms of its leadership, slightly falter in the middle of the nineteenth century or merely fail to reach its fullest potential at a time when, socially, everything seemed to be in its favour – an ordered society, an expanding nation and an agreed moral programme led by a young queen bringing decorum and good sense to the throne? Did Evangelicals fail to see that their theology needed continuously to be brought into contemporary settings? Did they overlook the necessity to produce men capable of administering and representing the Church at the highest level? They were magnificent in mission, at home and abroad. They were renowned for their saintliness but did they neglect scholarship and social involvement? Admittedly, they were not completely without scholars and theologians of standing. One such was the Rector of St Michaels, Cornhill, Henry Wace, who later became Dean of Canterbury. In 1889, he mounted a challenge to Huxley, a leading scientist–agnostic of the day, and wrote with authority of one who for a number of years had been Principal of Kings College, London. But, generally speaking, Evangelicalism in those days was not strong in scholarship and it tended to avoid real involvement in the government of the Church: 'When men like Hoare and Ryle began to attend Church Congresses they had to face a storm of criticism and even to endure being called in derision "Neo-Evangelicals".'[4]

An exaggerated sense of denominational loyalty caused most

of them to refuse to accept invitations to occupy Free-Church pulpits and they were not noted either for their cheerfulness or for their involvement with the world of art. These were sad reflections on the somewhat unbalanced attitude of Evangelical Anglicans, who appeared to exhaust their energies in contending for the faith, as doctrinally and liturgically expressed in the Thirty-nine Articles. At the time under review they, quite naturally, directed their main energies into safeguarding the Reformed Faith and preventing, as best they could, the efforts of those whom they saw as seeking to bring Anglicanism closer to Rome. This stand inevitably made them, in earlier times, suspicious of their brethren, particularly in the convocations of the church. Unconsciously, they set up barriers and retreated into safe, evangelical strongholds.

The most important of the corporate antagonists was the Oxford Movement, which saw itself as the restorer of some of the High Church interpretations of the seventeenth century and earlier. Furthermore, Romanticism in art in the nineteenth century renewed interest in medieval Christianity, whilst the Catholic Emancipation Act of 1829 brought about a situation in which it was feared that many Anglicans would join the Roman Catholic Church. Liberalism had so frightened many in the Anglican Church in the middle of the nineteenth century and the Oxford Movement self-confessedly sought to stem that tide, with Newman (himself once an Evangelical), Pusey and Keble, its leaders. Much bitterness arose in Anglicanism, especially following the departure for Rome of Faber and Newman and in 1865 the very Protestant Church Association was formed (in 1950, with the National Church League, to become Church Society). In very broad terms, the Association's ideals were to maintain the Protestant ideals of faith and worship in the Church of England.

The Tractarian or Oxford Movement had made such inroads into the Church that in 1904 'The Royal Commission on Ecclesiastical Discipline' was set up to inquire into 'breaches or neglect of the Law relating to the conduct of Divine Service in the Church of England and to the ornaments and fittings of the Churches' and to devise remedies. Evangelicals were not slow to provide evidence; in 1906 the Commission reported unanimously that the law of public worship was too narrow and the machinery for discipline had broken down. The recommendations were ambivalent – practices repugnant to the teaching of the Church

3

were to cease, vestments were legalised and a long drawn-out process of Prayer Book revision was initiated, culminating in the defeat in Parliament in 1927 and 1928 of the bill to introduce the Revised Prayer Book. Thus, the essential comprehensiveness of the Anglican Church was amply demonstrated, with all its tensions and frustrations, its limitations and its dangers. Compromise was inevitable and, indeed, required on all sides.

With the death of Bishop Ryle in 1900, the effective leadership of Evangelicals passed into the hands of the saintly and erudite Bishop Handley Moule of Durham who had succeeded Brooke Foss Westcott, a scholarly theologian and writer of New Testament commentaries. Earlier, Moule had been Principal of Ridley Hall, Cambridge. His influence, until he died in 1920, was benevolent and compelling (but he shrank from controversy). 'He laid down with tremendous emphasis that if his hearers were to be worthy of the name Evangelical they must preach the Evangel, and that Evangel was "the unsearchable riches of Christ" (Eph. iii.8).'[5]

Handley Moule, quietly sure and firm in his stand as an Evangelical, could yet command the respect and affection of those in other schools of thought:

Canon Body and men of his school had been brought up to speak a different ecclesiastical language to Dr Moule but soon 'misgivings' gave place to 'enthusiasm'. They found (as one of them put it) that 'so long as there was real spiritual conviction and true sense of our Lord, the Bishop could lay aside his own views and see things in question from that standpoint'.[6]

But, if there was one person who, more than another, captured Evangelical hearts, Anglican and otherwise, in the early years of the century, it was Bishop John Taylor Smith. He was no scholar but his warm personality and mellifluous voice captivated all (or almost all) including Queen Victoria, who made him an Honorary Chaplain. Already a diocesan missioner in Sierra Leone, in 1897 he was consecrated seventh bishop there and it seems that the 'Old Lady', just before her death, had suggested that Taylor Smith, at a suitable opportunity, should be appointed Chaplain-General to the Forces. He had served with the Ashanti Expedition in 1895–6 and, in 1901, took over the spiritual responsibility for the Armed Forces, a post which he held until his retirement in 1925.

It is not difficult to see how John Taylor Smith became the beau-ideal of Evangelical Anglicans at large and almost all non-

Anglican Evangelicals, including even the Christian Brethren, were prepared to overlook his gaiters and all they symbolised, in their enthusiasm for his simple, direct faith, salted with his delightful sense of fun. To all Evangelicals, he had the standing of an English bishop, his voice was deep and sonorous, he was a master of the epigram and he loved that ecumenical Evangelicalism represented by movements like the Scripture Union. In 1905, he presided at the opening of the mission in London led by the American Evangelist–revivalist team of R. A. Torrey and his musical partner, C. M. Alexander.

In the early years of this century, the flight from Victorianism was in full swing. Church attendance had fallen dramatically, scientific rationalism and the intellectual cults of Shaw, Wells and the Bloomsbury set ran like an incoming tide into every river and every tributary of national thought and life. In the latter part of the nineteenth century, Matthew Arnold, typical of the despondency among intellectuals of the aftermath of Victorianism, had written, in *Dover Beach*:

> The Sea of Faith
> Was once, too, at the full, and round earth's shore
> Lay like the folds of a bright girdle furl'd.
> But now I only hear
> Its melancholy, long, withdrawing roar,
> Retreating, to the breath
> Of the night-wind, down the vast edges drear
> And naked shingles of the world.[7]

The early part of the twentieth century was caught in the full flood of the results of Darwin's hypothesis and Huxley's dogmatic science. Almost all the great writers of the period which followed reflect the rationalism, the humanism, the pessimism and the agnosticism which were the natural result of the blight of Darwinism. Hardy, Yeats, Galsworthy and Virginia Woolf were all children of an earlier age of unbelief. The average man went on in happy abandon of all the old church-based belief and life; pleasures galore were on offer as alternatives. Thus, Evangelical Anglicans were pressed on all sides, not only offering their alternative to secularism and rationalism but also committed to preserving the fabric of the Reformed Faith against what they took to be the rising damp of biblical criticism from within the Church. There was also the ever present tendency by many to move the Church to an Anglo-Catholic stance. Yet another storm was about to break, to challenge, even further, the foundations of life – a world war of undreamt-of proportions.

However, socially and outwardly there was a brief interlude – the Edwardian afterglow of the glorious Victorian summer. All seemed so settled, with plenty of cynicism and lightheartedness in the balmy air. 'It is tempting to think of that time as serene and pleasant. Innumerable broadcast plays set in those days represent the sun as always shining; it is always summer; there are always strawberries and cream on the lawn; Gerald is at Eton and Michael is just finishing his first year at Oxford.'[8]

In all this, the Anglican Church was seeking to maintain its hold on the hearts and minds of an outwardly satisfied people. Evangelicals were, of course, preaching the gospel of grace, appropriated by faith, seeking at the same time to preserve the doctrinal edifice against the new 'modernism'. As ever and perhaps increasingly so, Evangelical Anglicans saw themselves as having a vital part to play in maintaining the essentially Protestant nature of the Church and the scriptural emphasis of her ministry. In all this, they had the Church Pastoral-Aid Society and Church Society (Church Association) to aid them in their endeavours and they had a few church dignitaries to give them leadership and vital encouragement, Handley Moule being the most outstanding. On the other side of the evangelical coin, when they found the going hard inside the Church, they could always go to the Keswick Convention for refreshment of the flagging spirit. Some felt freed from the domestic strain in missionary endeavour and others threw in their lot with the Scripture Union and the Children's Special Service Mission, where denominational loyalties and other problems could conveniently be forgotten. However, in parochial life, sharp divisions were drawn between evangelical parishes and the rest, the former becoming rallying points for miles around, thereby increasing the spirit of partisanship.

The Christian Church could not hope to be exempted from the impact of the First World War. The Kaiser's War, as it was called, became the watershed of modern history and the map of Europe had to be redrawn. As the lights went out all over the west, a long night drew on. The Empires of Austria–Hungary and Germany were to be dissolved, their monarchs, together with those of Russia and Turkey, brushed aside. New states, like Yugoslavia and Czechoslovakia, were born.

In this cataclysm, millions died throughout Europe, including

750,000 of the flower of British manhood. In September 1914, shortly after the outbreak of the conflict, Thomas Hardy asked, somewhat wistfully:

> What of the faith and fire within us
> Men who march away?[9]

Catapulted into the mud and blood of trench warfare, away from the settled ways of the old country, Christian faith was tried as never before, with physical and mental endurance stretched to the limits. Was it possible still to believe in a God of love? Was Jesus Christ a reality (or perhaps even more so to some), in Flanders? Siegfried Sassoon, typical of the 'squirearchy' of the age which was rapidly passing, issued a *cri de coeur* in one of his poems:

> O Jesus make it stop.[10]

In his extremity, the soldier had turned back in his mind to some semblance of a faith, at least, which he had absorbed in earlier days. A war which had started in high hopes of a quick battle or two to make young men feel good, quickly deteriorated into endless carnage, bitter resentment and a healthy loathing of war and all it stood for. Epitomising the debonair soldier of 1914, Rupert Brooke wrote:

> Now, God be thanked Who has matched us with His hour
> And caught our youth, and wakened us from sleeping.[11]

In a few years this mood completely vanished and was replaced by the tones of Wilfred Owen, who was killed in action a week before the Armistice. In his 'Anthem for Doomed Youth', he wrote:

> What passing bells for those who die as cattle?
> Only the monstrous anger of the guns.
> Only the stuttering rifles' rapid rattle
> Can patter out their hasty orisons.[12]

However, this was, people were told, 'the war to end war', to create 'a land fit for heroes to live in'. It was, as it turned out, a cruel and bloody war, with gas being used for the first time and shell-shock becoming a common tragedy. Varying degrees of Christian faith, in millions of men and woman, were tested as by fire. Many men carried their pocket Bible or New Testament with them into battle and there were few who did not pray, at some time.

Bishop Taylor Smith was in charge of spiritual rations for the Armed Forces and set about recruiting sufficient chaplains of different persuasions but insisting that they were men with a spiritual mission for those facing privation and death. 'He wanted his chaplains – and he himself set them an example – to present the religion of Christ to the soldier as something which was both desirable and attractive, as well as being an absolute necessity to a full complete manhood.'[13]

Taylor Smith was a man of strong, evangelical conviction but although, in later life, he appears to carry no direct weight in the counsels of the Anglican Church, in overseeing his chaplains he was kindly and understanding. He fostered a real unity of purpose among them. To the ordained men going abroad with the British Expeditionary Force in 1914 he wrote a warm-hearted message and using his well-known epigrammatic style, he counselled:

> Tell of His birth at Bethlehem – Emmanuel – God with us!
> Tell of His death at Calvary – God for us!
> Tell of His heavenly gift at Pentecost – God in us![14]

At the outbreak of hostilities, Taylor Smith appealed to the bishops to spare their best clergy. He turned down some who volunteered who were manifestly unsuitable and then he asked the Archbishop of Canterbury, who immediately responded, to help in making up the deficiency. Inevitably, there were criticisms of such an unashamed Evangelical that he had only appointed men of his own persuasion and colour. Roger Lloyd was of the opinion that:

The difficulties of becoming a chaplain were still greater if the priest happened to be a known Anglo-Catholic. Bishop Taylor Smith, the Chaplain-General, was hardly sympathetic to such and had no glimmering of understanding of their position. The war was but two months old when Lord Halifax sniffed out the scandal of this discrimination and he, the English Church Union and the *Church Times*, started to give tongue. First he tackled Lord Kitchener, who sent him a most cordial but non-committal reply. Then he wrote to the Chaplain-General. He said that soldiers were now civilians in uniform, and should have the same religious privileges in the army as they enjoyed at home.[15]

In his reply, the Chaplain-General wrote:

Having to cover all sorts and conditions of churchmen in the Army and with a desire to help all and hinder none, I make it a rule to appoint Catholics – men who will not be party men, but loving and considerate to all. An extremist is out of place in the Army.[16]

Interviewing candidates for chaplaincies, Bishop Taylor Smith often asked the question – 'If you had five minutes and five minutes only to spend with a man about to die, what would you say to him?' He had the gift of using vivid, if sometimes naive, illustrations. Stories against Taylor Smith were often coloured by what was called 'Anglo-Catholic naughtiness'.

Lord Halifax, well-known for his strong High Church position, went so far as to suggest that the Chaplain-General should be removed from his post. In spite of this fierce antipathy, Taylor Smith always saw the best in his Anglo-Catholic chaplains, many of whom were drawn from the communities at Mirfield and Kelham. A typical remark, on appointing a new chaplain, was one which the Chaplain-General made regarding a colleague in the next brigade: 'He is Father Conran (one of the Cowley Fathers) and you'll like him. He loves our Lord and His Church.'[17]

John Taylor Smith frequently visited front-line trenches and hospitals. His humanity was always bubbling to the surface and he lost no opportunity of commending his simple faith to all he met. However, criticisms from Lord Halifax and others continued and the Archbishop of Canterbury, in a successful effort to appease, appointed as Deputy Chaplain-General, a moderate High-Churchman, apparently bringing the rather acrimonious antagonism to an end.

'The Bishop', as he was often called amongst all Evangelicals, was always gracious, courteous and understanding. Not surprisingly, he understood and appreciated Evangelicals more than Catholics but, within his lights, he did his best to hold the balance. His *A Soldier's Prayer*, millions of copies of which were issued to the troops, has become part of our Christian heritage:

Almighty and Everlasting God, by whose grace Thy servants are enabled to fight the good fight of faith and ever prove victorious: we humbly beseech Thee so to inspire us that we may yield our hearts to Thine obedience, and exercise our wills on Thy behalf. Help us to think wisely; to speak rightly; to resolve bravely; to act kindly; to live purely. Bless us in body and in soul, and make us a blessing to our comrades. Whether at home or abroad, may we ever seek the extension of Thy Kingdom. Let the assurance of Thy presence save us from sinning; support us in life, and comfort us in death. O Lord our God, accept this prayer for Jesus Christ's sake. Amen.[18]

There were other chaplains who hit the headlines during the war, notably 'Tubby' Clayton, who went to France in 1915 and founded Talbot House, a soldiers' club at Poperinghe, near the front line. As a result, Toc H, in the post-war period, sprang up in many parts of England, catering for men of all denominations. The other 'popular' *padré* was the Rev. G. A. Studdert-Kennedy, affectionately known as 'Woodbine Willie'. Neither of these men was an Evangelical but they made a distinctive and colourful impact on the man in the front line. Despite the brave efforts of some, the Church of the war period, if truth be told, had very little to offer, speaking only generally in the realm of the spirit and it found itself engulfed in the holocaust of Flanders. Men invented a kind of sub-Christian folk religion. They talked of their 'lesser Calvaries', 'little Christs', and swore they saw an angel at the battle of Mons.

Millions of men and women were away from home and, as the war dragged on, life itself was seen as very transient; the old ties were loosened and a rash independence threatened to overtake the individual: 'There was also the grimmer reason, too familiar now for pretence of concealment. Why should anything be grudged to the men who could never know, when a leave ended, whether they would see another?'[19] As Alan Wilkinson pointed out, during the war sexual relationships became more casual and by 1918, the illegitimacy rate had increased by 30 per cent.[20]

Life itself was held as a very passing experience and the stark reality of death was brought into sharp focus by the awful happenings in Flanders, on the high seas where the U-boat menace became a nightmare and in such a tragedy as Gallipoli, a landing which failed and which discredited Winston Churchill. Death on every hand might have represented an extra dimension of opportunity for Evangelicals. 'The evangelical emphasis upon death as a moment of judgement, and the revival of Catholic rituals for dying and burial made the deathbed of crucial religious and moral importance; the pathos of the deathbed was believed to be morally purifying.'[21]

Prayers for the dead also became generally acceptable in the Church but were opposed by Evangelicals, led by Bishop Chavasse and Bishop Knox, who were, however, thought to be out of touch with popular sentiment. Bereavement was in fact, sweeping away much of the latent Protestantism of the English people. Much mere sentiment and false theology characterised the general thinking of the average person and it is not surprising to find that a popular text for memorials was John 15.13, 'Greater love hath no man than this that a man lay down his life for his friends.'

It would appear that the strange currents of secular thought, the internal struggles with rationalism, liberalism and ritualism had somehow robbed the Church of its power and Evangelical Anglicans, holding aloft the pure gospel of redeeming grace, found themselves fighting a desperate, spiritual battle to the backdrop of whining shells and to a foreground of machine-gun fire:

But all this meant that the national existence was colouring the mind of the churches rather than the other way round; and they had little to bring to the war except what they had been giving for years in peace. Not that this was valueless; example and influence did not fail . . . But again it was far too much a question of the individual fibre of the chaplain, not the panoply of the church. Save for some admirable exceptions, the army chaplain was to the mass of soldiers a kind, cheery person, who saw to their needs in cigarettes and chocolate, often served them in canteens, and gave them occasionally a bit of the old lost civilian life in some hearty hymns and a brief address.[22]

Undoubtedly, the idea of killing, even for 'King and Country', represented a major problem for Christians in time of war and, at the start of the First World War, many Evangelicals were pacifists, being willing to serve only in the Red Cross or the R.A.M.C. As the war lengthened, a number changed their mind and served in a combatant role but it is true to say that, although war produces much heroism and self-sacrifice, and also a strengthening of character in many, it is a time which drains moral and spiritual resources. It places a strain on home ties, interferes with general progress and also weakens actual church life.

By and large, the Church of England was solidly behind the war effort of 1914–18 and the clergy, if they did not go away into service life, encouraged their parishioners to do so. Echoes of the Rupert Brooke heroics are to be found in the stand made by many parochial clergy. Here is an evangelical example:

The war was almost welcomed, as calling forth a more adventurous manhood. 'National prosperity', it was claimed 'had been sapping the virility of three generations and Science might have seemed to have done much to have turned us into a lesser breed than that of the men of Waterloo'. Mr Sinker had no doubts about the war effort – he spoke about it as a 'holy war for the Allies', 'the Cross against the Sword, Right against Might'. He regarded Satan as standing at the Kaiser's right hand. He criticised 'those who delay too long to put on the King's uniform', and in fact ran a two division league table for those streets that had the highest percentage of enrolments per rated house.[23]

Something of the sapping of the vitality of the spirit and the frustration of the Church at large is echoed by the experience of this parish:

In 1916 the nation was called to a National Mission of Repentance and Hope: in each parish a body of lay persons called 'The Bishop's Company' was to be formed to be an active group of interceders, evangelists and workers. Mr Sinker, who discerned the beginnings of revival in the war experience, was an enthusiast for the mission and became a bishop's messenger sent that autumn to enthuse other parishes for the work. There was much talk, some planning but little came of this initiative. Rather the work of the church was forced to contract because of the loss of man-power – and when peace came it proved impossible to restart some of the temporarily abandoned activities.[24]

All in all, the personal faith of Christians was tested in the perils of war, as never before or after; some lost what faith they had and others came through with theirs strengthened and deepened. But those who took an easy-going interest in Christian things or only belonged to their Church in a nominal way, who had but a nodding acquaintance with divine truth, were unlikely to find the assurance of eternal life in the face of disaster and death. Similarly, if they survived the experience of the battle-field, those who were offhand and lukewarm were less likely to return to milk and water offerings in their home churches.

In 1916, a questionnaire was issued to the Armed Forces covering religious experience and needs. It revealed an appalling lack of knowledge of Christianity, an antipathy to the Churches and the fact that service life militated against Christian beliefs. This caused the religious leaders to take stock and endeavour to meet the challenge. In 1916, the National Mission of Repentance and Hope, earlier referred to, was inaugurated by the Archbishop of Canterbury, Randall Davidson, addressing a large congregation in his cathedral. As was found in Stafford-shire, the mission achieved little, only serving to emphasise the drift away from organised religion. However, one result was that evangelisation was placed at the top of the agenda in the Anglican Church.

After Darwin and others had persuaded earlier generations that we were constantly evolving to higher forms of existence and experience, the full impact of the First World War came as a devastating blow. Humanly speaking, what remained? Oliver Lodge, a leading physicist, had declared that original sin was completely outdated; Bernard Shaw in *Androcles and the Lion*, tried to demolish the doctrine of the atonement; but, on the other hand, men in Flanders were raised to the position of more than human, mortal heroes. No wonder the national mood in 1918 was disillusioned, unrestrained, light-hearted, carefree and fatalistic. The overthrow of authority, that pillar of the Victorian era, was a slow process but it was considerably hastened by the shattering experience of total war. It was as if the war gave one mighty push to an edifice already slipping in the wrong direction before the conflict began:

What was conspicuous in the thought of pre-war years was its void of any-thing that could be described as faith. The old creeds hardly maintained the semblance of their authority among educated people; nobody who mattered would have dreamed of citing Scriptural authority in philosophic or scientific discussion, and in fact there were Anglican churchmen, often in distinguished posts, who would cheerfully reduce to folklore not only Genesis but the Resurrection.[25]

This view of a secular historian helps us to understand something of the position of Evangelical Anglicans in the early years of the century. The war added extra dimensions to the old problems whilst 'Higher Criticism', in its most extreme form, by reducing the Bible to the level of ordinary literature, sought to remove the miraculous from the faith. Wingfield-Stratford is very sweeping in his conclusion:

For the time, at any rate, in culture and philosophy, in social and international affairs, organised Christianity had practically ceased to count, nor had anything come in its place capable of restraining the tendencies that were now palpably driving mankind to the alternative forms of suicide represented by an international and a class war of annihilation.[26]

However, the saintly Bishop Moule took a more godly view of the War and its aftermath:

The Great War is not only the biggest struggle of the nations ever seen; it carries with it, from our God, a call of earnest warning: but of Divine Kindness too. He is not afflicting us for nothing, or carelessly deferring the victory of a righteous cause. He wants us to be fit to be trusted with triumph and peace. This means that He bids us turn from our evil ways.[27]

On the other hand, many leading figures in the Church felt that the nation was too divided and distracted by the terrors of war to make a meaningful response to the 1916 National Mission. There was, for a variety of reasons, a slump in religion, both Evangelical and Catholic, and it seemed that the whole Christian Church was on the horns of a serious dilemma. Without doubt, there was a need to evangelise, to renew life and to engender real hope for the future but the Church was too debilitated by the pressures of combat as yet to undertake that task. Yet the realisation of national need remained firm and, in 1918, after commissions had done their work in examining the Church's needs, a report was issued, with a foreword by the Archbishop of Canterbury, indicating that in every diocese, with something similar in every deanery, an evangelistic council should be appointed. Heavily underlined in the report was this call to commitment: 'We desire to see as the means to this concentration a further call from the Archbishops to the Church, summoning it, by the all-powerful aid of the Divine Spirit, to nothing less than the evangelisation of England and the English people.'[28]

Reasonably, it might have been expected that here was a clarion-call to which Evangelicals would have made an instant and leading response but there is little evidence of such a reaction. Suspicion and preoccupation with defending the gospel must account for this lack of evangelical initiative in evangelisation. Perhaps is was the recurrent negative stance of Evangelicals which prompted the comment: 'Between 1900 and 1914 the Anglo-Catholics were worth all the hatred they got and much more than a match for it. They had something to offer; their opponents generally had not.'[29]

Theology must always lie at the heart of the Church's faith and life. Differences of emphasis and interpretation have always shown themselves in denominational differences but, when it comes to authority, Evangelicals have consistently stood their ground on the basis of Holy Scripture, allowing neither Reason nor the Church herself to interpose an extra or *supra* authority. Both scriptural authority and Reformation doctrine in the Church had been whittled away in the early part of the century but some theologians, at least, were eventually working through the wilderness towards firmer ground. Horton Davies, the church historian, provides an interesting assessment of the ebb and flow of doctrinal and theological emphasis over the early decades of the twentieth century:

It seems that a penitential piety becomes credible only when the doctrines of original sin and the holiness of Divine Love are stressed. It is only when the Incarnation is stressed that the importance of sacramental practice is acknowledged. Only when the doctrines of the Cross and Resurrection are emphasised is it felt by faith that 'the sufferings of this present world are not to be compared with the joy that shall be revealed'. It is a theology of grace

14

alone that elicits the adoration which is the heart-beat of corporate Christian worship and the joyful song of souls in pilgrimage. This was to be more fully appreciated by the theologians of the second three decades of the century.[30]

For a long time, the Anglican Church had been drifting from its scriptural and traditional moorings and the First World War provided the ultimate storm. Bishop Stephen Neill summed it up when he said that war had 'shattered the dream of human progress' and it would be fair to say that the Church of England at large was not exempted from such disillusionment. The change, from a settled, secure Victorianism to a jaundiced, bewildered and emptied Georgianism, was complete. 'The three major modes of thought in the nineteenth century – Romanticism, Liberalism and Evangelicalism, together with their counterparts in the Church of England – were all weighed in the balance between 1914 and 1918 and found wanting.'[31]

Wilfred Owen, the most lastingly famous poet of the war, had been reared as an Evangelical and was contemplating ordination when he went off to become a soldier. Admittedly, the kind of Evangelicalism which he experienced was very diversified in his parents. His father, Tom Owen, sang in Gilbert and Sullivan:

After one such concert, he was asked by the Secretary of a Seamen's Mission if he could sing to an audience of sailors in some dockland hall in Liverpool. He agreed and was such a success that the Mission authorities asked him whether he would be prepared to help as a voluntary worker. He had none of his wife's evangelical fervour, but was happy to take on the task of distributing tracts about the docks for the contact it gave him with ships and sailors.[32]

But Wilfred Owen's own war experience was, perhaps, typical of many:

Through his experiences of war, his understanding of God and of Christ became more ironic and more profound, richer and wider in scope than anything he could have received from his evangelical upbringing.[33]

So the First World War ended in a mood of exhaustion, physical, mental, moral, spiritual and financial. The tank, lumbering across the trenches, the cries of 'Gas' and consequent fumbling for gas-masks, the withering effect, literal and symbolic, of machine-gun fire, together produced a ghastly waste of life and spelt out the very end of the old civilisation, possibly even the close of western civilisation, in a long death-throe, not yet ended. The Church of England, debilitated, disillusioned and divided, had to set about the task of inward renewal and rebuilding. Could Evangelicals, custodians of the Reformed Faith, advocating new birth and salvation, rise above lesser things and mere controversy, to proclaim the gospel of the grace of God in a stricken land? Could they, in the process, counteract the jingoistic sentiments of 'O valiant hearts who to your glory came'? This hymn became immensely popular at Armistice Day services throughout the country. Its author was Sir John Arkwright and it was ultimately included in *Hymns Ancient and Modern Revised*, published in 1950. One verse displays fine poetic achievement combined with orthodox faith:

> Long years ago, as earth lay dark and still,
> Rose a loud cry upon a lonely hill,
> While in the frailty of our human clay
> Christ, our Redeemer, passed the self-same way.

However, to most, if not all, Evangelicals, who view Calvary as standing completely alone, the next verse is offensive:

> Stands still his Cross from that dread hour to this,
> Like some bright star above the dark abyss;
> Still, through the veil, the Victor's pitying eyes
> Look down to bless our lesser Calvaries.

Sadly, this verse obscured the unique nature of the atoning sacrifice of the Son of God, always the centre of evangelical proclamation and it typified the confusion which total war had engendered inside and outside the Church.

2
The Defensive Years

AFTER THE SLAUGHTER of a world war, Britain, eventually and substantially, placed her faith in the League of Nations and 'no more war'. This kindled a special brand of liberalism and humanism and many Christians, modernist and conservative, Catholic and Protestant, were hopeful that we would be able to pick up the pieces and rebuild a decent way of life in church and society. However, Evangelicals realised, better than most, that there would always be 'wars and rumours of wars' until the second Advent. In fact, as the years went by, suspicion, in thinking men and women, of recurrent failure hardened into a conviction that, despite political artefacts and the best will in the world, there was a persistent maggot in the human apple.

How, then, did Evangelicals respond to the heady days of optimism, recovery and resettlement? Within their own circumscribed church communities, they continued to preach the saving grace of God, appropriated by personal faith in the Lord Jesus Christ; they conceived the means of grace much more in terms of the weekly bible study and prayer meeting than in the sacrament of Holy Communion and they eschewed, on the whole, anything like real social concern and involvement. A good number of young men, evangelical and otherwise, hardened by life on the western front, went to theological college and, meanwhile, the faithful sought earnestly to guard the flame of biblical inspiration and the guiding light of the Thirty-nine Articles. However, it has to be stated that, in the early post-war years, the nadir of evangelical influence in England is to be seen: 'But for the moment, Evangelicalism was reduced to a level of less repute and less influence in the Anglican world than at any time in the preceding hundred and fifty years.'[1]

Why had this happened? Had the cross-currents of Darwinism and Tractarianism of the previous eighty years so battered the ship that it was, as Stephen Neill avers, a sorry sight? Or, must it be concluded that Evangelicalism, always standing for the *status quo* in authority and doctrine, was constantly chafed by the modernist, the liberal and the sacerdotalist alike, so that the movement was reduced to caring for its own skin? It appeared to fail to respond in any way to the novelties of twentieth-century experience, at least in those traumatic first twenty-five years. The evangelical traditionalists (or conservative Evangelicals) were forced to take on the revolutionaries of one kind or another and thus there was a tendency for them to retreat into ghettoes of one sort or other, building up from within wherever possible.

In the immediate post-war years, the National Assembly of the Church of England (known as Church Assembly) was being re-formed and, emerging into the limelight, appeared a King's Counsel and leading Evangelical, Thomas Inskip, later to be knighted and afterwards created the first Lord Caldecote. He was appointed a member of the influential Provisional Standing Committee of Church Assembly and from then on was to play a decisive part in the shaping of Church history. He was established as a leading Evangelical but within an overall structure of hierarchical government in the Church, which many thought had an 'old guard' look about it and was overdue for reform. The mood of discontent was not confined to the Services, where home-coming men criticised generals and politicians alike, but it overflowed into the Church:

In January 1919, Archbishop Davidson toured France and Germany to hold conferences with the chaplains. He found an extraordinary mixture of suggestions, on the one hand for equalizing clerical stipends and for covering the land with companies of mission priests, and on the other even for the organising of a general strike of chaplains who would refuse to come home until their demands for the radical reform of the 'official elements' in the Church were met.[2]

So the remorseless process of change and liberalisation was at work within the Church and Archbishop Davidson, always a moderate with an uncanny ability to sit on the fence (in a states-manlike way), had a difficult role. He preferred the easy way out of problems but, one way and another, he had guided the Anglican ship of state through the war years and from the Edwardian summer to the economic blizzard beginning in the late twenties, just when the famous Revised Prayer Book had been finally thrown out by Parliament. Reform of one sort or another was in the ecclesiastical air. Had not Davidson initiated the very investigations into doctrinal matters which eventually led to the Prayer Book controversy?

There were many new doctrinal currents in the wind as well.

One of the most far-reaching and popular of these was the new liberal theology of the Kingdom of God coming visibly on earth, as a product of church growth and the betterment of man:

The radical revision of the orthodox conception of man's destiny as well as the redefinition of the role of the Church is fully contained in the exposition of the key concept of the new theology – the Kingdom of God. This was the characteristic concept of Liberal Protestantism throughout the present century, and none was held more tenaciously by Christian Laymen in our time who found in it the sanctification of their secular vocations as service for Christ in the world. And this, despite the fact that Schweitzer's *The Quest of the Historical Jesus*, appearing in English translation in 1910, had entirely shattered the view that the Kingdom of God was the earthly establishment of a kingdom of social betterment by insisting that it was a supernatural and world-denying kingdom to be inaugurated imminently by the Messiah.[3]

Evangelical Anglicans and Evangelicals in general had not, in those days, either come to accept their Christian mission in society as such or to emphasise the Christian ethic of work, then temporarily forgotten, so they were very frightened of reference to the Kingdom of God. They did not see the Church as a mustard tree, with the birds lodging in its branches, and they found it difficult to accept their leavening influence in a non-Christian set-up. However, to be fair to Evangelicals, it was unpopular in pulpits to declare that the Church's mission was to pluck brands from the burning and translate them into the Kingdom of the Lord Jesus, for liberalism held firmly to the view that the Kingdom would come to earth under the influence of the Great Teacher and his followers. Evangelicalism preached that the Kingdom would be welcomed by believers when it came in visible form on the personal return of the Saviour. The full error of liberal theology and the preaching of a merely social gospel was to be revealed in the thirties with the run-up of Hitler to the Second World War, but in the meantime it held considerable sway.

A variation of liberalism was to be found in Immanentism which reinterpreted 'the fall' and many other basic doctrines, asserting that God was everywhere to be found and that social justice was to be the main outcome of Christianity. R. J. Campbell, originally a Congregationalist at Oxford, was successively a minister at Brighton and the City Temple in London before becoming an Anglican and eventually a canon in Chichester. He was one of the leaders of this new kind of theology and a prolific writer. Inevitably, his reinterpretations were seen by many as denials:

Campbell's most scandalous statement, however, was his redefinition of sin as a blundering search for God, as contrasted with the Biblical conception of rebellion against God. He was perhaps unfortunate in the examples he chose. He wrote: 'The man who got dead drunk last night did so because of the impulse within him to break through the barriers of his limitations to express himself, and to realise more abundant life.'[4]

It is not difficult to see that these new variations or aberrations of the faith found powerful allies in politics, particularly among socialists, and theology soon became rather a matter of ethics. In the meanwhile, conservative Evangelicals had few scholars, a dearth of intellectuals and, as yet, no eloquent advocates of orthodoxy. A notable exception, however, was found in Edmund Arbuthnott Knox, who had held a Fellowship at Merton College, Oxford, and was Bishop of Manchester from 1903 until 1921, being a contemporary of Handley Moule. Perhaps the greatest contribution made by Knox to the evangelical emphasis was found in his dynamic preaching but he wrote a powerful account of the Tractarian movement, contrasting it with what he took to be the more healthy influence of Evangelicalism:

While in the early part of the nineteenth century there was a great revival of religion throughout Europe, that revival took two forms. One, the Evangelical was progressive, associated with humanitarian reforms and world-wide missionary enterprise; the other, the Tractarian, was reactionary, guided by romanticism and desire to re-establish the rule of the clergy over the laity.[5]

Not surprisingly, Evangelicals in the Anglican Church, although at first 'courted' by the Tractarians, who saw them as a potential ally in helping to purify the Church, in the nineteenth century had found themselves in bad odour with their High-Church brethren:

Partly through superficial acquaintance with Evangelical teaching, and still more for the very inadequate representatives of Evangelicalism in Oxford during the first half of the nineteenth century, even Newman, who owed his spiritual life to them, and Pusey, who believed that he loved them because they loved our Lord, were inclined to hold them very cheaply. Newman goes so far as to say in his *Apologia* that he had a thorough contempt for them, and Pusey complained that they condensed the whole Gospel into the two fundamental doctrines of nature and grace, that by nature we are corrupt and by grace we are saved. 'They attach no value' he adds, 'to the church, or the Sacraments, or repentance or good works. The narrowness of their system seems to identify them with Nonconformity.'[6]

Other Tractarians are represented as voicing more furious views

The defensive years

still of Evangelicals and one (W. G. Ward, 1812–82) as going so far as to suggest that, if the Oxford Movement had succeeded, it would have expelled Evangelicalism from the Church of England.

This somewhat extreme sentiment (and Ward held extreme Tractarian views) helps one to understand the polarisation of the two movements within the Anglican fold, the reverberations of which went rumbling down all the successive decades. At the least, it helped the Church to decide whether, in the ultimate analysis, it would choose to follow the Anglo-Catholic tradition in its revival of the Catholic ideal or stay with the Reformed Faith. This crucial question proved to be the touchstone in the defeat suffered by the Revised Prayer Book in Parliament in 1927 and 1928.

In summarising the work of Evangelicalism, in the face of Tractarianism and its long aftermath, Bishop Knox affirms that it brought to men the whole of scripture, not just selected fragments, and instilled not only holiness of life but missionary enterprise and philanthropy. Another view of Evangelicalism and its influence is given by Sir Edmund Gosse (1849–1928), librarian of the House of Lords and best known for his indictment of an upbringing among the Plymouth Brethren (as they were popularly called) in *Father and Son*. He writes: 'their ridicule of what was called "the dignity of the pulpit"; their active, breathless zeal in urging what they thought a pure faith on all classes of society, gave them a remarkable power over generous and juvenile natures. They were wealthy, they were powerful, they stormed the high places of society.'[7]

But opposition to Evangelicals could always be relied upon, for at times they were fierce, at others naive and they were other-worldly, appearing to be stand-offish. However, they maintained their faithfulness to holy scripture, the preaching of the gospel and the fellowship of all believers. But in the midst of this work the evangelical movement was vehemently attacked by the Tractarians, held up to contempt and scorn, and declared to be a form of 'Anti-Christ' worse than atheism! Such fierceness and bitter hostility persisted for many decades after Newman and Pusey were forgotten and is very sadly reflected in the 1970s and 1980s in the strife between Protestants and Catholics in Northern Ireland. Christians holding opposite, perhaps complementary, views seem to engender the strongest of personal animosity in every age.

21

Bishop Knox had a steadying influence on the evangelical cause and published *On What Authority?* sub-titled *A Review of the Foundations of the Christian Faith* at a time when the 'New Theology' abounded in many varied forms – the Social Gospel, a pragmatism searching for Christianity in life rather than in faith and the new modernism with its radical, destructive criticism of the Bible. Also, the quest for 'the historical Jesus' brought waves of scepticism and unbelief. By this time, in the Roman Catholic Church, modernism had been condemned in an encyclical *Pascendi* and also personally by Pope Pius X.

A kindred spirit with Edmund Knox, Bishop of Manchester, was found in Henry Wace, Dean of Canterbury from 1903 until his death in 1924. Significantly, Dean Wace gave his name to the headquarters (until 1979) of Church Society in Wine Office Court, off Fleet Street in London. He was a prolific writer for the evangelical press and twice published a series of these articles in book form, *Some Questions of the Day* (London, 1912). He called the series 'Evangelical truth, and of old English Church-manship' and they were first found in *The Record* which was, in fact, the first Anglican newspaper to appear, beginning on 1 January 1828. It was always strongly evangelical and one of its founders was the then Evangelical, John Henry Newman. In 1949, *The Record* was merged with the *Church of England Newspaper* (founded as the *Church Family Newspaper* in 1894). The *C.E.N.* has remained strongly evangelical in outlook, whilst carrying new and views of the whole Anglican Church. On the other hand, *The Church Times* (1863) was founded with the express purpose of furthering the aims and faith of Anglo-Catholicism. It has very considerably broadened its views and is now the most widely read Anglican newspaper. Many Evangelicals take both weeklies.

Wace's articles dealt with a wide variety of topics, for example, 'Sound and Unsound Criticism', 'The Gospel and the Political World', 'Ulster and Home Rule' and 'The Scout Movement'. One on 'Evangelical Principles' neatly defines the word 'Evangelical':

The purport of the term Evangelical as applied to a school or party in the Church has thus always been the same. It has designated a body of ministers and laity who have held as supreme principles of the Christian faith the authority and power of the Word of God, applied by the Spirit of God, and the free forgiveness of sins, with the gift of the Holy Ghost, in answer simply to repentance and faith, and as independent of any sacerdotal interposition.[8]

22

He then asked the question whether Evangelicalism needs 'revival among us'. He replied – somewhat defensively: 'perhaps a reckless criticism has weakened and obscured the preciousness and power of that Word, and its excesses are urgently in need of restraint.' Accordingly he affirmed that evangelical truth, 'above all identified our faith and practice with that of (the) Evangelists and Apostles'.

The general climate of post-war Britain soon changed to one of unease and disenchantment, leading to despair and depression. Thomas Stearns Eliot, one of the greatest poets of the English language, had summarised it all in his poetically revolutionary epic *The Waste Land*, published in 1922. In this, he described, in his own enigmatic style, the feeling of desolation and futility which gripped the minds of thinking people. A few years later, he signalled his conversion to Christianity with the publication of his first religious poem, *Ash Wednesday*, and he remained friendly with the Bloomsbury set, who tried hard to tease and taunt him out of his faith but failed utterly. He was dubbed the 'Anglo-Catholic baritone' but there was much in Eliot's writings which could have appealed to Evangelicals, for example in *Murder in the Cathedral*, in which he described the martyrdom of Thomas à Becket:

> A Christian saved by the blood of Christ,
> Ready to suffer with my blood.[9]

Furthermore, he trenchantly satirised the easy-going, middle-class life of the twenties in his famous lines from 'The Rock':

> In the land of Lobelias and tennis flannels
> the rabbit shall burrow and the thorn revisit;
> the nettle shall flourish on the gravel court
> and the wind shall say,
> 'Here were decent, godless people,
> their only monument the asphalt road
> and a thousand lost golf balls.'[10]

Significantly, Roger Lloyd heads one of his chapters: 'The Waste Land after the War':

The long hurricane of the 1914–18 war had blown itself out, but for many years to come there would be little peace in the world and no enchantment in the air. By Great Britain the storm had been ridden, and we had just managed to master it, but at the cost of the sacrifice of the most promising lives of a whole generation, whose loss crippled the next twenty years.[11]

Attempting an evaluation of the years which separated the two wars, Lloyd described them as a 'dark corridor of the twenty shabbiest and most disastrous years of English history.'

The same remarks might well be applied to the Church of England and specifically to Evangelical Anglicans, who appeared to have little to offer to the Church at large. They were in their evangelical strongholds but, in terms of influence and achievement, they reach something of a nadir, particularly in the twenties. However, some would contend that the founding of the Bible Churchman's Missionary Society in 1922 and the defeat of the Revised Prayer Book in 1927/8 were evangelical landmarks, as indeed they were, and cause for rejoicing. So far as the B.C.M.S. was concerned, its formation was the result of a rather drawn-out controversy dating, in the C.M.S., from 1912. 'In the decade before 1922 there had been a steady hardening of differences, ecclesiological as well as biblical, and sweet reasonableness was in short supply.'[12]

Questions had arisen as to co-operation with those in the Anglican Church who held more liturgical or even a more sacramental view and a group of clergy in the North of England, which in 1923 became the Anglican Evangelical Group Movement, expressed concern at official reaction to the greater spirit of co-operation:

They were perturbed at what seemed to them to be an introverted and defensive attitude within the evangelical party. Taking 'the mind of Christ' as the supreme authority for thought and life, they welcomed what they called 'the positive results' of biblical criticism, trusting the Holy Spirit to sort out the gold from the dross. They also coveted greater freedom in worship.[13]

It was insisted that there was no sacrifice of scriptural principle but that greater fellowship within the Anglican Communion in missionary enterprise was called for. The issue at one time turned on the difference between 'friendly relations' and 'co-operation'. Much was made of the significance of the 'Eastward position' at communion, which was adopted by some, where it was the normal custom. So the controversy developed as to how comprehensive the C.M.S. should be: whether, in fact, the liberal Evangelicals and the conservative Evangelicals should divide.

The controversy began with issues of liturgy, the sacraments and the ceremonial but soon came to hinge on the inerrancy of Scripture. But it was still hoped by the majority of C.M.S. adherents to provide a basis for 'unity and brotherly co-operation in the work of the Society'. The Book of Common Prayer and the Thirty-nine Articles were held up as a unifying factor. However, there were deep divisions within the ruling bodies of the C.M.S. and delays occurred in reaching unanimity. Without waiting to see the outcome of the work of a sub-committee, commissioned to bring everyone together, a group of about thirty clergy and laity met in London and, after prayer and heart-searching, decided on 27 October 1922, to form the Bible Churchmen's Missionary Society. As a rider, it was agreed that the decision should not be implemented until after the meeting of the C.M.S. General Committee in November when, it was hoped, acceptable solutions would be forthcoming, thus preventing a split.

The C.M.S. sub-committee affirmed the Society's 'unwavering acceptance of the supreme authority of Holy Scripture, in all matters of faith and doctrine'. Some members of C.M.S., at the subsequent meeting, tried to amend the statement by deleting the words 'in all matters of faith and doctrine', presumably because they thought the words to be *qualifying* rather than *confirmatory*, as indeed they were intended to be. As someone pointed out later, if the amendment had been adopted, C.M.S. would have laid itself open to the charge that it did not accept that faith and doctrine were ruled by Holy Scripture!

The statement went on to confirm belief in the deity of the Lord, His atoning death and the absolute reliability of his teaching as recorded in the New Testament. In the event, the split resulted from disagreement on whether the words,'and we believe that His teaching, as recorded in the New Testament, is free from error, and that His authority is final', safeguarded the doctrine of Our Lord's infallibility as a teacher. No less an Evangelical than G. T. Manley, writing in the *Record* later (8 February 1923) averred that they did but there were those who felt that the two words 'and utterances' should be included after 'His teaching'. Liberals protested at their inclusion, 'on the grounds that they would "rule out modern critical views as to the 110th Psalm and the Book of Jonah" '.[14] But the ultimate withdrawal of these two words, seen originally as an extra doctrinal safeguard, proved decisive and the formation of a new society was settled. All hope of reconciliation had now disappeared and preparations for the organisation of the Bible Churchmen's Missionary Society went steadily forward.

The results of the split, apparently on a relatively slight matter of tightness of wording on the authority of Scripture, reverberated throughout the mission field and the supporting Churches throughout Britain. Three vice-presidents, four honorary governors and, initially, only two serving missionaries, resigned. Charges and counter-charges were issued by the rival factions. Someone, wishing apparently to remain anonymous, described the whole affair, after the split, as a 'game of theological tennis'. The whole matter was left 'on the table' for several years until, the dust of controversy having settled, Wilson Cash, General Secretary of C.M.S., wrote to E. L. Langston on 22 November 1926:

We adhere to the Committee's Minute of November 1922, and we shall not attempt to modify it in any way, partly because we are persuaded that it is not through credal statements that confidence is secured and partly because we are convinced that rightly interpreted this Minute absolutely establishes the integrity of the Society's faithfulness to God's truth . . . Perhaps it will assist you and others who are doing so much to help the C.M.S. if I put down a few statements as to what I believe with all my heart to be the true facts about the position of the Society.

1 The C.M.S. stands today, as it always has stood, for the unique inspiration of the whole Bible.

2 The C.M.S. believes in the true and essential Godhead of our Lord Jesus Christ, and only accepts candidates who believe in this truth.

3 The C.M.S. believes that Jesus Christ on the Cross made a full, perfect and sufficient sacrifice for the sins of the whole world, and requires this faith in all its missionaries.

4 The C.M.S. accepts, and has never denied, the absolute truth of all our Lord's words and teachings.

5 The C.M.S. never has denied nor does it send abroad missionaries who do deny the Virgin Birth of Our Lord.

6 The C.M.S. aims, in all its work, at the individual and personal conversion of men to God through the saving grace of our Lord Jesus Christ.

The real test of a missionary society must be the blessing which God graciously gives to the work undertaken in His Name, and anyone who reads the records of C.M.S. work in recent years will at once see how abundantly God has blessed and is blessing it.[15]

Although, in the eyes of some, C.M.S. was sometimes showing signs of modernism in its publications, its deputation secretaries and its choice of candidates, it would be facile and irresponsible to think that the formation of B.C.M.S. represented an exact split between conservative and liberal Evangelicals since it was much more difficult to define the exact *casus belli*, for its seeds were sown in seemingly minor issues and flowered in outwardly unimportant clusters of words:

The defensive years

In the early years of the century, Evangelicals suffered gravely through the disagreement between the more liberal and the more conservative wings of the party. These difficulties came to a head in 1922, when a group of those who had been supporters of the Church Missionary Society broke off and formed the Bible Churchmen's Missionary Society. Division had struck the evangelical cause at its most sensitive point. Probably separation had to come: and in the end the result has been a strengthening and extension of Anglican Missionary work.[16]

This is a generous and fair assessment of the outcome but, at the time, Evangelicalism suffered a severe blow by another unhappy division. In due course, B.C.M.S. did excellent pioneering work in Burma, Baffin Island, Western China and other areas. Eventually, the new Society trained men for the home ministry as well and made its own distinctive and far-reaching contribution to conservative evangelical Anglican life. So far as C.M.S. (founded in 1799), was concerned they were the first church society to endeavour to go into all the world with the gospel. They had John Venn, of the Clapham Sect, a leader of the Evangelical Revival, as their first president and it would be fair to say that the Society, despite the ups and downs of nearly 200 years, has remained consistently and thoroughly evangelical and never more so than in the present day. On the face of it, this makes the founding of B.C.M.S. regrettable. However, one must take comfort from surveying, as a whole enterprise, the joint work of the two Societies. The total missionary endeavour of C.M.S. and B.C.M.S. was much greater than before and one can see the overruling hand of God over the seemingly unpleasant split. And at least, those who remained in C.M.S., as well as those who formed B.C.M.S., retained their membership of the Church of England.

To the average Evangelical not directly concerned with the dispute the split between C.M.S. and B.C.M.S. was most embarrassing. A parish that had enthusiastically supported C.M.S. found itself torn by a desire to remain loyal to the old missionary society and a wish to support the new evangelical venture. Bishop Taylor Smith epitomised in himself the dilemma, for had he not been a devoted C.M.S. missionary bishop and was he not now the evangelical bishop to whom very many looked for a lead? He was very distressed and most embarrassed by questions put to him wherever he went. At parochial level, at least one parish decided to deal with the problem by abandoning its interest in C.M.S., having nothing to do with B.C.M.S. and switching its African interest to the Ruanda Mission, which had affiliation with C.M.S. but enjoyed its own inbuilt safeguards of independence and doctrinal purity.

It would be fair to say that, in accord with the spirit of Evangelicalism in the earlier part of the century, the early days of B.C.M.S. were characterised by the problems of being a small minority, of being much misunderstood and of developing a kind of siege mentality. Leading figures in B.C.M.S. have included Canon A. T. Houghton who, after a curacy in Tunbridge Wells, went to be Field Secretary of B.C.M.S. in Burma and was General Secretary of the Society from 1945 to 1966. He was succeeded by Canon Alan Neech who had spent the whole of his ministry in missionary service.

Another significant event of 1922, not just for Evangelicals, was the birth of radio. John Reith (later Lord Reith) was appointed Governor, he was a committed Christian with a Scottish Calvinist background and a very austere, severe outlook. Having been refused by both St Paul's and Westminster Abbey, the B.B.C. (as it became) more or less adopted, as its church, St Martin-in-the-Fields, from which services were regularly broadcast. Liberal theology and the social gospel held sway in the early twenties and this was certainly the hallmark of Sunday services broadcast from St Martins. A brief daily service was commenced on the 'wireless', as it was then called, bringing worship to those in hospital and confined to their homes but, inevitably, criticisms were voiced on all sides that broadcast services kept people away from Church.

There is nothing to show that Evangelicals were initially able to take advantage of the new medium. They regretted the milk and water offerings of the sermons preached but Reith, with his great integrity and sense of fair play, saw to it that the doctrinal stance of the B.B.C. in its early years, was neutral to the point of being insipid. There were no Evangelical Anglicans able to see and to seize the opportunity of broadcasting the gospel and they were slow to get on terms with those in authority at the B.B.C. The Rev. Dick Sheppard of St Martins was a popular preacher and attracted his congregation from the suburbs but he was hardly an expositor of the Word of God. The first broadcast service came over the air on Sunday 6 January 1924 (the year of the crossword craze from America and the British Empire Exhibition at Wembley).

The defensive years

Bravely reaching the churchless millions, the broadcast Sunday services were monochrome in content but provided great comfort for the bedridden and the house-bound.

3
Through the Waste Land

ONE OF THE most far-sighted but potentially highly inflammatory moves in Anglican circles in the early twenties was initiated by the leading Anglo-Catholic, Lord Halifax. It consisted of Anglican–Roman Catholic conversations at Malines in Belgium, held between 1921 and 1925 which, with the exception of the inaugural meeting, were all held with the cognizance of both Canterbury and Rome. During these conversations, agreement was reached that, if union could be achieved, it should be on the basis of the Pope being recognised as first in honour, that the Body and Blood of Christ were received in the Eucharist and that the sacrifice of the Eucharist was both real and mystical. Naturally, when news of these conversations reached Protestant circles in the Church of England, alarm bells rang, for predictably, the Anglican representatives at the conversations were all drawn from High-Church circles. In a letter to Archbishop Davidson, dated 24 January 1924, Sir William Joynson-Hicks (Home Secretary 1924–9) made the point:

Are we to suppose that your Grace regards persons holding the views of Lord Halifax, Bishop Howard Frere, Bishop Gore, and Dr Kidd as the only or truest representatives of the position of the English Church? If so, the position must indeed have changed. Why, for instance, was not the Bishop of Durham, or Bishop Chavasse, or the late venerated Dean of Canterbury, nominated? If, as your Grace assures us, there is no thought of weakening the position taken up by the great Anglican theologians of the sixteenth and seventeenth centuries, Lord Halifax, Bishop Frere and Bishop Gore are not the persons one would naturally think of as maintaining it.[1]

This was courageously and firmly put by one who, in the ultimate show-down on doctrine only a few years later, when the Revised Prayer Book was rejected, was to play such a leading part. Towards the end of his letter, Joynson-Hicks added this trenchant comment:

The best and most direct path along which we may approach the question of Christian unity is in the way of re-union with our separated brethren at home, and it is the strongest condemnation of efforts of this kind to secure union with Rome that not only are they absolutely futile, for Rome never yields a tittle, but that their success would destroy all hope of re-union with our brethren of the Free Churches.[2]

The primate's reply failed to answer this particular point. Joynson-Hicks, again courageously, returned to the charge and insisted that there could be no re-union 'unless and until Rome undergoes a similar change to that which we effected in the sixteenth century'. His watchword and one on which he and the archbishop profoundly disagreed was 'Rome is immutable'.

Doctrinal rumblings had been heard in the Church of England for many decades. Malines was only one: the Tractarian movement and its aftermath was a constant volcano and Randall Davidson himself, in a continuing process initiated by the 1904 Royal Commission on Ecclesiastical Discipline, tried to pacify his more Catholic elements and this eventually led to the bishops putting together a proposed new Prayer Book which the archbishop presented to the Convocations of Canterbury and York in February 1927. The proposals were approved by large majorities. The next step was presentation to Church Assembly for final approval, which was given on 6 July. The voting was:

	For	Against	
Bishops	34	4	(all from the southern province)
Clergy	253	37	
Laity	230	92	
	517	133	

The book had been put forward as 'optional', which, on the face of it, was a judicious move. However, the Eucharist rite took as its model Cranmer's first rite of 1549, which appeared to its opponents as a move back in the direction of pre-Reformation doctrine. The Reservation of the Sacrament, with all that that implied in possible 'adoration' of the elements, was allowed for. Baptism and matrimony were couched in more modern terms but the storm centre was undoubtedly the refashioning of the service of Holy Communion. However, the proposals failed to satisfy the more specific Anglo-Catholic elements who even saw themselves hindered in their 'progress' by the new services and they hoped that Evangelicals would defeat the new Book and thus save them from the opprobrium of opposing it. The House of

Lords, probably largely out of loyalty to the Archbishop of Canterbury, voted heavily in favour of the new Prayer Book but a different reception altogether was to be given to it by the House of Commons.

It is interesting to note, in passing, that in 1549, Parliament had authorised the 'First Prayer Book of Edward VI', which was taken into national use. In a way like the 1927 proposal, this first B.C.P. was a compromise, brought into being by the tireless labours of Cranmer and others, but it pleased neither the old traditionalists brought up on the Latin services who wished to change neither the doctrine nor the language nor those of a more extreme reforming mind who wished to change both doctrine and language, welcoming the English of the new order of Holy Communion, etc. Objections were then made to vestments, prayers for the dead, and other things, and the second B.C.P. came out in 1552, ordering the use of the surplice in place of vestments. Puritan objections to the B.C.P. were voiced early in the seventeenth century and eventually, after much controversy, the 1662 edition was authorised by the Act of Uniformity and it endured for over 300 years as the norm for public worship in the Church of England.

Parliamentary debate against the 1927 Prayer Book was led by Sir William Joynson-Hicks, ably supported by Sir Thomas Inskip, also later to become a Cabinet Minister. They represented formidable opposition and the protagonists of the Bill had no rhetoric to offer by comparison. The debate was, by and large, conducted with restraint and good manners. Sir William, who declared that he had been a witness at the Royal Commission on Ecclesiastical Discipline in 1905, spoke strongly against 'the adoration of the Blessed Sacrament' and referred to those who had been brought up on the Book of Common Prayer:

who would not wish to be offered a change of doctrine and who hate the idea of any alteration being made in that one part of the service of all others, the service of Holy Communion, which will bring it nearer to the medieval ideas which were abolished for us at the time of the Reformation.[3]

Sir Thomas Inskip, in support of Sir William, also used moderate language in speaking of 'The real tug-of-war . . . about that part of the Book, small in volume but supremely important, connected with the service of Holy Communion.'[4] He went on, at a later stage in the proceedings:

I feel that this is a grave moment for the House of Commons. The Archbishop of Canterbury has mentioned the fact that for 25 years he has occupied his high office. I wish I could give such comfort or solace for the last years of his tenure of his great office by granting him through the House of Commons this Book but I doubt if it is ours to give. We ought not to give – whatever veneration and affection and esteem can be given to the Archbishop are his already – and I ask myself, have we any right to give to any man, even a man greatly beloved, that which belongs to the nation and posterity. This House of Commons is going to write its name in history in a few minutes. Still for a few minutes we are asked to defend or to yield what some of us believe to be one of the ramparts of our national faith.[5]

Such eloquent, gentle but firm persuasiveness proved decisive in the lower chamber, the quiet patronising of the primate and the slow build-up being most telling. The Commons voted against the proposed new Prayer Book with a majority of thirty-three. The former General Secretary of the Protestant Reformation Society has written:

But if Convocation and the Church Assembly were ready to allow the Church of England's doctrinal position to be subverted by their new service book, Parliament was not. It is possible Parliament saw the issues more clearly. Its members were not subject to Episcopal pressure as the clergy and the lay members of Church Assembly were. They were free to make an independent judgement on the basis of the feeling in the country generally.[6]

The Church as a whole was staggered by the defeat and was reluctant to admit it. So the bishops set about making certain minor alterations to the text and the book was again presented to Parliament in the following year, 1928. It was then turned down by an even larger majority – 266 votes to 220. Thus, Evangelical Anglicans, largely through the staunch leadership of Sir William Joynson-Hicks, the older and more senior man, and Sir Thomas Inskip, achieved a notable victory for the continuance of the Reformed nature of the Church and for evangelical Christian Faith. They were actively supported in Parliament by many members, including Sir Arthur Hazlerigg. Inevitably, however, there was abroad an atmosphere of doctrinal indifferentism and, for instance, Inskip, for the rest of his political career, was dubbed as 'of Prayer Book fame' and Evangelicals were so often misrepresented as 'Low-Church controversialists'. Simplicity of worship was equated with purity of doctrine in the minds of the average citizen, whereas they were not always directly connected. Joynson-Hicks, Inskip, Hazlerigg and their friends were contending for the Reformed Faith, the Protestant repository of truth rather than fighting against candles and stoles. However, there is, obviously, *a* connexion. 'It is idle to imagine that liturgical change can be made without theological principles becoming involved. Liturgy is so much an expression of theology in worship that a change in one is almost certain to be reflected by a change in the other.'[7]

Randall Davidson, for twenty-five years Archbishop of Canterbury, was devoted to seeking a compromise in matters of doctrine. He realised only too well the problems of holding in balance the many twentieth-century strands of thought. He had seen the Royal Commission on Ecclesiastical Discipline of 1904 come forward with a list of illegal practices in the Church but took no action except eventually to bring forward the new proposed Prayer Book. At Malines, he had allowed himself to be drawn into an Anglo-Catholic pre-emptiveness and in 1922, with the Archbishop of York, he had set up his Commission on Doctrine in an attempt to accommodate Anglo-Catholicism. (It did not report until 1938!) Small wonder that Randall Davidson, although well respected for his statesmanship, was not exactly popular with Evangelicals. But the time of reckoning came when the House of Commons threw out the result of all these labours, judging, just in time, that the clock appeared to be in process of being put back to pre-Reformation days, with a suggestion, for example, that the Bread of the Lord's Supper should be venerated, if not positively worshipped, as the actual Body of our Lord.

The battle-cry of the protagonists of the proposed Book had been 'Trust the Bishops'. The question might have been asked 'To do what?' but within the Church the slogan nearly won the day. However, the Church had not reckoned with the strength of 'public' opinion, which did not wish to see the Church pushed back to pre-Reformation days, nor had the archbishops and the bishops realised that there was a very considerable 'grass-roots' feeling against the proposals. At a meeting held in London in 1927, just before the Parliamentary debate, 1,050 clergymen agreed on their opposition to the proposed Book and 600 others signified by post their allegiance with the protesters. It was by no means a small minority movement and the laity, both inside and outside Parliament, were very active in concert with their evangelical brethren among the clergy.

The headquarters of the Committee for the Maintenance of Truth and Faith, as it was called, was set up at The National Club (now merged with the Junior Carlton) at 12 Queen Anne's Gate, London, S.W.1 and other Members of Parliament to join the struggle against the Rome-ward move were Lord Carson, Sir Malcolm Macnaughton, Sir Samuel Roberts and Sir Charles Owens. Eventually the question was asked bluntly of the proponents of the Revised Book and voiced by Bishop Knox: 'Is God in the consecrated elements or is he not?' and the answer had to be given 'Our Church at the Reformation distinctly answered "No" '! No wonder the whole of the Evangelical Body – Anglicans and Free-Churchmen – welcomed the defeat of the 1927 and 1928 proposals as 'a great deliverance'.

Feelings in the Church naturally ran very high during the 1927/ 28 Prayer Book debate. Bishop Hensley Henson of Durham (succeeding Handley Moule in 1920) was heard to describe Evangelicals as 'an army of illiterates, generalled by octogenarians'. But we should note that, in 1928, Joynson-Hicks was sixty-three and Inskip fifty-two. The former was Home Secretary and the latter Solicitor-General. Joynson-Hicks became Viscount Brentford in 1929 and Inskip, Viscount Caldecote in 1939. Unquestionably, it was the influential positions in Parliament held by these two and their restrained but telling pleading which swayed their fellow members. But it was only a partial victory, for lawlessness in parts of the Church continued: 'Convocation illegally authorised the Bishops to allow the use of the revised Book during "the present emergency". Emergency and illegality have persisted to the present day. The outcry was the echo of dead themes.'[8]

It is worthwhile noting that publication of the Malines Report was delayed until 1928, three years after the meetings finished, for fear it should influence public opinion against the Revised Prayer Book, or so Lord Halifax reasoned.

Obviously, the defeat in the House of Commons raised the difficult question of the Established nature of the Anglican Church. Should it not be free to run its own affairs, many reasoned? On the other hand, Evangelicals were very glad of the safeguard provided by belonging to the National Church. Since that time, the Church–State issue has received attention from some quarters but greater emphasis has latterly been placed on the Church running its own affairs, for example General Synod passing the Alternative Service Book and the appointment of bishops being largely in the Church's own hands.

With the passage of time, the 1927 Prayer Book crisis was seen as a climax in theological controversy cloaked in a debate on liturgy and churchmanship, the State siding eventually with, and representing, 'the man in the pew'. Here is an over-simplification of the conflict as it undoubtedly was:

The last really discreditable outbreak of such sectarian strife was on the occasion of the debating of the Revised Prayer Book of 1928. It was most violent while it lasted, but it subsided with remarkable speed, and it is doubtful if we shall see any revival of it. When parties find that they have so much more in common than they once suspected, partisanship ceases to be.[9]

However, it may well be wondered how it has been possible, in the latter part of the same century, in such relative calm and compromise, satisfactorily to provide alternative services of Holy Communion. It is at this stage worth quoting from Archbishop Ramsey's sermon on his enthronement in 1961:

Here in England the Church and the State are linked together and we use that link in serving the community. But in that service and in rendering to God the things that are God's, we ask for greater freedom in the ordering and in the urgent revising of our forms of worship. If the link of Church and State were broken, it would not be we who would ask for this freedom who broke it, but those – if there be such – who denied that freedom to us.[10]

The influences brought to bear on the Anglican Church since the Oxford or Tractarian Movement were many and varied. Evangelicals felt hard pressed and, after the rejection of the proposed Prayer Book, in something of an isolated position. They had won a notable victory but they were made to feel out on a limb, even discredited, in Anglicanism. So they found their fellowship in the realm of the spirit and increasingly with their Free-Church brethren and, as ever, the Keswick Convention was a great rallying point. The only common ground between Evangelical Anglicans and Anglo-Catholics was in defending the Church against the inroads of liberalism and modernism. The Anglo-Catholics claimed, in addition, that they were reviving the forgotten rich heritage of medievalism, in all the arts, within the Church.

Not unnaturally, at the time of the Prayer Book debate, the relative and special appeal of Anglo-Catholicism was brought to light but it has always been generally recognised that High-Churchmen are not as numerous as their opposite numbers, although their clergy are generally better organised and certainly more vociferous in the affairs of the Church. In 1928 it was shown from, 'An analysis of the figures . . . that the twenty-one churches of an evangelical character (in the Metropolitan area) which had the largest attendances had twice the number of worshippers that the twenty-one Anglo-Catholic churches with the largest attendances could show.'[11]

It is, of course, generally recognised that Anglo-Catholicism emphasises the authority of the priesthood and the Church rather than that of the Bible, but it would be foolish to think that the Anglo-Catholic does not love his Bible, for many are staunch members of the Bible Reading Fellowship and read the Scriptures privately and daily. Yet, the defeated Prayer Book emphasised the desire of a Church drifting from scriptural moorings to lean more heavily on mysticism and the traditions which the Reformation rejected. Joynson-Hicks summarised the view of Evangelicals concerning the 1662 Book of Common Prayer:

In our present Prayer Book we have, not the book of a party but of the whole Church: a book which seeks to promote unity, because all can join in its services; and above all a book whose teaching in all its parts is in full harmony with the revelation which God has given to us in the Bible of His purposes for us.[12]

The ten years which separated the end of European hostilities and the new Prayer Book rejection represented a period of heroic evangelical effort to preserve the Anglican Church in its Reformed state. Society itself, reeling under the blows of a terrible and bloody war and drained of many of its resources, was seeking desperately to find a way out of 'The Waste Land', 'worm-eaten with liberalism' as Eliot had himself declared. Rationalism and humanism were very popular with the intelligentsia and, within the Christian Church, the full force of the Oxford Movement was found in the potential Anglo-Catholicism of the defeated Prayer Book and all the undercurrents which went swirling outwards from that time. As in the days of Wilberforce and Shaftesbury, Evangelicals were nobly and effectively led by laymen, now by Joynson-Hicks and Inskip – men for their times as their Victorian forebears had been. But in episcopal fields, the main leaders were E. A. Knox of Manchester, until he retired in 1921, and F. J. Chavasse of Liverpool, who retired in 1923.

The questions of authority and access to God continued to dominate the thoughts of churchmen. The Evangelical and the Catholic were still very much at odds, as ever.

On the question of access to God the controversy between Tractarians and Evangelicals may be concisely summarised thus: 'The Evangelical takes the words of our Lord: 'No man cometh unto the Father but by Me' (St John xiv.6) without any supplement or addition. The Tractarian adds to them the qualification: 'through the Church'. Whence follows the enquiry 'What is the Church?' 'Where is it to be found?'

Again the Evangelical teaches that we enter the Church through living union with Christ. The Tractarian teaches that we are admitted into living union with Christ through the Sacraments of the Church.[13]

In spite of this clarity of thought and strong emphasis on the gospel, the post-war years appeared to find the Evangelical Anglican poorly equipped and hardly motivated to spread that same gospel. Any war of the proportions of that of 1914–18 must weaken the whole fabric and therefore the effective witness of the Church and it is not surprising to find the decade which followed one of an uphill struggle for those surrounded by widespread disillusionment. Most of the new efforts to bring the Christian ethic, with or without true Christian faith, into the new society were sponsored by the Higher Critics, the social reformers and the liberals. Evangelicals got on with their parochial work as before:

The main strength of the Evangelical movement has always been in the parishes. Evangelicals have not produced many great scholars, nor have they had many representatives amongst the higher clergy. The latter fact is not perhaps so urgent as it appears to many. The normal Evangelical minister does not seek great things for himself. His primary desire is to win souls for our Lord Jesus Christ, to build them up into the worshipping church, and to train them for Christian witness and service. He is happiest in the pastoral work of the parish, offering Christ as the one who can supply all needs and satisfy every soul. The parish is the sphere where this great ministry must be carried on, and it has been found to provide abundant and fruitful scope for God-given energy.[14]

That being so, it is hardly surprising to find a general lack of evangelical archdeacons and bishops. It is both the strength and the weakness of Evangelicalism that it has concentrated on spreading the gospel and has had little time left over for taking part in the counsels of its church at deanery, archdeaconry and diocesan levels. The emphasis of post World War Two Evangelicalism is now different, but it was to take many years before efforts were made to repair the omission of an impact on the government of the Church.

4

Continuing Nadir

I T IS, of course, difficult to assess the real value of the Protestant and Evangelical victory represented by the defeat of the Revised Prayer Book of 1927/28. Many would assert that it was a major triumph for the maintenance of the Reformed Faith of the Church of England, as by law established, and also for the Book of Common Prayer with its Thirty-nine Articles. Unquestionably, those two White Knights of the political scene, Sir William Joynson-Hicks and Sir Thomas Inskip leave, for all time, an example of what can be done in Parliament by men of commitment prepared to stand up and be counted. The detractors of Evangelicalism, numerous as ever, were quick to write off the victors as 'Low-Church controversialists', whilst those determined to follow the Rome-ward path within the Anglican fold were undeterred and even glad about the defeat of the new Prayer Book. All in all and reviewing the years which followed, it must be conceded that the triumph was rather hollow and produced something of a stalemate for Evangelicals. Did it give a dull character to a long period of pietism, a turning inwards in a defensive exercise? Sadly, it is true that, after Bishop Handley Moule of Durham, Bishop Chavasse of Liverpool and Bishop Knox of Manchester, Evangelicals lacked this kind of leadership and their influence overall in the Church was on the wane. They had few intellectual or scholarly minds to their credit, little social concern and a paucity of literature. However, they were on excellent terms with their brethren in the Free Churches and their missionary endeavour was on a high note.

For example, the China Inland Mission (later to become the Overseas Missionary Fellowship) was at the height of its influence in China before the Communist revolution. A remarkable Anglican missionary family was seen in the Houghtons, five out of eight children becoming missionaries. These included Canon A. T. (Tim) Houghton of B.C.M.S. and Bishop Frank Houghton of East Szechwan. Frank was a gentle gifted poet and hymn writer who married the daughter of Bishop Cassels of West

China. He had begun his missionary service in 1920 and four years later was appointed principal of a Chinese theological college but, in 1926, nationalistic violence in China prevented his return and he joined the U.K. staff of C.I.M. Perhaps his best known hymns are: 'Facing a task unfinished' and 'Thou who wast rich beyond all splendour'.

In 1937 he was consecrated bishop of a Chinese diocese as large as England and Wales and in 1940 he became General Director of the Mission, leading it through the war years to its rehabilitation in South East Asia as the Overseas Missionary Fellowship. At the age of fifty-eight he became vicar of St Martin's, Leamington Spa. Frank Houghton was fairly typical of a godly, gifted generation of Evangelical Anglicans in the full-time ministry of the Church which had a very great influence in evangelical circles generally, where their stature was undoubted but which carried, not surprisingly, little direct influence in the main body of Anglicanism. The victory of 1927/28 had not yet overflowed into positive action but it was a very significant one for a group of 'frightened people' and eventually encouraged them to make strategic advances. There was a distinct rise in evangelical morale in the 1930s – a stirring of the spirit.

Hensley Henson, one of the best known twentieth-century bishops, who succeeded Handley Moule at Durham, referred, disparagingly, to Evangelicals as 'semi-dissenting'. A High-Churchman in his earlier years, he later adopted a more moderate position but wrote coldly and unsympathetically of the evangelical position: 'Hidebound by its Calvinistic dogma and by its connexion with Dissent, the Evangelical party was never really at home in the Church of England. It achieved much in the sphere of social reform, and in the conduct of foreign missions, but ecclesiastically it counted for little and achieved nothing.'[1] This comment was fair in that evangelicals very often failed to think in corporate terms or indeed of the visible Church at all, being inclined to view the Church of England as the best 'ship from which to fish', that is, in which to preach the gospel, and this attitude persists with a minority.

One of the longest serving Archbishops of Canterbury, Randall Davidson, resigned in 1928 at the age of eighty, having occupied the primacy for twenty-five turbulent years. At an early age chaplain to a former archbishop, he married one of the arch-bishop's daughters and became confidential adviser to Queen Victoria. No churchman can have exercised more influence in this century on Church and nation than Randall Davidson. Essentially a cautious chairman rather than a great leader, he was careful to see appointed only 'moderate' bishops with the exceptions, as he would have conceded, of Bishop Gore of Oxford, leader of the Anglo-Catholics, and Bishop Knox of Manchester, the head of the Evangelicals and famous for his missions on Blackpool sands. Gore resigned in 1919 and Knox in 1921. Davidson had planned that a new primate should be in the chair before the Lambeth Conference of 1930 and his resignation had therefore nothing to do with the rejection of the proposed Prayer Book.

During these years there was one figure who became the antagonist alike of the Establishment, Anglo-Catholics and Evangelicals, and that was Bishop Barnes of Birmingham, a mathematician and a scientist, and an outspoken champion of the evolutionary view of the origin of man; he claimed a freedom to restructure Christian theology on that basis. Barnes was equally hard on those who held to the doctrine of Transubstantiation and those, Evangelicals among them, who at that time saw the Darwinian evolutionary theories as being in opposition to the Sctiptures. He saw man as descended from the apes but Barnes was not easily pigeon-holed. At a conference of modern churchmen he preached a sermon in which he gently chided them for allowing their modernist enthusiasms to take them too far, and for attempting to shuffle from under some of the foundation doctrines of the Faith but he was, he said, an Evangelical!

Bishop Barnes was for many years to remain a stormy petrel of the Anglican scene but certainly never accepted by Evangelicals as one of their number. In 1947 as Bishop of Birmingham, he published his notorious book. *The Rise of Christianity* (O.U.P. 1948), which by its wild negations of so much of the Gospel narrative and its unscholarly procedures and unscientific assumptions made many wonder how he could conscientiously remain a bishop in the Established Church. However, Barnes remained as Bishop of Birmingham from 1924 until 1953. He represented the ultimate in negative criticism during the earlier part of his episcopacy but he lived to see the eclipse of most of his theories by the return of orthodoxy. His influence, however, on a whole generation of churchgoers, was very considerable.

In 1928, the new archbishops, Cosmo Gordon Lang at Canterbury at the age of sixty-four, and William Temple at York, then aged only forty-eight, addressed a pastoral letter to the Anglican Church, which exhorted clergy and people to a renewal of life and power, stressing the need to study the Gospel of Christ as revealed in the Bible and in the Creeds which set it forth.[2] This ought to have pleased all the evangelical hearts in the Anglican fold. Lang brought with him to Canterbury a good all-round experience – the academic life, big parishes and twenty years as Archbishop of York. However, his primacy was rather undistinguished, which adjective could not be applied to the work of William Temple, who was translated to Canterbury in 1942. Temple was an ardent educationalist and social worker who had been very active in the work of the Student Christian Movement in its heyday. He concerned himself with all social, economic, international and ecumenical questions but he remained independent of party, in religion and politics. Unfortunately, he was only at Canterbury for two and a half years before he died.

But the spiritual vacuum continued and Evangelicals had no national answer; the nation as a whole seemed drained of inner resources; orthodox Christian faith and churchgoing continued to decline. Every kind of alternative 'enjoyment' was on offer, the wide open spaces called jaded citizens out of town to 'the church of the open air' and, perhaps worst of all, unemployment, which was nil during the 1914–18 war, two million in 1921, and in January 1933 reached three million. The early thirties were times of national depression, epitomised by the dole queues. Commenting on the fundamental changes experienced in the national ethos, Horton Davies writes:

Three cataclysmic factors have radically changed optimistic imperialistic Edwardian England into the sober, realistic, country of today. The first was the horrifying impact of two World Wars. The second was the change from an opulent centre of empire spanning the seas to the leading partner of a freely associated British Commonwealth of Nations, with the passage of the Statute of Westminster in 1931. The third is the institutionalization of the concept of social justice in the development of the Social Welfare State. In consequence of this searing and apocalyptic revelation of the two World Wars, the humanists committed themselves to a greater humaneness, and the optimistic liberal Christians began to think again about that destructive selfishness in man which an older theology has called original sin, and of man's desperate need of the transformation of a Divine grace. Theology . . . became more realistic, knowing from bitter experience that man is both crucifier as well as redeemable.[3]

The Church was witnessing the slow demise of the older

liberal theology and, very gradually, the revival of an orthodox understanding of man's innate sinfulness, with an insistence upon the necessity of redemption. Thus, the evangelical emphasis on the gospel of Divine grace was gaining ground under pressure from outside factors coming, ever so slowly, to the fore. 'The fundamental doctrines of Evangelicalism are no monopoly of the party, they are not certain peculiar views held by them exclusively and by no others. That which differentiates them is not a distinctive essence but a distinctive emphasis.'[4]

Now it became increasingly possible, with the march of events, national and international, political and theological, for the evangelical Christian to gain a hearing, if only he could involve himself more in human affairs and if only he would warrant recognition because of his intellectual standing and his humanity. Regrettably, during these decades, Evangelicals lost much of the attractiveness which they had in Victorian times and the negative attitude of a life-denying Puritanism asserted itself. 'The appeal of beauty has on the whole made but little impression on Evangelicals. In their nature is much of the Puritanism which sees in beautiful things merely the snares of the evil one, a siren voice luring them from the stern pathway of duty.'[5]

During this long nadir of Evangelicalism, with its inevitable retreat into pietism, no strictly conservative evangelical bishop was appointed but the liberal evangelical movement, represented by the Anglican Evangelical Group, supplied a number of bishops between the wars – Perowne of Worcester (1931), Hunkin of Truro (1935) and Woods of Lichfield (1937). Lord Brentford (Sir William Joynson-Hicks) died in 1932, so there were few evangelical spokesmen left. Nevertheless, a most important contribution was made by Dr Griffith Thomas, sometime Principal of Wycliffe Hall, Oxford, and later Professor of Systematic Theology at Wycliffe College, Toronto, when he wrote *The Principles of Theology: An Introduction to the Thirty-nine Articles* (published posthumously in 1930). Although the work is now considered to be rather dated in appearance, it diligently devotes a whole chapter to each of the Articles and has established for itself a place as a classic of evangelical literature. As Dr Packer points out in his preface Thomas had earlier (1904) published a 'Protestant exposition of basic Christianity, Prayer Book style', which he called *The Catholic Faith*. Dr Packer remarks:

It is clear that in convictional terms Thomas was an evangelical before he was an Anglican (which was as it always should be); but it is also clear that his reason for being and remaining an Anglican was his certainty that by historical and theological right real Anglicanism is evangelicalism in a pure form. Within the Anglican fold he saw himself and those whose views he shared not as party eccentrics who needed to beg for toleration, but as mainstream churchmen recalling their benighted brethren to a true Anglican identity.

The year 1928 witnessed a most significant event in the founding of the Inter-Varsity Fellowship of Evangelical Unions, the I.V.F., later to become the U.C.C.F. (Universities and Colleges Christian Fellowship). The movement, undenominational in character, was to become of very great importance to Evangelicalism as a whole and, in particular, to Evangelical Anglicans, giving them many of the factors which they had previously lacked, viz. in-depth scholarship, academic influence and literature.

The formation of the I.V.F. grew out of the Cambridge Inter-Collegiate Christian Union, founded in 1877. The Student Christian Movement was founded after the C.I.C.C.U., from which it became separated in 1909. The split eventually came when S.C.M. was asked the pointed question: 'Does S.C.M. consider the atoning blood of Jesus Christ as the central part of their message?' to which the reply came: 'No, not as central although it is given a place in our teaching.' So, the break was made and at a post-demobilisation meeting in Cambridge in 1919 plans were laid to form the I.V.F. which has remained traditionally conservative Evangelical ever since.

After several annual conferences and even after the appointment of a travelling secretary, the Rev. H. Earnshaw Smith, later to become Rector of All Souls, Langham Place, the Inter-Varsity Fellowship of Evangelical Unions was eventually and officially formed through receiving into membership the Christian Unions at Oxford, Cambridge and a few other universities.

Norman Grubb, who had won a Military Cross in the First World War, was a leading light in the formation of the I.V.F. and quickly saw that a Christian Union was necessary, as he put it, 'not only at Cambridge but at every university in the world' and in 1919 he said: 'God gave me the clear vision of the I.V.F. that was to be.' Its aims were very clearly stated and have remained the same to this day: 'Loyalty to the truths of God's Word and a soul winning work among unconverted students.' The intrinsic and dynamic value of the I.V.F., from an Evangelical stand-point, is twofold: first, the countless number of converts to the Christian faith arising from the work and witness of the constituent Christian Unions, many of whose members have gone on to occupy positions of great influence, having built up their faith whilst at college and, second, the extensive publishing programme instituted by the I.V.F. (later Inter-Varsity Press and sometime Tyndale Press) which began in a small way in the early thirties and continues to this day. It would be fair to say that the I.V.F. (U.C.C.F.) has been a most vital part of the world-wide Evangelical Anglican scene for the best part of this century. Its members have shared in the shortcomings and weaknesses of traditional Evangelicalism but they have positively enriched mainstream Anglicanism as a whole. In their earlier days, members of the I.V.F. had often little use for the established churches, they eschewed involvement in society, they tended to be life-denying rather than life-affirming and they had little culture. Moreover, they tended to know all the answers. Their Tractarian or High-Church brethren had a better doctrine of the visible church and,

they found a split caused by the Pharisaism of the Evangelicals and sought, by correction of Protestant error, to restore the unity of the Church. No fair historian will deny that the Evangelicals, in their zeal for the salvation of individuals, had sharply distinguished between the 'saved' and 'the lost' and were often too confident of their power to discern between the two. Nor can it be denied that they attached to salvation not only belief in a definite body of doctrine, but also abstention from practices thought to savour of worldliness.[6]

Such comments were never more apposite than when applied to the young men who, in increasing numbers, were being converted to the Christian faith through such interdenominational agencies as the I.V.F., Crusaders and the Scripture Union, the highest percentage of whom became committed Anglicans. A factor in the 'holier than thou' attitude, which characterised the Evangelicalism of these para-church movements, was the involvement of large numbers of the Open Brethren, who tended to have a very 'black and white' idea of who was truly saved and what the saved ought and ought not to do. The Evangelical Anglican and the Plymouth Brother (as he was originally called) were happy to join forces in the leadership of Crusaders and Scripture Union and, besides being united in holding all the tenets of evangelical faith, took a rigorous view of keeping themselves separated from the world, differing only over baptism and confirmation and sharing a strong concept of the invisible church. Equally, they shared a suspicion of the ceremonial and the sacramental. It was in these movements that Evangelicals were increasing in the thirties and the Anglican Church was the first to benefit, both numerically and in vitality. In Bishop Knox's judgment:

So long as Evangelicals were in opposition to lifeless dogmatism and to shameless immorality they could not justly be accused of 'splitting the church', for separation from evil and formalism is an essential characteristic of Christianity. Christ cannot be followed except by crossbearers, and crossbearers cannot expect to be popular or even to escape notice.[7]

Certainly, in the two decades which separated the two world wars, Evangelicals were offering a sure foundation for the bewildered, a peace for the disturbed in mind, and, as well as a present salvation, an assurance for the future. They did not change their tune with the times and many sirens did not lure them from their anchorage. According to Roger Lloyd:

No historian will ever be able to write happily about English history between 1919 and 1939, and it would be hard to find any other period of twenty years in which more people were unhappy, or more people also believed that their unhappiness was neither necessary nor of their own making, but due to some betrayal of the powers-that-be, the custodians and vested interests of the old order, or to the indifference of God himself. thus a weary nation which is not given time to rest and recover after long strain is bound to feel.[8]

Although the flood-gates of a new morality had not yet been opened, overt immorality was more easily tolerated and divorce was definitely on the increase; there were twice as many divorces in 1939 as in 1922 and nearly ten times as many as in 1912. An advanced liberalism, which John Henry Newman once described as 'the half-way house to Atheism', had tried to rob the Christian faith of the miraculous and of the strength of its morality. As Newman said, the liberals preferred 'intellectual excellence to moral'. But liberalism and its successor modernism had, by the early thirties, largely become a spent force, leaving something of a vacuum in Anglicanism which Evangelicals, largely through their non-church agencies, were eager and able to fill. Moreover, some of the old antagonism between Anglo-Catholics and Evangelicals began to fade: 'Protestants saw that many indubitably Catholic theologians were laying more and more stress in their teaching on the Bible, while their own theologians were

46

enthusiastically exploring the authority of churchmanship.'[9] The drawing together of the differing evangelical bodies and of the churches was greatly helped by the Bible reading systems of the Scripture Union (founded 1879) and of the Bible Reading Fellowship (founded 1922), the latter being mainly Anglican in orientation.

During the late thirties, the idea of the Parish Communion was gaining ground, set in motion by a book of that title.[10] The view was expressed that, with the secular world impinging on the Church, it was wholly desirable to demonstrate to that world the essential and rounded nature of the Church and her ministry. 'It is one with the Church of the Scriptures, and one with the primitive Church of the first three centuries, and as such should be conscious of its separation from the world and its position of privilege in the divine scheme of things.'[11]

But Evangelicals, as a whole, would have none of it at that time. For them, the Parish Communion appeared to emphasise the Eucharist at the expense of the preaching of the Word. Much later, Evangelical Anglicans were to see that, under the dictum of 'no sacrament without the word', the two could effectively be combined, with the enrichment of both. Forty to fifty years after the start of Parish Communion or Family Communion, as it is often called, it would be hard to find parishes, other than in some scattered rural communities, which did not have that kind of service, at least as an occasional alternative to the more traditional pattern of 8 a.m. Holy Communion and 11 a.m. Mattins. Evangelicals have mostly been able to adopt the new formula without diluting their ministry of the Word.

Gabriel Hebert of the Kelham Community was just about the founding father of the movement of the Parish Eucharist or Parish Communion and the time of this service was seen as 9 a.m. or 9.30 a.m., with, if possible, parish breakfast following. Great difficulty was experienced at first for 9 a.m. in many districts was sacrosanct as the time for Sunday breakfast at home!

Those who practised Parish Communion saw it as the central act of worship of the people of God, deepening the meaning of the sacrament in a vision of communion, offering and fellowship. The churches were at that time mainly Anglo-Catholic and insisted on fasting before the service. However, they viewed the service as a sacramental showing forth of the one sacrifice of Christ and also of the offering up of the members of Christ's body in union with Him to be a 'reasonable, holy and living sacrifice to

God' – in other words it was a sacramental expression of the Church's common life in Christ.

Hebert and his associates did not see the Parish Eucharist as a panacea for all the problems of the local church but, somewhat naively, they hoped it would heal party divisions. After all, they reasoned, did not the Evangelical see as his chief service of worship a memorial of the Lord's death? Parish Communion did not see itself as a ritualistic movement and its pioneers hoped it would greatly improve on the 11 a.m. Eucharist *without* Communion – a mere spectacle – which was current in some churches at the time. Hebert and his followers felt that as preaching the gospel would be involved at Parish Communion it would unite Catholics and Evangelicals. However, as the years went by some Evangelicals saw two dangers in the emphasis on this service. They felt that it could trivialise the service of Holy Communion as 'a weekly trip to the Communion rail' and they considered that the service tended to exclude rather than encourage the curious and those who have been described as 'God's irregular army'. But opinions differed widely on that subject.

It is interesting to note that the Anglo-Catholics who fathered Parish Communion did not wish the service to be sung – they felt this to be too distracting. Evangelicals would, of course, have agreed. Very high hopes were held for the Parish Eucharist – too high, as it turned out – but the concept of the Church as a 'virtuous circle' of prayer, fellowship and service was, perhaps, slightly ahead of its times.

The changing patterns of parochial life were made against the background of an increasing population and a decreasing number of clergy but the laity had not yet been called upon properly to exercise a real ministry in the Church. Again according to Roger Lloyd:

In 1905 there had been 19,053 clergy in active work. In 1914, the figure had dropped to 18,180. In 1922, it was 17,162. In 1930 it was 16,745. Thus in the twenty-five years from 1905 to 1930 the number of clergy at work had dropped by 2,308; and in the same period the population had increased by 3,000,000.[12]

Not only had the population increased but so had the Church's awareness of her social responsibility to campaign for better housing and other amenities. As a generalisation, but not too wide of the mark, one might say that Evangelical Anglicans who, in the 1920s, were campaigning against Anglo-Catholicism, were now making a stand for the spiritual essentials of the faith against those who, in putting forward the social gospel, appeared to equate Christianity with social justice rather than with belief in Jesus Christ. And the Great Depression of 1929–32 was just the right soil in which to sow the seeds of 'social' Christianity. Simultaneously, the pacifists were on the move and Canon Dick Sheppard of St Martin-in-the-Fields founded the Peace Pledge Union which claimed 80,000 adherents in one year.

Hitler was on the march in Europe but the mood of the British public did not change to one of alarm. A paralysing hedonism mixed with cynicism characterised social life but, politically, the easygoing optimism of the period was occupied with curing ills at home (or trying to) and the Church of England, led in this respect by William Temple, the Archbishop of York, was endeavouring to give a lead. But there was no Dr Barnardo even, let alone a Wilberforce or a Shaftesbury, to give an evangelical emphasis. Yet the evangelical churches, dotted around the country, every few miles in the big conurbations, were full, sermons lasted twenty minutes to half an hour and it was the custom to go several miles to church, if necessary, to hear an evangelical preacher. Evangelical Anglicans continued to be zealous either in their own churches or in the numerous organisations which flourished outside the established churches, for there was no doubt that a common evangelistic purpose was the easiest way of drawing together the Evangelical Anglican with his brother in the Free Churches. It wonderfully concentrated the soul, whereas in the local church there were many down to earth, distracting matters to be dealt with. At least, within their own environs, Evangelicals rose above the spirit of the age:

The essence of the spirit of the thirties was not apathy but inertia: an incorrigible *immobilisme* in State and Society, a structural resistance to change, and especially to any radical improvement. Far from being apathetic, opinion of many kinds was exasperated and despondent, made so by repeated experience of inability to impose any effective control either on politics or on the sheer course of events. Consciences were deeply stirred, but they could find no outlet in constructive action. The sense of helplessness and drift that resulted may explain the escapist flavour of the most fashionable cults. What appealed most was 'getting away from it all'.[13]

There was a sense in which Evangelicals got 'away from it all' by concentrating themselves into spiritual confines, whether parochial or para-church, such as Christian Unions, Missions, Crusaders and the like. However, the average evangelical parish, in the mid to late thirties, was content with 1662 mattins and evensong and congregations at *both* were up to capacity – churches comfortably full, with rather more young people there in the evening. Those parishes with good I.V.F. connexions were probably using, mid-week, an excellent three-year Bible Study Course issued by I.V.F. entitled *Search the Scriptures*, edited by G. T. Manley and written by leading Evangelicals. This series made an outstanding contribution to intelligent knowledge of the scriptures and represented the first major break-through by the I.V.F. in nurturing evangelical 'scholarship' and communication. Dr Douglas Johnson, for so many years the chief executive of the I.V.F., was a man of very far-sighted vision, always believing that evangelical influence should be paramount at academic and theological college level. He was not a committed Anglican, being much happier in the interdenominational milieu, but he had an immeasurable influence, indirectly, on the Anglican Church. Essentially a modest man, he knew how to choose his leaders in every sphere and G. T. Manley, one of his earliest finds, was no exception. Vicar of St Luke's, West Hampstead, in the early thirties, Manley was a Senior Wrangler at Cambridge, for some years Fellow of Christ's College and Mathematical Lecturer of Magdalene College. At a later stage and in an entirely different field, Douglas Johnson 'harnessed' the wealthy influence of Sir John Laing in furthering the work of the I.V.F. At about this time and still early in their publishing history, I.V.F. brought out two books which made their contribution to evangelical thought, the second being relatively lightweight: these were, *In Understanding Be Men* (1936) by T. C. Hammond and *Valiant in Fight* (1937) by B. F. C. Atkinson. Canon T. C. Hammond was Principal of More Theological College, Sydney and Dr Basil Atkinson was under-librarian in the University Library at Cambridge.

Whereas earlier generations of Anglicans had tended to draw the lines between 'High', 'Broad' and 'Low' Church, all being held within the comprehensiveness of Anglicanism and for several centuries within the confines of the Book of Common Prayer, the lines were now drawn doctrinally rather than liturgically or, to be more specific, in terms of attitudes to the Bible. On the far right were the Obscurantists, but these were mostly to be found amongst strange non-Anglican sects. 'The Authorised Version was good enough for St Paul and it's good enough for me' they were alleged to have said. Next to them were the

Fundamentalists, inclined to reject scholarship and certainly militant in opposition. They would have been quite well represented in the thirties amongst Evangelical Anglicans. Taking a central position we find the conservatives, conserving all that was best in the past, open to all genuine scholarship and gracious in advocacy. On the extreme left were the modernists, destructive, denying the miraculous and emptying the gospel of all but human connotation. Occupying the position between modernism and conservatives were the liberals, who accepted that the Biblical texts were amenable to critical study either of a more radical or a more reverential fashion. Many men and women called themselves (and still do call themselves) 'liberal Evangelicals' but admittedly the lines were difficult to draw and they still are because the liberal and conservative Evangelicals so often found they had very much in common:

In the 1930's a new type of Evangelicalism began to make its appearance – neither liberal nor conservative in the earlier sense of these terms; entirely open to the ideas and methods of modern scholarship, not greatly interested in the old controversies about ritual and ceremonial, but standing firmly in the great biblical tradition of the Evangelical Fathers with its emphasis on justification by faith, the obligation to holiness, and Christian assurance through the work of the Holy Spirit.[14]

This same emphasis on scholarship was increasingly to be seen in the work of the I.V.F., fathered by Dr Douglas Johnson. The long 'bottoming-out' trough of Evangelicalism was coming to an end and a very positive contribution was being indirectly made to the life of the Church of England at its grass roots.

Evangelical Theological Colleges became full and many of those in high office in the Church became concerned over the undue influence of Evangelicals! (They need not have worried about this.) As Horton Davies remarked:

The date given for the beginning of the demise of liberal theology and for its replacement by Biblical theology is 1933. This may seem the less arbitrary when it is remembered that Karl Barth's *Commentary on the Epistle to the Romans* appeared in the English translation by Clement Hoskyns in 1933. That event signalizes the impact on British theology of both Europe's greatest twentieth-century theologian and a great English Biblical scholar.[15]

It is important to remember that Karl Barth (born in 1886) was a potent influence about the time of the First World War and afterwards in the theological life of Germany. He stood out as a beacon light, questioning the secularisation and the liberalism of

51

the Church under the shadow of both Kaiser Wilhelm and Adolf Hitler. As he joined hands, in his polemic against liberalism, with the philosophy of Soren Kierkegaard, the Danish philosopher (who died in 1855), Barth re-emphasised, almost re-introduced, the fundamental and, by some, diluted truths of Evangelicalism – sin, grace, justification, forgiveness and resurrection – though he remained suspect by many an Evangelical.

Perhaps this notable Christian prophet of our century, Karl Barth, drove away the last vestiges of a tired, watered-down theology; he thundered denunciations of man's confidence in man, he opposed Nazism with all his eloquence but, being a Swiss citizen, he escaped direct confrontation. He underlined the sufficiency of scripture, the fall of man, the need for Divine Grace and the uniqueness of Jesus Christ in his life, death and resurrection. The thirties belonged to Barth theologically although English theology was, at the time, hesitant to take very much direct notice.

It was the day of European dictatorship – Communism, Nazism and Fascism. Young intellectuals like the poets Cecil Day Lewis and W. H. Auden went off to Spain to drive ambulances in the Spanish Civil War. Recalling those days in *A Thanksgiving*, Auden sang:

> Then, without warning, the whole
> Economy suddenly crumbled:
> there, to instruct me, was *Brecht*.
>
> Finally, hair-raising things
> that Hitler and Stalin were doing
> forced me to think about God.
>
> Why was I sure they were wrong?
> Wild *Kierkegaard*, *Williams* and *Lewis*
> guided me back to belief.[16]

Clearly Auden owed much to both Charles Williams and C. S. Lewis and, although he would certainly not describe himself as an Evangelical, he was a believing Christian, a prophet of his times and an intellectual. There were many like him, who began with hopes of Communism, Humanism or mere intellectualism and who, in the thirties and forties, came into an orthodox Christian belief. Some, without following any particular path of Evangelicalism, were claimed by Evangelicals in the nicest possible way as 'fellow travellers', none more so than C. E. M. Joad, the philosopher who later became famous as a member of the original 1941 'Brains Trust'.

It would be too much to say that the rediscovery of Biblical orthodoxy in the thirties was the immediate panacea for all the ills of the Church but it was, at least, the start of a revitalising power in a moribund situation and it marked an expansion of evangelical influence which was to continue, unabated, for many decades. Again, in the words of Horton Davies:

It was not too much to say that the return to Biblical orthodoxy in England meant the recovery of the Church's soul. The authority of the Biblical revelation, which was both doctrine and life, replaced the uncertainties of human ideals and experiences. The Bible became the source, not the confirmation of religious experience. Theology stressed the objectivity of the Divine deeds for the salvation of the human race.[17]

The rediscovery of the Bible and the return to Christian basics and, dare we say, in general terms, to evangelical orthodoxy, had long-term and germinant results throughout the world:

In rediscovering the Bible, they found it to be the Book of the People of God, and they learned that their intellectual and critical study of it needed to be nourished by devotion through worship. Whatever the explanation, it became clear that Bible, Church and Liturgy are three witnesses to the recreating Word of God, Jesus Christ, and that they belong together.[18]

Another potent European influence upon Christianity in the thirties and a generally unfavourable one was Sigmund Freud, an atheist Austrian physician and psychologist whose views produced what became known as 'The New Psychology'. He endeavoured to bow God out of human thought by asserting that the Heavenly Father was only our way of compensating ourselves for the lack of personal responsibility and effort. He equated all activity with sexual drive. One of his disciples, Carl Jung, a Swiss, had also concentrated on the solution of human problems by mental effort. He declared that the world could be divided into the extroverts and the introverts and held that there were four primary functions of the mind: thinking, feeling, sensation and intuition. At least, unlike Freud, he allowed God a place but the new psychological views caused the Church a lot of problems – possibly the worst since Marx and Darwin. Evangelicals reacted strongly against much of the new psychoanalysis, although later admitting to some of its beneficial results. Too often in the past people had been dubbed as either 'mad' or 'sane' but the new study showed up the complexity of the human mental condition.

An I.V.P. paper-back of this time was entitled – significantly – *The Menace of the New Psychology* (1939) by J. S. Conn. It was not one of I.V.F.'s best publications.

Progress was being made in the thirties with evangelical theological colleges. The London College of Divinity had been founded as long ago as 1863, fourteen years before Ridley Hall, Cambridge and Wycliffe Hall, Oxford, founded by the same Deed of Trust. In 1970, L.C.D. was moved to Nottingham and became St John's College. But in 1932, Oak Hill College, Southgate, came into being and also Clifton Theological College (merged in 1972 with Tyndale Hall to become Trinity College, Bristol). With St John's, Durham (founded in 1909), these six colleges made an impressive evangelical contribution to the Anglican Church.

It may well be wondered what sort of people Evangelical Anglicans were in the years before the outbreak of the Second World War in 1939. They were, above all, a separated people and their contact with non-Christians was minimal. They *belonged*, as little as possible, in ordinary society and their sub-culture was of their own making. They did not go to the theatre or to the cinema, they did not, on the whole, go even to family dances nor, if they could avoid it, to parties outside their own communities. They bought their citizenship at a minimum cost, contributing little or nothing to political life or social well-being. They regarded the ordained ministry and missionary work as the highest calling, then medicine and teaching, with everything else as poor 'also rans'. Their concept of 'full-time Christian service' meant that you had not really 'arrived' until you were a 'full-time' minister in the church. The Evangelical Anglican was a very moral person, he paid twenty shillings to the pound, was hard working and a sound family man. On Sundays, he wore a dark suit and went to church two or three times; he was generally a teetotaler and socially ill at ease, except with his own kind. He had his own jargon, talked of things being 'top-hole' or 'wizard' and referred to other Evangelicals as either 'sound' or 'keen'. He liked sport and, in fact, many excelled in university sides. It was very unusual to find the Christian Unions at the 'Varsities' (as they were called) without a few 'blues', 'purples' or whatever. 'Muscular Christianity', in this latter form, was one of the light-hearted jibes the Anglo-Catholics and the liberals levelled at evangelical religion in the universities. On the other hand, the evangelical young generally shunned the more difficult side of sport – the social aftermath – and never went to a pub. Between the sexes there was a proper reserve, proper that is for those times; young men, generally, were advised to see as little as they could of the opposite sex and many married late or when they felt it was 'about time', only indulging in kissing after engagement. Evangelical Anglicans were devoted to their 'in-groups' but they had, even within these groups, little time for art and literature; it seemed as if their taste in poetry was limited to A. A. Milne and their musical appreciation to Gilbert and Sullivan (Shakespeare was just about allowed in the theatre, particularly if the play was being studied at school!).

Reflecting on an Evangelicalism of the nineteenth century and hoping for a thoroughgoing re-emphasis on positive faith and life, the Archdeacon of Norwich (now the Bishop of Thetford) wrote:

They were giants in those days; combining, *of course*, natural advantages with a strong sense of God's grace in all creation, and the serious Victorian reverence for art and civilised culture, before these words became as debased and devalued as they are today. It did not last long; but while it lasted it was a golden age. Perhaps its message for tomorrow is that evangelicalism can and must be world-affirming, in the sense of *God's world*; even whilst it is world-denying, in the sense of fallen human society organised apart from God.[19]

Ever since then there was a remarkable inclination, happily now on the wane, for Evangelicals, Anglican and Free Church, to be 'anti-life' rather than 'pro-life'. They took refuge from the harsh facts of life in their evangelical ghettos, they evangelised more by shouting texts from a distance and they eschewed everything except what they conceived as the 'spiritual' side of life. Also, they took a strange kind of refuge in the Pauline commentary: 'For consider your call, brethren; not many of you were wise according to worldly standards, not many were powerful, not many were of noble birth; but God chose what is foolish in the world to shame the wise . . . ' (I Corinthians, Ch. 1, verses 26/27 R.S.V.)

Somehow between-the-wars Evangelicals inclined to the view that they were excused culture, scholarship and intellectual exercise on religious grounds and they felt exonerated from loving God with their minds. It was all part of their 'backs-to-the-wall' attitude.

The Evangelical Anglican loved a good sermon and often travelled many miles with his friends to a 'keen' church. Only exceptionally was he prepared to throw in his lot with a middle-of-the-road church in order to exercise a ministry there. The result, particularly in the 'Bible Belt' around London, was that evangelical churches became preaching centres, crowded with 'Sundays-only' people, particularly young people, from other parishes.

In the run up to the Second World War, with the age of liberalism and modernism at its death, evangelical orthodoxy was in the ecclesiastical air, influential writers were about to make a very significant contribution to the faith and the shadowy period of Evangelicalism was coming to a long-overdue end. The transformation of society on earth appearing an unlikely possibility, the community of the redeemed was impelled to advance.

5
The Turning Tide

Two specifically evangelical youth movements rose to positions of remarkable influence in the thirties, viz. the Children's Special Service Mission and the Crusaders Union. Both were seen at their most influential in the work of their summer (and to a lesser extent Easter) camps which were used to evangelise and then build up in the faith thousands of boys and girls from lower and upper middle-class families. These societies were non-denominational in character but inevitably they worked more in the direction of the Anglican Church than elsewhere and far-reaching results were eventually to be seen in men being ordained who owed their conversion to the camp work of C.S.S.M. and Crusaders. Most of the leaders in these organisations were ambivalent regarding their churchmanship, for they saw their work among the young as freeing them from too much involvement with their own Churches and yet they saw themselves always as part of 'the handmaid of the Church' and working towards the goal of active Church membership for their converts. Perhaps they would have fretted in a wholly denominational environment but being Evangelicals and always feeling at home in a truly ecumenical setting founded on the gospel, they were able to work most happily with these movements outside their own religious milieu and to bring back, to the Anglican Church in particular, a not inconsiderable 'harvest home'.

For a long time there had been Scripture Union Camps but, as the work of its sister organisation, the C.S.S.M., expanded, so the latter flowered into what were called Varsities and Public School Camps (V.P.S.C. for short and even 'Veeps' to the really initiated). These camps took many forms – canvas, house parties and Broads cruises but one of the most far-sighted and far-reaching enterprises was led by the Rev. E. J. H. Nash, who, at the age of thirty-three, gave up his work as chaplain of Wrekin College (a Martyrs Memorial Trust School) to work full-time for C.S.S.M. and S.U. Immediately, he organised camps at Claysmore School, Iwerne Minster, Dorset, which continue to this day, the mantle of Elijah having fallen on the Rev. David Fletcher. The keynotes of Iwerne were always very simple bible teaching and pastoral care through strongly developed friend- ships at all levels. Attendance was by invitation only and limited to boys at major public schools, at least boarding schools. The unofficial, *sotto voce*, slogan of the 'Bash Camps' (Bash being the very affectionate name given to E. J. H. Nash) was 'key boys from key schools' and, whilst this strategy of creating a patrician, elitist Christian society was criticised by many, the results were most remarkable and, in themselves, a powerful answer to the critics. It is, in fact, worthwhile highlighting four leading Evangelicals who were converted through 'Bash Camps', viz. Canon Michael Green, formerly Principal of St John's, Notting- ham and now Rector of St Aldate's, Oxford, the Rev. Dick Lucas, the Bishop of Liverpool (the Rev. David Sheppard) and the Rev. John Stott. All four men have had a lengthy and fruitful ministry in key centres, in university missions and beyond and it would be impossible to attempt any kind of evaluation of the scope of their ministry, deriving, under God, from this single evangelistic agency. John Stott became a 'camper' just pre-war, the others post-war; David Sheppard, with John Dewes, another convert through Iwerne, opened the innings for the Cambridge University team, both subsequently playing for England. John Stott had been head-boy at Rugby School and was the son of Sir Arnold Stott, chief physician at Westminster Hospital. They were a very distinguished generation. Needless to say, however, some professing an evangelical conversion either lapsed into unbelief or moved over to other forms of churchmanship. Examples of leading clerics from strongly evangelical backgrounds who moved to an Anglo-Catholic or broader churchmanship are to be found in the Archbishop of York, John Habgood, the Bishop of London, Graham Leonard and the late Bishop of Guildford, David Brown. Both Graham Leonard and David Brown came, it is understood, from quite hard-line evan- gelical backgrounds. When one searches for 'traffic' in the opposite direction, it is not easy, although Prebendary John Pearce, Chairman of Church Society through several troubled years, is a shining example.

All the major public schools were reached by the careful, thoughtful and dedicated work of the Iwerne Minster Camps represented by 'Bash' and his assistants. Their follow-up work was outwardly very low-key but meticulous and yielded dividends in the number of committed Christians going into the Anglican ministry and into the professions, notably teaching. Of course, they had their in-groups and their jargon, 'campers' being the title earned by those attending Iwerne. Although, they tended, at Oxford and Cambridge, to create elitist groups for the furtherance of the work of the camps, they were sufficiently out-going as well; for instance, in providing four successive presidents, in the thirties, for the Cambridge Inter-Collegiate Christian Union, including Basil Gough, who afterwards became Principal of Clifton Theological College, and Dick Knight who became, successively, headmaster of Oundle and Monkton Combe. They were not men of straw; by and large, their faith endured – and developed.

So far as Crusaders were concerned, their contribution goes back much further, the Union of Bible Classes having been founded in 1906 by the Rev. A. C. Kestin, an Anglican returning from missionary service in India. Among notable Evangelical Anglicans becoming Christians in Crusaders we find the Rev. Dick Rees (now deceased), a full time Evangelist in the Anglican Church, the Rev. Michael Saward, Area Dean of Ealing, London, and the Bishops of Lichfield (Keith Sutton) and St Albans (John Taylor).

The influence of Crusaders and the beach missions of the Children's Special Service Mission is well illustrated in the early life of Canon Max Warren, described by many as a liberal Evangelical:

As was common in London suburbs, there was in Upper Norwood a Crusader class for adolescent boys in secondary schools. Through his attendance at this when possible, and then in the summer holidays through his association with the Children's Special Service Mission led by his brother at Eastbourne, Max came under the strong influence of one of the most vigorous evangelistic movements of that period. Both the Crusaders and the C.S.S.M. were largely the products of lay leadership and this fact may well have helped to develop in him that profound respect for the Christian layman which he never lost.[1]

Max Warren was always primarily interested in overseas missionary work but it was as a boy at Marlborough College that he found direction for the whole of his life.

In his teens he committed himself, by an act of personal surrender, to Jesus Christ as his Saviour and Lord. He had grown up in a family entirely dedicated to the service of Christ but it was through the Crusaders' Union and the Children's Special Service Mission that he was led to discover his own identity and calling as a Christian disciple. He never ceased to be grateful for what these two evangelistic movements had done for him.[2]

In the thirties and forties, both V.P.S.C. and Crusaders were typically evangelical; male dominated, authoritarian and middle class, Crusaders limiting its intake to public and private schools (theoretically those unreached by Sunday Schools). 'Bash' Camps were dominated by the bachelor outlook of their charming mentor and relationships with the opposite sex were viewed with some suspicion, being categorised as danger along with motor bikes and the business world.

Recalling the famous, it is worth noting, *en passant*, that Canon Bryan Green, for so long Rector of St Martin's, Birmingham, was for two years a missioner on the staff of C.S.S.M., during which time he conducted a mission in the North of England assisted by two young men who later became famous as Bishop Trevor Huddleston and Bishop Mervyn Stockwood. All three, in their differing ways, have since been evangelistic in their work but only Bryan Green has, it would seem, remained evangelical in outlook, although even he has not been really acceptable in the bosom of Evangelicalism. Other notable figures in the Anglican scene who latterly developed a healthy regard for Evangelicals would include Bishops Cuthbert Bardsley, John Bickersteth and Oliver Tomkins.

It is important, at this stage, to bring into our consideration of the evangelical scene, a man who, although not an Evangelical any more than he was a Catholic, had a great influence on Evangelical Anglicans and was, in fact, taken into doctrinal partnership by many Evangelicals. I refer to C. S. Lewis, whose influence on orthodox Christianity was quite remarkable. Born in 1898, reared as a nominal Christian, he became a committed Christian in 1929. He describes his experience in inimitable style:

The fox had been dislodged from Hegelian Wood and was now running in the open 'with all the wo in the world', bedraggled and weary, hounds barely a field behind. And nearly everyone was now (one way or another) in the pack; Plato, Dante, MacDonald, Herbert, Barfield, Tolkien, Dyson, Joy itself. Everyone and everything had joined the other side.[3]

He also describes himself experiencing a feeling of checkmate and paints the actual moments of conversion thus:

I was driven to Whipsnade one sunny morning. When we set out I did not believe that Jesus Christ is the Son of God, and when we reached the zoo I did. Yet I had not exactly spent the journey in thought. Nor in great emotion. 'Emotional' is perhaps the last word we can apply to some of the most important events. It was more like when a man, after long sleep, still lying motionless in bed, becomes aware that he is now awake.[4]

Lewis restated with vigour, colour and charm all the essential truths of the Christian faith. After the long night of humanism and liberal thought he re-established, by use of popular language, the doctrine of original sin; he called people back to basic beliefs and stressed the ethical content of true Christianity. He was certainly among the greatest intellectuals of this century – at least of the orthodox kind – he refused to accept any truth second-hand and he abhorred the shibboleths either of Evangelicalism or of anything else!

I have always in my books been concerned simply to put forward 'mere' Christianity, and am no guide on these (most regrettable) 'inter-denominational' questions. I do however strongly object to the tyrannic and unscriptural insolence of anything that calls itself a Church and makes teetotalism a condition of membership. Apart from the more serious objection (that Our Lord Himself turned water into wine and made wine the medium of the only rite He imposed on all his followers), it is so provincial (what I believe you people call 'small town'). Don't they realise that Christianity arose in the Mediterranean world where, then as now, wine was as much part of the normal diet as bread?[5]

(He was actually replying to some American readers of his books.)

Four years after his conversion, Lewis published his first positively Christian book, *The Pilgrim's Regress: An Allegorical Apology for Christianity, Reason and Romanticism* (Geoffrey Bles, 1933). His next important work came in 1938, in the form of a novel, *Out of the Silent Planet* (Bodley Head), then in 1940 one of his two most important books appeared, *The Problem of Pain* (Geoffrey Bles) and went through many editions, becoming a classic on the subject. So great was his general appeal that in the years 1940 and 1941 he served in the Royal Air Force as a lecturer on Christianity, becoming a popular speaker with chaplains, both evangelical and otherwise. In 1941, he gave twenty-five talks over B.B.C. radio. These were soon published, first as *Broadcast Talks* and then as the major part of *Mere Christianity*. Shortly afterwards, Lewis's most popular work was published: *The Screwtape Letters* (Geoffrey Bles), and became a bestseller. Suddenly, in the space of a year or two, all the great truths of Christianity, including those of an actual devil and the personal return of our Lord, had become intellectually acceptable. Further broadcast talks followed in the war years and in 1947 his other major work appeared, *Miracles* (Geoffrey Bles). Later he wrote children's novels of Christian emphasis and in 1951, reflecting on his other-worldly attitude, declined the offer of a C.B.E.

It would be impossible to estimate the influence of C. S. Lewis either on Christians or on Anglicans or on Evangelical Anglicans. It was certainly immense and the advent of his many writings gave Evangelicalism an opportunity to come really alive again, both in the pulpit and in its writings. He would not have subscribed to the ˏexactitudes of every evangelical question – on the atonement he thought there were many ways of understanding and expressing it – but it was his firm orthodox Anglicanism and biblical emphasis which came as a whole summer of fresh air to a war-beleagured Britain in the 1940s.

Hitler's war was seen by some as a continuation of that of 1914–18, for only twenty-one years of peace intervened and for part of that time the German war machine was terrifyingly on the alert if not on the march. So the familiar pattern was re-vamped; total war-effort, food shortages, thousands of men and women in uniform, etc. The big differences were the absence of trench warfare and the arrival of large-scale bombing. Church services were held under the threat of death from the skies and very many clergy were, as before, in uniform. Evangelicals had a new bishop in Christopher Chavasse of Rochester, appointed in 1939 from St Aldate's, Oxford, where he had been mainly concerned with the care of evangelical undergraduates. But, regrettably, he never had the whole-hearted support of Evangelicals:

He was suspect all round among Evangelicals. His support of opponents of the Revised Prayer Book had led Liberal Evangelicals to treat him as a Conservative Evangelical, and everything else he had done, apart from his stand with them over the 1928 Controversy, made him suspect to the Conservatives. It was true of Christopher, as it had been in his father, that he was no Evangelical in a party sense. Evangelicalism was a school of thought and a way of life, rather than a party flag to be waved or a ditch in which to hide and in which to take a final stand.[6]

However, the new Bishop of Rochester was still hailed from every direction as a good choice. The popular press recalled that C. M. Chavasse played wing three-quarter for the St Helens Rugby League team and that he was the son of the late Bishop of Liverpool:

The item of news on his appointment which most intrigued the general public was that the new Bishop had never been to a theatre in his life. This confession he had made at the Evangelical Conference earlier in the year. 'I have never been to a theatre, and I was never taught to dance. I should not be happy if I went to the theatre now, but I would not mind if my children went.'[7]

His confession was typical of that generation of Evangelicals.

Christopher Chavasse was a forthright, vigorous leader and just the man to help point the way out of humanism:

He quoted with approval Dr Temple's words: 'If the security of the nineteenth century, already shattered in Europe, finally crumbles away in our country, we shall be more and more pressed towards the theology of Redemption.'

The Church as a whole was greatly impressed by his latest utterances and the *Church Times* published his views in a sermon entitled 'The Theology of Redemption', in which the Bishop described the failure of 'Christian Humanism'. In a more generous than usual leading article we read: 'The Bishop belongs to the younger category of English prelates; that is, he is still under sixty. His mind is vigorous and alert. He makes experiments, some of which occasionally threaten to undermine the unity and integrity of the English Church. But together with this impetuosity of spiritual youth goes, in his case, a theological outlook on the world in general, derived from the simple doctrine of the Bible which stamps him as a genuine religious leader.'[8]

Even William Temple, Archbishop of Canterbury, who died in 1944, came, near the end of his life, to abandon his liberal Catholicism and hopes of a new Christian order through social change. The whole theological outlook had moved and Chavasse gave a paper to his Diocesan Conference entitled 'Evangelism in War-time', thus setting the ball rolling for his chairmanship of a *Commission on Evangelism* which resulted from a Church Assembly resolution of 1943. He had thus begun the detailed examination of a subject which was to absorb many remaining years of his life, and to issue in the much-praised, bestseller report *Towards the Conversion of England* – a remarkable document.

The Second World War dragged on with devastation of property and loss of life as never before, though battlefield casualties were, mercifully, less than in the earlier conflict. The atomic bomb was the most awful of the new weapons and was only seen in the Far East to end the war there. Roger Lloyd summed up the Church's reaction to the Second World War as follows:

Of the reaction of the Church of England to the war of 1939 there seem to be few dramatic tales to tell. Insofar as the clergy represent the Church, they were in a position, because of the kind of war it was, to take a much fuller share in the general suffering of the people, whether in uniform or out of it.[9]

Another powerful war-time literary influence came from the writings of a Congregational minister, D. R. Davies, who left the ministry,

to devote himself full time to educational activities on behalf of the Labour movement, and finally became an Anglican vicar, [he] analysed his disillusionment with liberalism in theology as follows: 'Christian Liberalism has had four consequences in the social and religious life of our time: (1) a false estimate of human nature; (2) the practical banishment of the other-worldly element in the Christian Ethic; (3) the denial of the uniqueness of Christianity; (4) the secularisation of life and religion' (*On to Orthodoxy*, p. 13).[10]

Davies, a dynamic and convincing writer, was a man for the polemic and the cutting edge. His book *On to Orthodoxy* made a big impact on a world fed on the sour milk of liberalism and now plunging into another war. He declared that he knew beyond any further possibility of doubt that humanism is a false faith and that Christian liberalism is an aberration and an abortion! He had, as he put it, 'boxed the whole compass', of the inter-war years through pacifism, socialism, Marxism, liberalism, etc. Many of his generation, sickened by the failures of mankind resulting in two world wars, turned to despair but some, like Davies, turned to a sound evangelical faith, fulfilled in experience:

As we have already seen, man carries his sinfulness up through every phase of his growth. He can only transcend his nature of original sin by a Power outside. Every man must, therefore, be born again, must himself experience the grace of God. He must pass through the inner spiritual revolution of conversion . . . [11]

Like C. S. Lewis, D. R. Davies also emphasised the need for underlining the truth of the return of the Lord in glory: 'As a life-long socialist, even, I am convinced that the rejection of the hope of heaven by the masses has not improved their prospect of heaven on earth . . . I am convinced that a re-emergence of eschatology is the greatest need of our world today.'[12]

So the fatal optimism of the thirties was passing; powerful minds were being brought to bear on the Christian verities, and recalling Christians (and churchmen at least) to proclaim a more evangelical faith.

Davies made another powerful and scintillating contribution to the cause of orthodoxy, three years later with the publication of *Down Peacock's Feathers* (Geoffrey Bles, 1942). This took the form of a reappraisal of the General Confession in the light of contemporary experience. His writing continued to dovetail in with that of C. S. Lewis and their thoughts on human personality, as intensified by the Christian faith, were very similar. His style was compelling and almost as brilliant as that of Lewis:

Nothing – absolutely, literally nothing – can 'allay the eternal restlessness of mortal man'. There is no thicket in which he can hide himself from storms of self-accusation; no shore that cannot be washed by the recurrent tides of brooding awareness. The sense of guilt is universal in time and space. The jauntiest and cockiest of generations and individuals sense its Damoclean presence.[13]

Yet another very gifted writer had now arrived on the scene in the person of Dorothy L. Sayers. Her broadcast series of plays *The Man Born to be King* (Gollancz, 1943) made a very considerable impact on wartime Britain as did her series of newspaper articles on the Creed. In October 1941, she gave an address to the Public Morality Council in London which was later printed in booklet form: *The Other Six Deadly Sins* (Methuen, 1943). Her utterances and writings were widely respected:

The three most successful apologists for Christianity in England have all been lay members of the Church of England. They are: T. S. Eliot, the distinguished poet, dramatist, man of letters, and author of *The Idea of a Christian Society*: Dorothy L. Sayers, author of a superb study of the doctrine of creation entitled *The Mind of the Maker* and of the strikingly successful cycle of radio plays, *The Man Born to be King*: and Professor C. S. Lewis, who held the chair of Mediaeval and Renaissance Literature at Cambridge University. Lewis seems to be the only Anglican layman whose sermons have been published and are to be found in the volume, *Transposition and Other Addresses*.[14]

Evangelicals made good use of both Dorothy Sayers and C. S. Lewis because, in fresh style, they restated the cardinal truths of the faith. They tended to ignore T. S. Eliot, mainly because they had, as ever, little taste for good poetry and poetic drama. But by this time, Evangelical Anglicans had at their command some very convincing literature with which to go into battle, earlier having had to be content with the Weymouth (1929) and Moffatt (1935) Bible translations as enlightening aids to preaching the gospel. And soon, they were to be armed with two new 'versions' of the New Testament. One was the Revised Standard Version (Thomas Nelson, New York, 1946) which came as a breath of fresh air acclaimed by Evangelicals and which quickly became a bestseller. The other 'version' was strictly a paraphrase and, initially, made only of the Epistles. It was made by J. B. Phillips and again this was often reprinted (*Letters to Young Churches*, Geoffrey Bles, 1947). C. S. Lewis contributed an excellent introduction in which he sought to answer the ever-present minority who resist change of any kind:

There are several answers to such people. In the first place the kind of objection which they feel to a new translation is very like the objection which was once felt to any English translation at all. Dozens of sincerely pious people in the sixteenth century shuddered at the idea of turning the time-honoured Latin of the Vulgate into our common and (as they thought) 'barbarous' English. A sacred truth seemed to them to have lost its sanctity when it was stripped of polysyllabic Latin, long heard at Mass and at Hours, and put into 'language such as men do use' – language steeped in all the commonplace associations of the nursery, the inn, the stable, and the street.

He went on to emphasise that the Greek of the New Testament is not a 'literary' language:

The same divine humility which decreed that God should become a baby at a peasant-woman's breast, and later an arrested field-preacher in the hands of the Roman police, decreed also that He should be preached in a vulgar, prosaic and unliterary language.

This 'rediscovery', as it were, of the Epistles, placing them in ordinary book form and the similar presentation of the whole of the New Testament in the R.S.V., led to a resurgence of bible reading, even in public places, on the bus and the train. The tide of positive, full-orbed, Bible-based, intellectually satisfying faith was coming in and, in a few years, was to be at the flood. It was fully Evangelical but did not always originate from evangelical minds.

Meanwhile, the ecumenical century was well under way. In 1942 the British Council of Churches had been formed but, three years before, the decision had been taken to form the World Council of Churches. However, the war intervened, delaying the inauguration until 1948. At an earlier stage, there were two branches of world ecumenical activity, known as 'Faith and Order' and 'Life and Work', their concerns being different but harmonious: 'When, in 1938, the decision was taken that the two wings of the ecumenical movement should join together in a World Council of Churches, no doubt at all was felt as to the person who should preside over the Provisional Committee appointed to bring the World Council of Churches into being.'[15]

That man was William Temple, whose sudden death in 1944 was such a blow to the Church of England. He is described as 'the greatest ecumenical personality of this age'. By contrast, the Evangelicals of that day, as a whole, were ill at ease in such an ecumenical environment, feeling, at that relatively early stage of the movement, that the lowest common denominator of doctrine would prevail and, sadly, would preclude emphasis of the fundamentals of the faith. By and large they were right, for the reductionist method has so often characterised the work of the W.C.C. However, the basis of membership agreed was 'Churches which accept our Lord Jesus Christ as God and Saviour', which, with hindsight, ought to have given Evangelicals a good toehold but in practice effective co-operation was found to be difficult and the Ecumenical Conference at Amsterdam in 1948 was sadly unable to find an agreed form of service for the celebration of Holy Communion, so each community held its own service.

All through the years of the Second World War there were significant pointers that the mood of contemporary man was changing from blind optimism and Godless endeavour to a more God-conscious mood. Perhaps it was the imminence, just across the Channel, of a very hostile, ruthless foe or perhaps it was the sense of destiny which the leadership of Winston Churchill engendered or, again, it may have been the horrors of nightly bombing which struck terror into people's hearts:

When the full uncensored history of these years has been written, the survival of this little island within five minutes range of enemy aircraft, surrounded on two sides by enemy occupied territory, and on another by enemy infested ocean, will be something for which no historian who ignored the Law of the Almighty in the affairs of men will be able adequately to account. Let us consider some of the miracles of Divine Providence . . . [16]

Hugh Evan Hopkins was at that time a vicar at Redhill, having earlier served as an I.V.F. travelling secretary. He recalled the words of a godly King in his Christmas broadcast of 1940:

'Put your trust in God as I do . . . ' I said to the man who stood at the gate of the year: 'Give me a light that I may tread safely into the unknown.' and he replied, 'Go out into the darkness and put your hand into the hand of God. That shall be to you better than light and safer than a known way . . . '

In other quarters of the globe where the conflict raged there were godly and positively evangelical men in command; for example, in Malta during that island's darkest hour, General Dobbie, who once said: 'I could not face life without Christ and I pity from the bottom of my heart those who are trying to live without Him', General Wingate with the Chindits in Burma (a somewhat enigmatic figure) and, in the Far East, not always rising above the corruption that surrounded him, General Chiang- Kai-Shek who, in 1938, had broadcast: 'Let us bravely go with Jesus to the Cross, to seek the everlasting peace of mankind and the renewal of our nation.'

Hitler had overrun Europe by the middle of 1940 and the British forces had a miraculous escape from the beaches of Dunkirk. Churchill warned that only relatively few could be safely evacuated but, in the event, most of the men were safely brought home in an Armada of little ships, hurriedly pressed into service, low cloud protecting the evacuation. 'Not only was the sea smooth, but the tide practically stationary, and the task which no-one could anticipate without apprehension became, not a victory but a miraculous deliverance.'[17]

There followed months of anxious waiting for the next blow. Equipment had been left behind in France and England was, in human terms, at the mercy of an all-conquering enemy. But the Hand, which caused the sea to be flat and the tide at a standstill at Dunkirk, was again at work:

After the evacuation, the time Hitler had set beforehand for the invasion (of Britain) was September 16–20 when the tides are such that attempts to swim the Channel used to take place. The weather there is always calm, and there is a harvest moon. But the Unseen Hand intervened, and gales sprung up on the 17th and continued till after the 29th. The invasion boats, collected at many points on the opposite coast, had to be taken into harbours, where they made good targets for the R.A.F., but many were swamped on the way. The Germans then announced that Providence had favoured the British twice and that we were totally unworthy of such favours. We had only to wait for the November and December fogs, for which the Channel is well known, to get our desserts. But, for the first time in living memory, there were no fogs that winter in the Straits.[18]

Meanwhile the Battle of Britain produced our 'finest hour', about which Lord Dowding, of Spiritualist convictions, in command of Fighter Command at the time, commented: 'I say with absolute conviction that I can trace the intervention of God, not only in the battle itself, but in the events that led up to it.'

Surely such events and such sentiments ought to have led to a national revival of the Christian faith centred on redemption theology and the grace of God, to be pioneered by Evangelicals. People were facing death in the United Kingdom as never before or since; 43,667 civilians being killed during the blitz of 1940 and 1941. When all these factors are considered, no minister of the gospel ever had conditions more favourable to the preaching of the message of Christian salvation but no great movement towards God is recorded in the annals of the Church. The Second World War dragged on in the same way as its predecessor but, mercifully, with fewer casualties to Britain on the field of battle.

The passing of the Butler Education Act in 1944 provided for compulsory morning assembly in schools and the leaving age was raised to fifteen (effective from 1947). But more importantly: 'The Christian devotion of teachers, or of parents, could no longer be relied on. Christianity had to be propped up by legislative enactment. The British people were to show that they were more concerned with this world than with the next.'[19]

The erosion of Christian capital from national and family life had continued unchecked since Victorian times. Family prayers were only held by the few, church-going was always on the decline and morality had been sapped by two world wars. Parental influence on children had fallen and the Sunday School movement, at its height in the early years of the twentieth century was on the wane. Compulsory morning assembly was therefore seen as a favourable attempt to restore religious influence on children.

Another world war caused the Church of England to consider the really pressing need that existed to bring the nation, adults and children, to God. The long-awaited findings of the Commission on Evangelism were published in 1945 and called *Towards the Conversion of England* (Church Assembly). It had been a painstaking exercise, with *ad hoc* committees labouring on relevant aspects:

1 Modern Agencies for Evangelistic Propaganda.
2 Evangelism in Advertising.
3 Priests in Industry.
4 The Return of Men and Women from War Service.

Christopher Chavasse of Rochester, chairing the Commission, had done a delicate and difficult job with thoroughness and courage;

From his earliest days Christopher Chavasse viewed the Ministry as primarily evangelistic. Without evangelism the Church must die. This did not mean that he under-valued a pastoral ministry such as that encouraged by the parochial system. Far from it. But he saw the dangers of a pastoral ministry which fed the hungry sheep who looked up to the church and ignored the vast multitude which were too 'fed-up' even to look.[20]

The 172-page report was given a most enthusiastic welcome in the press. At a Press Conference, Chavasse had said: 'First, the adventure of the Church into the field of publicity must stand comparison with the high standard demanded for secular and professional undertakings. Otherwise the Church will only advertise its own 'frowsty' failure and confirm the popular impression that it is out of date.'[21]

After surveying the then current situation, 'moral depravity', humanism, scientific rationalism, too much 'education', scepticism, etc., the report defined 'The Gospel', went on to examine the parts to be played by clergy and laity and then to set out the ways and fields of Evangelism. At its outset, the Report had defined 'Evangelism'; 'To evangelise is so to present Christ Jesus in the power of the Holy Spirit, that men shall come to put their trust in God through Him, to accept him as their Saviour, and serve Him as their King in the fellowship of His Church.'

From an evangelical viewpoint, the report was a masterpiece of clear statement, not only on the needs and means of Evangelism but also on the essential doctrines of the faith, e.g. original sin, the cross, redemption, new birth, conversion, etc. However, there were criticisms voiced by hyper-critical evangelical agencies that the bibliography, lacking as it did, much reference to strictly evangelical writings, only emphasised the paucity of that kind of material available. Evangelicals, apart from the works of someone like D. R. Davies, had, to some extent, to rely on C. S. Lewis for literature. In fact, the report was as near non-sectarian, non-party, as it could possibly be:

But this final view was not shared by numbers of High Churchmen who damned the Report as sectarian and originating exclusively from the Evangelical school. In answer to this charge it was shown that 'of the seven members of the drafting committee four were definitely High Churchmen', and further that the criticism voiced by the Evangelical newspaper the *Record*, with evidence from the Report, pointed to a bias *in the opposite direction* from those objected to by Anglo-Catholics.[22]

These reactions, sadly, only emphasised two immutable facts. One, that many Anglo-Catholics tend to keep outside the mainstream of the Anglican Church, and the other, that Evangelicals come in different shades of opinion, some obstinately refusing ever to be satisfied. For that kind of Evangelical, there are really only two solutions; one, to break away and with kindred spirits form a new denomination or, two, to transfer to a non-episcopal, free-church ministry. Significantly, that trenchant free-church scholar, Dr Nathaniel Micklem had this to say: 'If this report had been issued by the Church of England in the eighteenth century instead of the twentieth there would be no such thing as the Methodist Church today.'[23]

The report was in great demand, being reprinted monthly for eight months. Christopher Chavasse was also much sought after as a speaker and there was a move to appoint him Director of Evangelism in the Church of England. Perhaps the finest sermon he ever preached was in Oxford, on the occasion of the 400th anniversary of the martyrdom of Latimer and Ridley, in 1955:

In a remarkable way the three Oxford martyrs symbolise in their respective persons the three different aspects of the Reformation in England. Cranmer stands not only for the whole religious revolution but also for the ordinary men and women who so largely composed it. The Reformation was first and foremost a popular movement. Nicholas Ridley, Bishop of London, was confessedly the leader of the English reform against Transubstantiation and the Mass, for the Reformation was a movement back to the scriptural and primitive truth. 'Honest' Hugh Latimer was the greatest English preacher of his own and perhaps any day and he was the prophet of the Reformation.

From those Reformation Martyrs has come the Church of England, the Protestant Reformed religion which has expanded into the world-wide Anglican Communion. If the wick of the Reformation candle was the Anglican doctrine of Holy Communion, then the wax of the candle was the Word of God given to every man, woman and child in their mother tongue.[24]

The paucity of evangelical writing in the first half of this century applies, in the main, to the field of apologetics, ethical issues and the communication of the gospel. Also, Evangelicals appeared to have little real appreciation of their position as members of the visible church; at that stage they found the inclusiveness of the Anglican fold too difficult a matter to embrace. However, in the field of doctrine, there had been some substantial contributions. In 1929, *The Atonement in History and in Life* was published (ed. L. W. Grensted, S.P.C.K.), giving a scholarly survey, both biblical and historical, by over a dozen writers, dealing with a subject central to all theology. The final chapter, 'The Preaching of the Cross', was written by Christopher Chavasse, then at Oxford:

as Isaiah proclaimed, the first work of the servant of the Lord was to preach 'Good News' of deliverance to exiles. This work Our Lord, in the synagogue at Nazareth, claimed as being at length fulfilled in Himself, save that the deliverance was a greater one from the bondage of sin. When therefore at Nazareth, He accepted this very word 'Gospel' as expressing his ministry, the context shows that He came to preach 'Good News' to those who were exiles in the 'far country' of alienation from God; and His own description of His redemptive work as a 'ransom for many' is explained from this picture, ever in His mind, of the exiled children of God. The burden of His message was therefore one of Atonement . . .

Another symposium of importance had appeared in 1939 under the title *The Evangelical Doctrine of Holy Communion* (ed. A. J. MacDonald, Heffer). Again the volume was well researched and, both doctrinally and historically, wide ranging. The work concluded:

The present volume is a real contribution to the study of eucharistic doctrine. Such a book is greatly needed. It will help to restore the balance in the sacramental teaching of today, and will do much to refute the charge, sometimes brought against Evangelicals in the Church of England, that they produce few scholars and are uninterested in theology.

Evangelicals, in the decades covered by the chapters of this book so far, tended to be strong in doctrine and they saw their primary duty as keeping the Anglican Church on a straight path in accordance with the Reformed Faith. Other issues, by comparison, did not receive much attention.

Roger Lloyd, the church historian, saw the years 1914 to 1945 as one continuous war, with peace intervening somewhere in the middle but he describes the whole period as 'The Nondescript Years'. This is not a title which should be applied by the Evangelical Anglican for, although there were low patches, a general decline in outward fortune and, from time to time, the bitterness of strife, the Lord God was, as ever, Sovereign over all and was providing the Body of His church with fresh vigour, through youth movements and literary achievements, to counteract the deadening influences of the years of rationalism and liberalism. Towards the end of the inter-war years, Evangelicals were being revived, which meant that, in due course, the whole of the Anglican communion and the Free Churches might well feel the invigorating breath of revival.

6
Towards the Conversion of Many

THE OLD LIBERALISM, through rinsings of humanism represented by a mixture of the League of Nations, St
Martin-in-the-Fields and the ideologies of dictatorship,
was by the end of the Second World War, largely discredited.
Writing at the height of the conflict and then ignorant of atomic
bombs, D. R. Davies made an interesting prophecy regarding
the European Economic Community and spelt out the endless
human dilemma:

> The world never stands still nor remains the same. Being a dynamic creature,
> man will invent new social structures. This will happen anyhow. But the new
> structure, like all the others, will prove to be temporary. Like all the others,
> it will contain within itself the seeds of its own destruction. The new order in
> Europe will be another makeshift solution of man's problem. In no sense will
> it be a radical solution. Of course, it is important that Europe should discover
> the best makeshift that is historically possible. European federation of inde-
> pendent sovereign states will be infinitely better than German hegemony. A
> regional organisation of Europe would be still better than federation of
> sovereignties. All this is of great importance, and the Church should do all
> in her power to bring about the best possible.[1]

Any consideration of theology and the Christian Church in
Britain in the post-war era must include some reference to the
indirect influence of German pastors and theologians, for the
Christian Church in Nazi Germany had experienced a baptism of
fire and had to re-think its position. There was Pastor Niemoller,
a U-boat commander in the First World War, a leading opponent
of Hitler, who was imprisoned for his faith, Dietrich Bonhoeffer,
the rather liberal theologian ('Jesus – the man for others') who
suffered death at the age of thirty-nine for his anti-Hitler
resistance and, in particular, the great Christian prophet, Karl
Barth, who, although a Swiss national (giving him a certain
immunity in Nazi Germany), held academic posts in Germany.
These men and many others, of course, had reacted violently
against the outrageously nationalistic humanism represented by
Nazism and, in all cases, were made to suffer, Niemoller,

Bonhoeffer and Barth to the various limits possible. Karl Barth, refusing to take an oath of allegiance to Hitler, was stripped of his academic positions and moved to Basle. Barth's object was to lead theology away from what he believed to be the fundamentally false outlook of modern religious philosophy, with its positive attitude to science, culture, and art, its sympathy with mysticism and its stress on experience and to bring it back to the principles of the Reformation. It was to be a return to the prophetic teaching of the Bible, of which he believed the Reformers were the most authentic exponents. He was described as the outstanding Protestant theologian, and perhaps the most notable Christian prophet of our times.

What became known as Barthian and Biblical theology had its influence throughout Europe during the war years and later, but Britain was slow to react to the new emphasis, although one can fairly easily discern the sound of many waters running in the decades 1940–60 and spelling out the complete overthrow of the old liberalism, humanism and rationalism. Barth, from his theological position, loathed them all; T. S. Eliot, as the greatest poet of his age, wrote philosophically against them and C. S. Lewis, as a scholar, put the point of view of Christian orthodoxy almost beyond contradiction. They all saw the emptiness of the old hypercritical, barren and destructive doctrines and they were all unconsciously helping Evangelism to its feet. Some feared a return to Fundamentalism, with its unthinking Biblical literalism, whilst others found fault with Karl Barth, who was, at the very least, a most disturbing element at the end of a theologically difficult age, at a crisis point in history itself, when Adolf Hitler threatened a new Dark Age in Europe. In the thirties, Barth had introduced 'The Theology of the Word of God' and it helped parts of the German church, at least, to resist the dominance of Nazism. It also helped to lay the foundations of revived evangelical scholarship which was seen in the fifties.

In the war years, however, Evangelicals hardly knew what to make of the new Barthian and Biblical theology and we find a very ambivalent attitude in the early publishing programme of the Inter-Varsity Fellowship. T. C. Hammond stated:

The Reformed Theology, which Barth conceives himself to adopt, is, in the words of the same writer, 'the clear antithesis to that form of teaching which declares that man himself possesses the capacity and the power to inform himself about God, the world and man'. It seems, then, as if a Barthian would regard the preceding pages as 'nothing but the more extraordinary

74

puffs of our own genius.' It may be so. At any rate, it would be dangerous to allow so stout an opponent to remain unassailed in our rear.[2]

Perhaps T. C. Hammond had in mind the anonymous wag who said that 'Theology was created in Germany, corrected in Scotland, abased in England and corrupted in North America.' His book was subtitled *A Christian Introduction to Apologetics* and represented almost the first scholarly evangelical attempt to grapple with a wide range of current theological, philosophical and scientific questions. It was long overdue.

Karl Barth had been a prodigious writer through the thirties and most of his works had been published in English. All through the war years and later he thundered his denunciation of Christians accommodating to the dictates of the State and in 1954, a collection of his post-war writings was, at last, very well received in this country. He bewailed the inability of the Christian Churches to have any great influence: 'It is a simple fact that the Christian Churches have not achieved this, nor has this been the meaning of their existence. Hitherto, no great light has proceeded forth from them to pierce the gloom of a Europe in decline.'[3] He insisted that the Christian Message for Europe in 1946 should be understood in 'the school of the Bible' and that the gospel of Jesus Christ was 'of free grace'.

It was difficult to categorise Karl Barth as an exact Evangelical but his magisterial style contributed markedly to the upsurge of the new Biblical orthodoxy and he was part of that steady stream of Christians which led, inexorably, to the resurgence of Evangelical Anglicanism in Britain. Sadly, Evangelicals tended to look for the flaws in Barth, as also they looked for the flaws in C. S. Lewis or J. B. Phillips. Some, alas, were prepared to write off anyone with a doctrinal 'hair out of place'. In England, they did not go so far as the Fundamentalists in America who held Bible-burning demonstrations when the Revised Standard Version of the Bible was published. Evangelicals as a whole always have a hard task in satisfying all who call themselves by that name. And as for their styles of preaching, they can range from the expository, graciously persuasive, intellectually viable to the dragooning, almost bullying 'take it or leave it' *attack*, where congregations may be forgiven for wanting to crawl under the pews for refuge. 'Faithfulness to the Word of God' is sometimes an excuse for being obtuse, very unattractive and even rude.

In May 1945, the Second World War had ended in Europe and, in August, following the dropping of the horrendous atomic bombs on Nagasaki and Hiroshima in Japan, peace was signed in the Far East. And so, civilisation, in its forward march, had carried with it the fashions of war. Within a few centuries, the development of the armaments industry from cannon balls to atomic bombs showed the awful potential latent within the process of scientific discovery. The mushroom clouds following the explosions of that summer of 1945 not only represented present destruction and the prospect of a coerced peace, but were to remain as a Damoclean threat still hanging over the whole world following the end of the Second World War.

Once, the Church was a check on human infallibility but when the Protestant Reformation in Europe threw off the papal yoke, that check vanished, as Davies points out. There followed four or five hundred years of human progress (or so some would claim) since the Renaissance inaugurated a period of development and human confidence, coupled with the neglect of divine rule. Eventually, nothing was thought to be beyond human reach and at the height of Victorian arrogance, Swinburne sang:

> Glory to Man in the highest!
> For Man is the master of things.

His contemporary, W. E. Henley, echoed his viewpoint in celebrating human competence:

> I am the master of my fate:
> I am the captain of my soul.

Whereas medieval Europe had been dominated by the Church, modern Europe was now ruled by an uneasy alliance of dictatorship, capitalism, communism and social democracy, with the Christian Church, Catholic and Protestant, forced to take a back seat, the mystique of politicians and bankers mesmerising the mind of modern man and the thin voice of Protestantism hardly heard.

And so, after six years of total war, in 1945 the Churches tried to get back to normal but, as people fought their way through shortages of food, fuel and furniture, the mood of Britain was one of frustration and disappointment. Spiritual capital had run low, traditional Christian morality had steeply declined and the age of the 'couldn't care less' had arrived. By 1947, divorces in the U.K. had risen by over 400 per cent compared with the 1938 figure. Meanwhile, T.V. and the 'fridge' were rapidly becoming household essentials and many saw the Welfare State as ushering in, with all the benefits, a decline in personal responsibility. The Anglican Church, Evangelicals included, had its back to the wall. However, although few Evangelicals could expect to be appointed to the archdeaconry or the episcopacy, at the centre of evangelical life in the West End of London, at All Souls, Langham Place, a curate was appointed in 1945 who was in due course to make a unique contribution to Evangelical Anglicanism; his name was John Robert Walmsley Stott. This young man of patrician charm became very popular at All Souls and when his vicar died in 1950, the unusual step was taken of appointing his twenty-nine year-old curate Rector of this famous church. The future of Evangelical Anglicans was so incredibly influenced by this persuasive and clear-sighted expositor of the Word of God (an Evangelical rather than an Anglican states-man), that the record of the next four decades must include very frequent reference to the work of John Stott.

In these immediately post-war years the stage of positive Evangelism was held by Tom Rees, not himself an Anglican but he attracted many Evangelicals of all denominations to his Saturday rallies at the Albert Hall in London. This went on for several years into the early fifties and was the means of many hundreds being won to the faith. The Evangelist, with his wife Jean, also founded Hildenborough Hall in Kent, a conference centre catering mainly for young people.

The need for Evangelism was commonly agreed by Christians but somehow little was actually being achieved. Writing of Bishop Christopher Chavasse in 1950, his biographer recalls:

Five years had gone by since the publication of the Report, 'Towards the Conversion of England', and his heart was heavy with disappointment. 'The laity', he said, 'not only accepted their responsibility, but even made valiant attempts to fulfil it. Their efforts, however, have so far proved abortive; partly because that quickened quality of spiritual life, essential for successful evangelism, has not yet been attained by a sufficient number of church worshippers, and partly because between the wars, we allowed to grow up a whole generation of church people ignorant of their Bibles and the fundamental doctrines of their faith.' But behind all that was the failure of the central authority of the Church of England to implement that section of the report which was designed to soften up the hard core of materialism and secularism through the use of mass media of communication. Not even a million pence of the million pounds proposed had been spent on advertising during the five years since the acceptance of the report.[4]

However disenchanted Christopher Chavasse, in one sense the leading Evangelical, was with the progress of Evangelism on a national scale, it was not for want of a general consciousness of the desperate need of the nation for turning to Jesus Christ which prevented any move from taking place. Indeed, the Lambeth Conference of 1948 focussed its attention on this very subject:

The supreme task of the Church today is to win the nations of Christendom back to the knowledge of God . . . and to take the good news to those who have not yet heard it. We call upon our people to engage in this campaign and to put themselves in training for it. God, in His mercy, has given to us in our conference a clearer vision of His will and purpose for His Church and of its mission in the world. To these we bid you dedicate yourselves.[5]

It is difficult to see why Evangelicals did not rise to the occasion and take the initiative on Evangelism. Were they so concerned with preserving their own purity of doctrine that they feared co-operation even in a matter on which they were leaders of the field, that of taking the gospel to the people? Or were they so occupied with their own 'parochial' affairs that they could have no time to spare for the higher counsels of the church? A positive answer to both of these questions must be near the truth.

There were some who queried whether the parochial system of reaching people was any longer valid and whether concentration of effort in specifically chosen and equipped centres was possibly the answer. Roger Lloyd:

But such large areas of modern life had moved out of their ken and reach, and their work had to be supplemented by an ever increasing number and variety of non-parochial ministries. Every year that passed made more plain the really acid fact that in every industrial centre, whatever the parish church did, whatever experiment it tried, however heroic the sacrifices of its people, the mass of 'the working class' would quite certainly and depressingly fail to respond in any significant way.[6]

There was one man at the centre of the Church's life who was unwilling to sit down under the difficulties of expanding the influence of the Christian faith by means of the parochial type of mission and that was Bishop William Wand of London, who mounted his Mission to London in 1949. For his 700 churches, he commissioned 155 missioners drawn from all over the country, he wrote the leading article in the *Evening News* for a week and, led by the band of the Royal Marines, he held a service at the Ideal Home Exhibition at Olympia, with Lord Rothermere of *The Daily Mail* giving it enthusiastic support. An Anglo-

Catholic, Wand set the Evangelical Anglicans a lesson in evangelistic fervour. But it has to be recorded that the mission had very little effect on the mass of unbelievers in the capital city. The faithful were drawn together and encouraged and some lapsed church members were wooed back into active life:

Nevertheless, in the calmly judicious perspectives of history, the Mission to London of 1949 was of great and real importance. Its timing gave it its significance. For too long the Church had supped the diet of failure and accepted the definitions of impotence. Here was a demonstration, staged in the battered capital city of the country, that church people had faith in the Gospel and in their mission to proclaim it, and that they did not intend to sit down tamely before the reproaches of paralysis. They could still organise a giant undertaking and carry it through. But above all it was a testimony to the faith, the courage, and the power of leadership of a great bishop, who was also a scholar and a prophet. (Roger Lloyd)[7]

Had the Anglican Church so lost its hold on the hearts of the people that, humanly speaking, no amount of internal effort was likely to reach the masses outside? Was some new bridge required to link the 'couldn't care less', easygoing firesides with the Gospel of the love of God in Christ Jesus? Was it necessary that an Evangelist should arrive on the scene, 'untainted', as it were, by the old traditions, one who could come to the life of Britain almost from another planet, speaking in tones unheard before from the pulpits of the land? The following years were, in fact, to unfold the answers to these questions and to show how new (yet old) methods of preaching could carry the unchanging Gospel to the hearts and lives of people caught up in the luxuries and tensions of the twentieth century.

Professor Arnold Toynbee, giving the Reith Lectures in 1952, described Britain as a 'post-Christian Society' but many 'God-shaped blanks' existed in the heart of man which man could not fill or even understand. In T. S. Eliot's *The Cocktail Party*, which he wrote in 1949, one of his characters (Celia) said:

'It's not the feeling of anything I've ever done
Which I might get away from, or of anything in me
I could get rid of – but of emptiness, or failure
Towards someone, or something, outside of myself:
And I feel I must – atone – is that the word?'

Man's sense of need often went unexpressed and almost always unresolved. What could take up the challenge; what, if anything, replace the Christian answer, from which people had turned away? Moral Rearmament, originally known as the Oxford Group when it came to birth under Frank Buchman in 1929, captured the minds of a good number of upper-middle-class individuals and exercised an influence greater than its numerical strength. Evangelicals generally rejected M.R.A. because it lacked doctrinal emphasis, concentrating rather on 'absolute honesty, absolute purity', etc. Oddly enough, Buchman had been converted at the Keswick Convention, twenty years before the Oxford Group took off under his leadership. In 1946 and in the following years an international assembly of M.R.A. was held at Caux in Switzerland. They spoke of being 'changed' and glossed over conversion to Jesus Christ and the necessity of the atonement.

Communism, in the post-war period, was seen as the great enemy of Christianity and Evangelicals were quick to react in seeking information on the exact nature of the Marxist faith. The Korean war was started by the Communists in 1950 and the United Nations Organisation, born in hope, to succeed the League of Nations at the end of the Second World War, was quickly put to the test. Berlin had been blockaded and the Christian way of life, for so long championed in the West, was seen in direct opposition to the tyranny of Communism, which deported millions to the slave-camps of Siberia.

Evangelicals prayed for revival, for they knew it had to come, if it were to come at all, from within the church. A revival of belief, a spreading of the flame of Christian testimony, with a consequent warming of the hearts of Christian people, was recognised as the only answer to the spread, world-wide, of militant, yet insidious, Communism. Spiritually breathless after the exhaustion of war, the Christian Church realised only too well the need to recover the lost ground but, sadly, little had come, either from Evangelicals or others, in response to the evangelistic call of the 1948 Lambeth Conference and the 1949 Mission to London. 'But immediately after a major war no Church can be filled with creative vigour. Before even the wind of God can blow right through it, there must be a preliminary period of reconstruction to correct the consequences of so giant a disturbance and a time of convalescent repose to heal bruised spirits.' (Roger Lloyd)[8]

Outwardly, the resources of the Anglican Church appeared to have declined quite sharply in the first half of the century. The following figures speak for themselves:

	Population (millions)	Clergy	New ordinations
1900	32	20,000	585
1949	45	15,000	362

To add to the picture, it must be said that the laity, although doing great work as churchwardens, Sunday School teachers and treasurers, were not yet being involved in the total ministry of the local church. The day of the lay elder and the pastoral team was still a long way off and Evangelicals had not yet been able to exercise a decisive influence on the way in which the local Christian community might permeate society.

The year 1948 saw the first meeting of the long-heralded World Council of Churches. This was opened in prayer by the new Archbishop of Canterbury, Geoffrey Fisher, and membership of the Council had, as its basis, confession of Jesus Christ as God and Saviour.

In this ecumenical setting, the Anglican Churches are sometimes seen to advantage as 'par excellence' the ecumenical Churches. With their own diversity and variety of tradition, they reach out in all directions, can find themselves at home with all manner of Churches and can to some extent serve as interpreters to one another of widely divided Churches both within and outside the ecumenical fellowship.[9]

Many have regarded the inclusiveness or comprehensiveness of Anglicanism as part of her spiritual glory but in the early days of the World Council of Churches Evangelicals, whilst gladly remaining members of the Anglican fold, were unable to make anything like a real contribution to ecumenical work and nearly twenty years were to elapse before they were able to see any real good in their non-Evangelical brethren. This inability derived from what was known as the siege mentality, the attitude of a depressed minority and the viewpoint which sees the necessity of subscribing to every punctilio of belief before a working agreement can be entered into. So long as this outlook persisted, there was little chance of Evangelicals becoming a really effective force in Anglicanism itself; thus they were ignored by main stream Anglicans as being unconcerned with the fate and future of their church. They were often 'black-listed'.

One of the most remarkable converts to the Christian faith of the post-war era was Professor C. E. M. Joad. Like so many of his generation, he travelled the road of faith in man's own ability to improve himself as civilisation progressed but he admitted:

It was because we rejected the doctrine of original sin that we on the Left were always being disappointed, disappointed by the refusal of people to be reasonable, by the subservience of intellect to emotion, by the failure of true socialism to arrive, by the behaviour of nations and politicians, by the masses' preference for Hollywood to Shakespeare and for Mr Sinatra to Beethoven; above all, by the recurrent fact of war.[10]

The year before the publication of this book, in which he traced his journey from atheism to Christian belief, he had written an article in the *New Statesman* which he entitled 'The Twilight of the Church'. He expressed alarm that the membership of the Church of England had declined from 3.39 million in 1939 to under 3 million in 1951 and after enumerating the acids of modernity he concluded: 'The church cannot, without absurdity, accommodate itself to all these changes. It cannot veer with every wind that blows from the laboratories.'

Joad was another example of the new intellectual Christian who was to lead powerful philosophical arguments for the rejection of Marxism, humanism and scientific rationalism. Initially, like so many of his generation, he had been bemused by the easy answers of George Bernard Shaw and had pinned his hopes on the cure of all social ills by a redistribution of wealth. Then he started going to church again, as if to return nostalgically to the words of the Bible and the Prayer Book and he was very considerably influenced by the writings of C. S. Lewis. In listing the ills of the Anglican Church to which he returned late in life as a new believer, he expressed great concern about the doctrinal decline of the church's ministry:

It is not clear what the Church of England today believes. In particular, there is a feeling that for years she has been fighting a losing battle against science, surrendering decade by decade under the growing pressure from science a few more positions, positions insisted upon in the past with passionate intensity as strongholds of the faith. That the elasticity and vagueness of the Church's creed have played no small part in the decline of its influence, the comparative popularity of the Roman Catholic Church which has made few, if any concessions to 'the spirit of the times' and has withstood the challenge from science, convincingly demonstrates. The Church of England, on the other hand, loses both of the swings of belief and the roundabouts of doubt.[11]

With Joad it was also his own personal failure, the inability to come to terms with life by himself that led him to recognise original sin as a fact, the need for Divine grace, forgiveness and power in Jesus Christ, the Son of God. With a charming modesty he described how he became a Christian of a very orthodox kind when, after doubts and hesitations, he became 'the diffident and halting Christian that I am'.

Dr Joad was not to be described as a 'precise' Evangelical but he affirmed the central doctrines of original sin and personal redemption in Jesus Christ as Saviour, Lord and God. Evangelicals rejoiced at his conversion, quoting from his writing on many occasions and seeing in him yet another welcome testimony to the failure of scientific rationalism and dialectical materialism, which had so captured the hearts of the intellectuals during the earlier years of the twentieth century. It seemed as if, one way and another, the path was being prepared for a dynamic upsurge, in the next thirty years, of the truths for which Evangelicals had always stood but which, either through a failure of nerve or through lack of vision, they had been unable previously to emphasise sufficiently at national level.

As if to revive a post-war Britain from the aftermath of war, 'The Festival of Britain' took place in 1951 and once again the evangelical voice of Christopher Chavasse was raised to insist on a Christian presence or witness for the event:

The Crystal Palace a hundred years earlier was built, he said, to house the arts and crafts of all nations, to show they all belonged to the same big family, for trade had become international. That was a time when British Christianity was at its height. But the present generation neither worshipped nor had faith. The churchmen of Rochester Diocese would during the festival year wear a silver cross on the lapel of their coats as a witness to that forgotten faith. At the same time the Church would see to it that the Festival would, *indeed*, show to the world the English way of life. It would be treachery to the British if that way of life was to be demonstrated to the world and including a fun-fair on Sundays, or if no place of prominence were given to the Bible. The British had been, in the classic phrase of the historian J. R. Green, 'the people of a Book, and that Book the Bible . . .'[12]

There is always a vociferous, backward-looking, hard-line element in Evangelicalism. It finds it difficult to co-operate and non-Evangelicals sometimes say that Evangelicals lack any empathy for their fellow Christians. This manifests itself in a failure to see the good points in another's make-up, in an inability to make the best of situations and in a consequent failure to seize on points of agreement as an opportunity to move forward in the fellowship of the Gospel. 'Come ye out from among them' has been the war cry. At worst, Evangelicalism is always meeting trouble half way and is disappointed, almost, if there is no battle. It combines all the worst elements of Puritanism with a rigid, legalistic attitude on liturgical and ecclesiastical matters. Happily, there are not now many 'hard-liners' left in Evangelical Anglicanism but in the early fifties and just after the Second World War they were still very much in evidence. Evangelicals lacked statesmen of the quality of Bishop Ryle of Liverpool and Bishop Knox of Manchester and they had to await the full arrival on the scene as a non-episcopal evangelical statesman of world-wide acceptance in the person of John Stott. Furthermore, Billy Graham, with all his American Southern Baptist overtones, was able, later on, to unify all the conflicting elements, apart from the Anglo-Catholic, in the spread of the Evangel and, in seemingly small ways, he infiltrated some of the unthinking rigidity of Evangelicals. Ruth Graham, his wife, arrived in England wearing make-up, so that became an immediately acceptable practice with evangelicals and when Graham quoted from *The Sunday Times*, Sunday papers (printed on Saturday, of course) became evangelically 'legalised'. Gradually the ungracious, hypercritical and insensitive attitudes of earlier generations of Evangelicals were being superceded, making them more loving, more gracious, more reasonable and, indeed, more Christian.

7
Flood-Tide of Evangelism

N O ACCOUNT of Evangelical Anglicans would be complete without reference to a man who left his imprint on the Anglican Communion through his work as an Englishman abroad and his name was Howard Mowll, Archbishop of Sydney and Primate of Australia. He was a man of massive proportions and commanding presence, as a young man president of the Cambridge Inter-Collegiate Christian Union, appointed Assistant Bishop of Western China at the age of thirty-two, Bishop of Western China at thirty-six and Archbishop of Sydney at forty-four. From his early days at Cambridge, he was always in great demand and he had the largeness of heart to match his frame. His fellow Australian bishops elected him as their Primate in 1957 when he was fifty-eight. Those were days when the diocese of Sydney had a habit, happily now overcome, of inviting to senior evangelical episcopal positions, Englishmen rather than Australians.

Rather more than either Bishop Chavasse of Liverpool or Bishop Knox of Manchester, both strong Evangelicals themselves, Howard Mowll commanded world-wide esteem among Anglicans and, of course, among Evangelicals:

There have been few who have spent so little of their working lives in England, yet have exercised so much influence on the Evangelical movement and on individual people at home. He so lived that he is greatly missed by people in all kinds of situations, both public and unsuspected. Bishop Moule of Durham was from 1900 until his death in 1920 the foremost figure in the mind of Evangelical churchmen in all parts of the world; Bishop Taylor Smith held this high honour after his death until he too died in 1938. Archbishop Mowll was the true heir to Handley Moule and John Taylor Smith in the twenty years from 1938 until his death in 1958. Both men had been his friends, men whom he had known and loved from his days at Cambridge; and he sought to follow them as they had followed the Lord. He came naturally and yet unconsciously to be to his generation what they had been to theirs.[1]

So compelling was his personality that, just before his ordination, there were clergy almost falling out with each other over obtaining his services and one lady going so far as to say that she would pay for a new curate but only if it were to be Howard Mowll! Ten days before he sailed for Canada he was ordained by Bishop Knox, with both Bishop Chavasse and Bishop Moule expressing their personal interest and good wishes. In China he married a missionary of his own age but, to their intense regret, they remained childless. However, they threw themselves into every work which came to their hands. Becoming Archbishop of Sydney in 1933, he attended the opening of the first meeting of the World Council of Churches in 1948 and he became an enthusiastic supporter of the movement in Australia. In a letter, he had written:

Some Christian people are frankly apprehensive about this whole move-ment. They fear that the basis of membership is not sufficiently Biblical. I would remind them what the basis is: a fellowship of Churches which accept our Lord Jesus Christ as God and Saviour. No one could listen to the addresses at Amsterdam without being impressed by the fact that they were each in their own way Bible expositions, with their emphasis on man's need of redemption and the offer of forgiveness, the necessity of judgment and the certainty of victory.[2]

Howard Mowll had listened to outstanding addresses by Karl Barth and C. H. Dodd, among others. His interest, however, was mainly in the missionary emphasis of the original W.C.C. meet-ings. Nevertheless, he attended the Central Committee meeting of the Council held in India in 1952 and combined this with an extensive missionary tour, embracing Malaya and Borneo as well as India. He was President of the Australian Council of the W.C.C. from 1946 to 1951 and for other periods. When not president, he was chairman of the Executive Committee.

Although a wholly committed Evangelical and a thorough-going Anglican, Howard Mowll found acceptance with a wide variety of churchmen and dignitaries in different walks of life. In the interdenominational circles of the Scripture Union he was made president on the death of John Taylor Smith:

He had a real love for colour and pageantry, and could not bear signs of drab or tawdry worship. Ritual and ceremonial were for him largely matters of taste, unless they had significance from a doctrinal point of view, and he was not averse to the ornate if it increased the sense of reverence and dignity in man's approach to God. But an act or form of worship which had a long record of theology and controversy behind it could not be placed on the same level. The test which he applied was shrewd, direct and practical; the one thing he wished to know was whether the doctrine behind the ceremony touched the honour of Christ. It was for this reason that the Eucharistic vestments were quite foreign to him, an extreme simplicity marked his conduct in a service . . . he never took the Eastward Position.[3]

Howard Mowll was as popular with Evangelicals in his generation as John Taylor Smith had been in his and, when he died in 1958, he had no obvious successor on the Anglican Episcopal scene.

During the rising tide of evangelistic emphasis which characterised the periods after the Second World War and which found its origins in a consciousness of the ground lost by the Church in the recent decades, the Archbishop of York, Cyril Garbett, gave a strong lead just five years after the 1948 Lambeth Conference with its emphasis on Evangelism:

In the struggle for the extension of the Kingdom of God the parishes are in the front line. If in the churches prayers were said regularly for the conversion of the people of the parish . . . if the Church Council gave time for discussion of plans for evangelism in their own parish, and its members went away with a real determination to work for its conversion, the good news of God and His love would presently spread.[4]

In answering the question 'What is our Good News', Cyril Garbett had outlined the four great truths which had to be proclaimed. First, the fact and love of God, His Lordship and power; second, man's recurrent failure is due to his inability, of himself, to resist evil; third, 'the Risen Christ' and fourth, the visible fellowship.

It might seem that the apparent failure of *Towards the Conversion of England* (1945), the call of the Lambeth Conference (1948), the Mission to London (1949) and Cyril Garbett's book (1953) were leading the whole Church (not just the Church of England) to the moment of evangelistic truth which was to come with the Billy Graham Crusades of 1954–67. God's answer was to come in a wholly unexpected way. On 20 March 1952, the American Evangelist had addressed leading Evangelicals in Church House, Westminster, and spelt out the needs, in no uncertain terms, for revival:

It was in the autumn of 1949 that Graham first attained prominence in the religious life of America. At this time his campaign in Los Angeles, originally planned for three weeks and then stretching into eight weeks with a total attendance of 350,000 people, stirred America to the realisation that a national revival was no longer a vague possibility.[5]

His personality appeared striking but not strident, emphatic but not in the least arrogant. He was thirty-five. 'The evangelist himself [was] – a young man, tall, virile, winsome, highly intelligent, genuinely humble, utterly sincere, whose gifted personality is wholly dedicated to the service of the Lord.'[6]

It was this man, without any of the authority and panoply of Anglicanism, with his decidedly American charm and a powerful Biblical emphasis, a loyal supporter of the World Council of Churches (although his Church was not), who completely captivated the hearts and minds of that influential audience in Church House, Westminster, and accordingly, a major evangelistic crusade was arranged for the spring of 1954. The chairman of the executive committee appointed to look after the 'Billy Graham Greater London Crusade' was Major-General D. J. Wilson-Haffenden, Financial Secretary of the Church Missionary Society. Leading Anglican supporters of the mission were Bishop Hugh Gough of Barking, Canon Tom Livermore of Morden, Canon Frank Colquhoun of Wallington and Maurice Wood, the present Bishop of Norwich, then Rural Dean of Islington and later principal of Oak Hill College. As the mission progressed, more and more Anglicans in high places were found on the platform and coach loads of church people from a very wide area, with their friends, came to the Harringay Arena. To quote John Pollock:

The year 1954 lifted the Billy Graham ministry to a new level through the historic events of Harringay Arena. Few who lived in England at that time can forget the atmosphere that came over the land. The Greater London Crusade, opened under suspicion and opposed by the press, ended three months later with Graham flanked by the Archbishop of Canterbury and the Lord Mayor of London in the largest outdoor stadium, as he preached the same unaffected gospel message.[7]

The 'All Scotland Crusade' took place in 1955 along with a return to London but this time to the Wembley Arena.

Too many churches, however, held back, debating the pros and cons of this evangelism instead of recognising their own opportunity. Had they grasped it, the sixties might have been as different for Britain nationally, despite the flooding in of secularism, as they were for the thousands who through the Crusades of 1954–5 found faith or vocation (the number of ordinands and missionary recruits shot up in the years following Harringay and Kelvin Hall).[8]

In no way was Billy Graham a self-assured man and he commenced his campaign at Harringay with all the natural concern of an ordinary or extraordinary man before a big occasion. However, two U.S. Senators, Stuart Symington and Styles Bridges, supported the Evangelist on the opening night:

And 'on the platform', he later exulted, 'were bishops of the Anglican Church and religious leaders from all over Britain. In the audience were members of Parliament and other leaders of British life . . . ' Over his next three months there, this accumulation of ranking converts included the First Sea Lord and the Chief of Naval Staff, the Admiral of the Fleet, and Sir John Hunt, leader of Hillary's Everest conquest the year before.[9]

Christianity became, for once, headline news; all the daily papers carried a review of the Crusade and men and women talked openly about hearing Billy Graham. The Archbishop of Canterbury, after one evening service, felt moved to comment, 'We'll never see such a sight again until we get to Heaven.'

Billy Graham was invited to meet the Queen Mother at Clarence House and then to have tea at Windsor Castle with the Queen herself, signalling the beginning of a friendship which was to last until the present time. Eventually, he had an audience with the Prime Minister, Sir Winston Churchill, then aged seventy-eight and by that time, a rather grumpy, irritable old man, in what Marshall Frady describes as 'that dim moroseness of his life's final long winter'.

An assessment of the evangelistic crusades of Billy Graham in Great Britain is no easy matter but in a quite dramatic way he captured the popular imagination, drew enormous crowds, enlisted the active support of very many churches of different denominations and was widely reported by the national newspapers. When asked how many converts resulted, Billy Graham found estimates difficult to make, as it was the number of *inquirers*, rather than converts to the faith, that was known. On the first night at Harringay 178 inquirers came forward and, after three months, counselling had been given to a total of 36,431:

Of these, approximately 75% were recorded as having made a first-time decision – that is acceptance of Christ as Saviour. The remaining 25% made other decisions, of which three were specified on the record card, Assurance of salvation, Reaffirmation of faith and Dedication of life.

Approximately 35% were men, 65% women. In both groups, just over half were young people under the age of 19, the largest age-group being, as one would expect, the 12–18. In the next age group (19–29) the number of men averaged 18% of the total, the number of women 15%. Those over 50 who recorded decisions varied week by week from 5% to 8% of the total.[10]

Billy Graham had insisted at the outset of 'Harringay' that his Evangelism must be church orientated and every inquirer without a church allegiance was passed on to a local church. About 90 per cent of those counselled claimed some connexion with a church although many of those could not remember the name of its minister. Inevitably, Anglican churches benefited most from the Crusade and a number of bishops expressed whole-hearted approval, among them being the Bishop of London, J. W. C. Wand, whose mission five years earlier had been such a bold and courageous idea, without yielding the results hoped for. He wrote in his diocesan magazine:

His aim was simple, to stab people broad awake, to make them face eternal values and to respond to the challenge of Christ. That this is not enough from the point of view of the church goes without saying. We tried to take people much further in our own Mission to London. But it is an essential first step and I never heard of any missioner who did not begin there.[11]

Christopher Chavasse of Rochester was another bishop who endorsed the Crusade, doubtless reflecting on his high hopes of Evangelism on a big scale expressed in *Towards the Conversion of England*, published nine years earlier. He wrote:

But it is the staggering response to the Mission which has been so striking. It shows that multitudes who are only on the fringe of the churches, and more especially young people (for remember that young people formed the majority of those who came forward after the meeting to yield their lives to Christ), are realising increasingly that in a world of wars and atom bombs God and His way are the only hope.[12]

Other enthusiastic bishops were C. A. Martin of Liverpool and P. M. Herbert of Norwich apart from H. R. Gough of Barking, who had been at the heart of things throughout.

Sir John Betjeman wrote appreciatively in the *Spectator* and Beverley Nichols, one of the most widely read journalists of his day, wrote in glowing terms in the *Sunday Chronicle*:

My Christianity is not an antiquarian luxury, it is a 20th century necessity. If the Gospels can't be translated into the slang of the street-corner then we might as well leave them to gather dust on the shelves of the library. And if Jesus is not a contemporary figure, he is nothing.[13]

One of the criticisms levelled at Billy Graham was that his message was merely 'fundamentalist'. In a few years, this word became the centre of a hot debate but it was, at that time, associated in English minds with an unthinking form of American 'bible-punching', 'hot-gospelling' and, inevitably, the opponents of Graham were quick to pin this label to him. 'Graham's fundamentalism was, by and large, the fundamentalism of the New Testament itself, with its sustained emphasis upon the deadly reality of sin, the saving and all-sufficient work of the cross, and the transforming quality of the new life in Christ and in the Church.'[14]

The final service of the three month long 1954 Crusade, with nightly attendance rarely falling below about 12,000, had to be held in Wembley Stadium, where 120,000 assembled. The Archbishop of Canterbury, Dr Geoffrey Fisher, attended and gave the blessing.

Almost incredibly, the recommendation, never carried out, in *Towards the Conversion of England*, that a large-scale publicity campaign be mounted, costing one million pounds, was, in fact, part and parcel of the Crusade and demonstrated the undoubted need to employ the media in any such venture. The actual advertising budget was, in fact, only just over £50,000.

One of the most spectacular converts at Harringay was the actress Joan Winmill who, for two years, played a leading role in 'The Chiltern Hundreds'. It so happened that on the particular evening Dale Evans, wife of Roy Rogers the cowboy film star, was giving her testimony and after Miss Winmill had gone forward, she was led into faith by Ruth Graham, one of the counsellors. Miss Winmill later played a leading part in the feature film produced by the Billy Graham Organisation, entitled 'Souls in Conflict'. Another very colourful convert at Harringay was Ernest Shippam, head of the world-famous meat and fish paste company. In a B.B.C. 'Lift up your Hearts' broadcast in 1960 he said:

At that time there were shameful things in my life, which I seemed powerless to eradicate. My home was unhappy; our business was my god; my church-going was merely in the pattern of my social life. Events led me to hear Billy Graham at Harringay. All I can actually remember him saying was this, 'If Christ could carry His cross to Calvary for you, can't you trust him with everything you have got?' The Holy Spirit made me realise my need. In a flash I saw what my life was like – and it was pretty rotten; and at that moment seeing the tremendous love of Christ for me, He also filled my heart with such love and trust for Him that I committed all to Him. It was an act of absolute and complete yielding to Christ.[15]

Such real-life stories could be multiplied many times and in answer to the question, so often asked, as to whether converts stand the test of time, Billy Graham was careful to point to the truth of the parable of the sower which, he contended, was still a true reflection of the reception of the Gospel. But a new openness, a new movement of the Holy Spirit had begun which was to eddy out to the furthest corners of the universal church, which was to make Evangelism a possible rather than an unlikely church activity and which, for some years, was to produce a new mood of active co-operation at least among all Evangelicals. John Pollock said, 'Billy Graham had released Britons from their reticence; it suddenly became easy to talk about religion. Tongue-tied English Christians had the opportunity of their lives, clergymen visiting in their parishes found that small talk vanished quickly. Billy Graham was the topic in homes, as in factories, clubs and public houses.'[16]

On B.B.C. 'Panorama', Malcolm Muggeridge described his reactions to Harringay and the closing moments of a service:

One or two first, and then the movement gathering momentum, as the choir sings quietly. I looked at their faces, so varied, so serious, and for me this was far and away the most moving part of the proceedings . . . This movement . . . gave every indication of being spontaneous and sincere, and the faces of the people gathered under the platform were touching in their sincerity and intentness.[17]

However, there was an element of seeming tragedy in the Billy Graham Crusades in Britain for, although they were well received by the press and the public at large, well supported by many churches, with over 80 per cent of the London churches backing the Crusades, the momentum could not be sustained. The Archbishop of Canterbury, Geoffrey Fisher, in anticipating the Coronation of Queen Elizabeth in 1953, had expressed the hope a year before that the reign of a new Elizabeth would usher in another Reformation similar in blessing to that brought about by the earlier Reformation. Everything pointed to such a possibility – men like Wand, Chavasse and Garbett had endeavoured to lead the Church of England in the direction of revival and conversion and here, within a decade of the earlier hopes, was a Christian mission the results of which far exceeded the hopes of all Christians. A year after Wembley, the Bishop of Chichester, G. K. A. Bell, one of the Church of England's most powerful ecumenical advocates, somewhat wistfully expressed conviction and hope that a new movement had begun. He told the American journalist Stanley High of *Reader's Digest* that:

of Billy Graham's great and enduring service to our country there can be little doubt. Spiritually, England was waiting for such a challenge. There are evidences all about, many in my own diocese, that clergy and laymen have been aroused by that challenge and that the message of the church to the nation is being given new force and authority.[18]

After the Billy Graham Crusades, not unnaturally an evaluation was attempted by all kinds of religious people and most certainly the Christian gospel and its proclamation was invested with greater possibilities and extra courage. Clifford Martin, who was Bishop of Liverpool from 1944 until 1966, when he was succeeded by Stuart Blanch, spoke of 'the general interest which the campaigns have aroused among people generally', and he went on: 'For example, members of business men's clubs are now willing to talk religion in a way that they were unlikely to do before.'

Undoubtedly, there were those Anglicans who felt a degree of shame that the Graham Crusades had been necessary to make parish churches aware of their responsibility to preach the gospel of redeeming grace in Jesus Christ, for it had to be admitted that for too long many Anglican churches had been offering a watered-down gospel and had been failing utterly to meet the needs of people in general. H. R. Gough, Bishop of Barking, who had been at the centre of the Billy Graham missions, in a letter to the *Church of England Newspaper*, commented somewhat ruefully:

A remarkable feature of evangelism in our country in the post-war years had been the emergence of numerous gospel halls and pentecostal missions which reflected, in part at least, the failure of the organised church to preach the gospel. If we had been preaching the gospel fully and faithfully these conventicles would not have come into being. People have come to our churches and have heard nothing but pious platitudes and moral exhortations and have gone away deeply dissatisfied.

Inevitably, there was some back-lash to the Billy Graham style of preaching and those who differentiated between fundamentalist and conservative standpoints were sometimes willing to dub the Evangelist as a Southern Baptist fundamentalist. But no-one went so far as to call Graham an obscurantist. One of those who led the counterblast, with his usual gusto and protesting defiance, was that stormy petrel of Evangelical Anglicanism, Bishop Christopher Chavasse, 'the senior evangelical bishop' of his time, as he called himself. Selwyn Gummer said 'He preached the Conference Sermon at Islington in January 1956 and with characteristic courage attacked the new fundamentalism which he labelled 'liberalism', the denial of historic fundamentalism and the breeding ground of a new and exclusive Bible sect of threatening danger to the Evangelical movement throughout the church.'[19] Chavasse was a natural fighter, unpredictable and slightly irritable, but he persisted in attacking the extreme forms which the Graham *style* of preaching might and did take, knowing full well that his outspokenness would give rise to some controversy. 'Here was the opportunity for the Evangelicals to dissociate themselves from the obscurantism which in the end would make them a laughing-stock and would, meanwhile, be a threat to the Anglican church.'[20]

Perhaps Chavasse was a little ahead of his time but in Evangelicalism, as he appreciated, intellectual viability of doctrine has to be held in balance with its scriptural purity, without ever wishing to tie up in precise packages all the minutiae of the faith. When Church Society was formed in 1950, joining together the Church Association and the National Church League, Chavasse was concerned lest the rather negative, Low-Church elements of the Association (formed in the wake of the Oxford Movement) would outweigh the evangelical and reforming zeal of the National Church League. He might well have wondered, as others have done since.

The Evangelical Alliance, which had been instrumental in arranging the Crusade, launched, in June 1955, the magazine *Crusade*, the editors being Canon Frank Colquhoun and the Rev. Timothy Dudley-Smith, now Bishop of Thetford. The cover of the first issue showed Billy Graham at Wembley with the Archbishop of Canterbury and the magazine was full of most helpful follow-up material after the previous year's crusade. The second monthly number of the new magazine carried a picture of Ruth and Billy Graham against a background of Windsor Castle and the issue concentrated on the 1955 visit of the Evangelist to Wembley ('Wembley in the Rain', as it was called). The event only lasted just over a week but no fewer than 23,000 made their way to the rostrum for counselling. Earlier in that spring, Billy Graham had been engaged at Kelvin Hall, Glasgow, in the 'All Scotland Crusade'.

There can be no doubt whatever that the Billy Graham crusades of 1954 and 1955 left their mark for all time on the Anglican Church. Hundreds, as a result, went into the full-time ministry of the church, churches were revived and added to, the idea of Evangelism was carried on for many years in the form of

94

parish missions by the Rev. Dick Rees and there was a new spirit of inter-denominational co-operation at the local level. But the *full* advantage of such an epoch-making occurrence was never taken: 'An element of classic tragedy is weaved into the Billy Graham story. God had sent a man and shown how He could use him with and for the Church. The Church drew back.'[21]

'Britain was greatly blessed through the Graham crusades in 1954 and 1955', Bishop Hugh Gough summed up in 1959, 'But to be honest, I think we missed what God intended for us. Many in the church doubted and even opposed, and as a result I fear the words must be spoken of this country, "Thou knewest not the time of thy visitation".'

8
Anatomy of Evangelicalism

YEARS AGO, the Anglican Church was described as the
Conservative Party at prayer and it is still true that
Christianity, as a whole, has been almost entirely
restricted to the middle class and, within the social spectrum of
that class bracket, Anglicans would occupy the top of the colour
band and the Salvation Army the lower end, with its influence
overflowing into the very poorest classes. Next to the Anglicans
but socially hardly distinguishable, would be the United
Reformed Church and the Methodists and, after that, the
Baptists and the Brethren. All four free church groupings have,
however, strong upper-middle-class elements although in no
case would they be so numerous as in Anglicanism. A little
lower, shouldering the Salvationists and after the main body of
Free Churchmen, we find the Pentecostalists and the Jehovah's
Witnesses. These generalisations, as indeed they are, inevitably
throw up local anomalies such as the Baptist Church at Sutton,
Surrey or the U.R.C. at Eastbourne or the Brethren Church at
Carshalton Beeches, Surrey, all of which would fall into a relatively high socio-economic grouping. But Evangelical Anglicans,
around the top of the social spectrum, are mainly 'white collar'
and, sadly, one would not find many 'blue collars', as one once
did, in Methodism.

Evangelicals are, of course, trans-denominational. In the
Anglican Church, both Anglo-Catholics and Evangelicals appear
to flourish in roughly the same social groupings but the latter are
seen at their strongest, it would seem, within a thirty-mile radius
of London; in other words, in the commuter belt surrounding the
metropolis, inhabited by the professional and managerial
classes. Evangelical Anglican strongholds are to be found, for
example, in Kent (Beckenham, Bromley, Orpington, Chisle-
hurst, Tonbridge, Tunbridge Wells and Sevenoaks), in Surrey
(Wallington, Morden, Ashtead, Woking, Ewell, New Malden
and Reigate), in Hertfordshire (Chorleywood, Barnet, and
Watford), in Middlesex (Northwood) and in Essex (Dagenham

and Harold Wood). These are but examples and for the rest of the country there are evangelical parishes of some strength in almost every city and town, sometimes several, as in Manchester, Nottingham, Norwich and Bristol, but in country districts the evangelical parishes tend *not* to be the 'rallying' points and often pass their days unnoticed. Coastal towns everywhere are well served by evangelical ministry, e.g. Cromer, Lowestoft, Folkestone, Worthing, Brighton, Eastbourne and Blackpool and the university towns of Oxford and Cambridge have always had outstanding evangelical witness, from the days of the seraphic Charles Simeon at Cambridge to the present day of Canon Michael Green at Oxford.

Brave efforts have been made to remedy the relative ineffectiveness in the past of Evangelicals in down-town areas and decayed city centres, Liverpool, Nottingham and York, for example, all having shown what can be done in such situations by bold, devoted and concentrated effort. In fact, St Michael's-le-Belfry, York, under the leadership of the late David Watson, became one of the 'show-pieces' of evangelical revival, where congregations of many hundreds are now the order of the day although only a few years ago that church, hard by the Minster, was on the verge of closure.

Evangelical Anglicans have always made a special appeal to students, the warmth of fellowship generated probably being the main factor. Nowhere is this more true than in the heart of London where the average age of the congregations at All Souls, Langham Place, Holy Trinity, Brompton and St Helen's, Bishopsgate, would be well below the national average. The other famous evangelical centre in London is St Paul's, Robert Adam Street, once St Paul's, Portman Square. However, if we focus attention on All Souls, Langham Place, literally opposite the B.B.C., we are at the very heart of Evangelical Anglicanism:

Today All Souls might also claim to be a pivotal church in the religious perspective of the nation. Every Sunday it has an enthused congregation of around a thousand, while every weekday it has an invisible one of half a million or so. The explanation is that the first congregation has come in person to have its batteries charged at the powerhouse of Evangelical Anglicanism, while the second consists of the listeners to Radio 4's Daily Service, one of the oldest-established programmes in the B.B.C. repertoire. The combination is piquant. For, while the All Souls style is outgoing and triumphant, the spirit of the Daily Service is a cool, intimate one, in which enthusiasm hardly seems at home. Yet the two have lived side by side for the past half-century, both, literally, serving 'all souls' in their contrasting ways.[1]

This probably represents a fairly complicated microcosm of the evangelical dilemma – a strong, vital position in the life of the national Church on which it seems impossible to capitalise to any dramatic extent. However, All Souls has remained for many decades the centre of Evangelical Anglicanism, being on the most friendly terms with the B.B.C., who appreciate that the daily service cannot very well be recorded and still retain its validity as a live act of worship. Furthermore, it is appreciated that an actual church setting is the only proper way of conducting a religious service over the air. The story of All Souls in modern times reads so as to give heartening encouragement to all Evangelicals.

The Rev. John Stott was Rector of All Souls, Langham Place, during the years 1950–75. In that time, he saw the congregation increase so as to outgrow the church buildings. During the Billy Graham crusades he urged all to pray and to attend the meetings. He emphasised the urgent need to help new converts and over 150 people were subsequently referred to All Souls where every effort was made to link them with the existing Nursery Classes for new Christians.

It is commonly agreed, not simply by Evangelicals, that the Rev. John Stott combines very remarkable qualities and gifts. He is especially gifted as a Bible expositor, whose clarity and presentation of truth is exceptional, he is always in great demand, world-wide, for Evangelism, conferences and conventions, spending a large part of each year outside the U.K., he has a remarkable charisma making him persona grata with all kinds of people and, because he is so widely read, he is a scholar in the best sense of the word. As a statesman on missionary work and Evangelism the Rev. John Stott is unique in that he combines a strong evangelical emphasis with the ability to appreciate other points of view which indeed he has done at the gatherings at Lausanne, the World Council of Churches, etc. He is the acknowledged leader of Evangelical Anglicans. To the Anglican observer, however, it would appear to be a pity that John Stott, appointed a chaplain to the Queen in 1959, did not take much direct part in affairs of state, either in the Church or in the nation. He has, of course, written some quite outstanding books, making original contributions to evangelical thought and he manages, as well, to be a Contributing Editor to *Sojourners*, a distinctly lively and different magazine published monthly in Washington, DC.

It is a socially conscious offering, including in 1980, for example, an article 'Vietnam: Our Unrepented Sin'.

Changes took place at All Souls in 1970 which are described by Raymond Luker:

At the end of the year the staffing pattern was to be altered in a unique way with the Rev. Michael A. Baughen being installed in the newly created post of Vicar 'to exercise the pastoral and administrative responsibility for the parish and congregation'. Because of legal problems, John Stott was to retain the title of Rector, but he would be free to pursue a more widespread ministry of reading, writing, missions and conferences . . . [2]

Eventually, in 1975, on the twenty-fifth anniversary of his institution as Rector, the Rev. John Stott resigned as Rector and the Crown duly appointed the Rev. Michael Baughen in his place, his predecessor assuming the original title of Rector Emeritus, thus enabling him to continue his supportive ministry at the church.

To read All Souls history of what happened next, it would appear that the Hand of the Lord reached down to work some mighty miracles. Somehow or other, three quarters of a million pounds were raised. A bulldozer waddled into the church, the floor was excavated to a depth of 13 feet, and a splendid new hall and other facilities were installed underground. [3]

Nowadays, the work of the church is quite decentralised during the week, up to about sixty-five fellowship groups of All Souls meeting in members' flats in central London for Bible Study, fellowship and prayer. Referring to the B.B.C. World Service there were the following comments:

So radio has made All Souls a worldwide church. But the parish remains the heart of its life. 'We're bursting at the seams again', says Michael Baughen. 'Though I don't think we can expand any more. We've just renovated St Peter's, Vere Street, and we're developing our closed circuit television over-flow facilities. But I don't think we can go much further.' [4]

All Souls, Langham Place, in the heart of the West End of London, continued to represent all that is best in Evangelical Anglicanism and the particular gifts of Michael Baughen (since appointed Bishop of Chester) in a very caring ministry appeared to complement those of his predecessor, John Stott. Not far away, St Paul's, Portman Square, now rebuilt in Robert Adam Street, once vied with All Souls as an evangelical 'powerhouse'. Since the days of the Rev. Colin Kerr as vicar, it has experienced varying degrees of favour but under Canon Harry Sutton it subsequently showed a quality of spiritual life which is bound to be significant in its future development. The relative newcomer to the London scene, in terms of evangelical witness, is St Helen's, Bishopsgate, where with the arrival, as rector in 1961, of the Rev. Dick Lucas, a remarkable ministry has been established, not only with students on Sundays but also with City businessmen at mid-week lunch-time services, which are always very well attended by those who work in 'the square mile', some of whom owe their conversion directly to St Helen's.

It would be difficult to overestimate the effectiveness of both All Souls and St Helen's as training schools for Christian service to be based on the parish church. Evangelical influence, mainly through non-ordained men and women thus, as a result, extends far and wide and these two churches are, in a way, 'theological colleges' for the laity.

If we turn our attention to actual theological colleges, we find that there are six of evangelical persuasion although two of these (Ridley and Wycliffe) have had what might be termed their theological ups and down and have therefore been inclined to vary in their evangelical partisanship. Furthermore, other theological colleges, for example Lincoln, would train a pro-portion of Evangelicals of different colours.

It is interesting to review the numbers of ordinands at the dif-ferent colleges and to note numerical progress within the overall position. The analysis is based on quota figures, which may be slightly exceeded or slightly lowered (a balancing factor).

	1970	1980	1983
Cranmer Hall (St John's College), Durham	47	50	75
Oak Hill, London	51	57	68
Ridley Hall, Cambridge	29	45	50
St John's College, Nottingham	71	80	96
Trinity College, Bristol			
(previously Clifton and Tyndale)	52	50	70
Wycliffe Hall, Oxford	30	50	65
	280	332	424
out of a total of	834	746	873

These figures must surely represent an Anglican grass-roots feeling in support of evangelical theology and, on the face of it, it is difficult to see how this could be resisted by the hierarchy of the Church in the need to create more bishops and archdeacons adequately to mirror the movement. Ultimately the Church must become the kind of Church required by the nation, represented by its total Christian constituency. Previously, St Aiden's, Birkenhead, now closed, carried some kind of evangelical flag and in 1958 there was a total of twenty-four colleges, twenty-one in 1970, now reduced by closure and merger to fourteen.

When it comes to finding openings as curates and vicars, Evangelicals have found that there have not been nearly enough livings within evangelical patronage to accommodate available clergy, with the result that they have had to go to parishes which may not have an evangelical tradition or, at least, not for very long. It is very much to the credit of Evangelicals in recent decades that they have been prepared to launch out into uncharted waters at a bishop's behest and, being willing not to alter the churchmanship of a parish, have taken the evangelical gospel, quietly and gently, into unfamiliar situations. By far the majority of livings (roughly 11,600 in all) are in the gift of the diocesan bishop, the crown, the clergy and private individuals, leaving only about 1,800 livings in the gift of patronage societies and trusts. Of these, about half are in the care of the evangelical Church Pastoral Aid Society (and associated trusts), Church Society, Simeon Trustees, etc. Often, in the past, an individual has decided that he or she no longer wishes to be responsible for a living and has handed over responsibility to a patronage society. Thus, it is quite possible for the 'furniture' of a church to have non-evangelical features, e.g. crucifixes, a survival from a previous patronage, and yet for the minister to be an Evangelical, appointed by a society to whom the benefice has been handed over.

Evangelical patronage societies would find it difficult to declare that, at any given moment, all their livings were in the hands of thorough-going Evangelicals since, inevitably, some clergy remaining in a parish for a long while might easily allow things to drift, for instance, into an arid Protestantism. Furthermore, although most of the incumbents backed by these evangelical societies would be expected to take a 'north end' or west position when celebrating Holy Communion, there would be some churches where the eastward position was the custom and the minister would not wish to upset custom by moving to another position. A further and more recent development, with the tendency to move the communion table forward, has been for the officiating clergy to face the congregation, thus taking a west-ward position. This is a move favoured by the younger evangeli-cal clergy and often the more charismatic of them bring the Holy Table to the chancel steps to become much closer to the congre-gation. All in all, it would be unusual to find an evangelical minister taking the eastward position when celebrating the Lord's Supper since that would imply a more priestly office – between God and the people – than would accord with evangeli-cal belief. But the patronage societies ensure, above all, that the man offered to a parish on the one hand is prepared to carry on the traditions of the parish, at least to start with, e.g. new or 1662 services, and on the other hand that the Parochial Church Coun-cil is going to welcome the man or men of the society's choice. There are men who consider themselves city centre clergy, others see themselves as working in suburbia or country districts and, it is not unusual for a clergyman to seek lighter parochial duties in the closing years of his ministry. But if, into the bargain, he finds that he is being offered three or four small villages, each parish with a separate P.C.C., he may wonder what he is thinking of taking on! With the amalgamation of small parishes there are now no really quiet separate country livings.

In spite of the strength of Evangelicals at parish level (about one-fifth), they are still not well represented at the level of arch-deacon and bishop but that has almost always obtained. The man in the very active parochial ministry may not see himself as being either fitted for or concerned with the administration of the Church and so the Evangelical may, unconsciously, have handed over the reins to the broad churchman or the Anglo-Catholic. Some years ago, the following assessment was made: 'Of the forty-three diocesan bishops, eight can be identified as uncom-promising Anglo-Catholics, and seven as uncompromising Evangelicals, seventeen should probably be classed as "high" rather than "low", ten as "low" rather than "high" and two perhaps would not object to the designation "liberal".'[5]

There is a tendency, noted by some evangelical clergy, for an evangelical bishop to broaden out on taking episcopal office but, whilst it must be admitted that inevitably some clergy change their theological position with the passage of time, episcopal duties do require that a bishop must become all things to all parishes. Certainly, no hard-line Evangelical could manage the overall duties of the episcopacy, which means that no such Evangelical is going to be satisfied with the 'performance' of an evangelical bishop. When the archepiscopal sees of Canterbury and York were recently held by Evangelicals, by Donald Coggan and Stuart Blanch respectively, all Evangelicals were inclined to 'throw their hats in the air' but not all of them realised the very difficult task which these two men had to perform. Clearly, they were not going to please the Anglo-Catholics anyway, so they were forced to take something of a middle path, with some inclination, wherever possible, in the direction of the Evangelicals. So, it must be admitted that during the tenure of Archbishop Donald Coggan and Archbishop Stuart Blanch, the Church of England did not become noticeably more Evangelical and, if anything, the Anglo-Catholics became more powerful, certainly more vociferous in General Synod. Both archbishops might be fairly described – at least by some Evangelicals – as liberal Evangelicals!

Not surprisingly, a number of young clergy who set out as either Anglo-Catholic or Evangelical may change their churchmanship and theology in the early years of their ministry and during the Billy Graham campaigns of 1954 and 1955 a not inconsiderable number of clergy became much more Evangelical, a few going so far as to say that they were converted at Harringay. Perhaps this is hardly surprising when it is appreciated that the years preceding the advent of Billy Graham were spiritually frustrating and barren for many clergy.

At the present time, twenty years after the analysis of Bishop Stephen Neill, although the episcopal personalities would be different, the same kind of mix of churchmanship would be discernible, although the descriptions of the different stances would be different. 'High Church' and 'Low Church' are now generally regarded as dated epithets but a few who would be regarded by their colleagues as, say, Evangelical would not themselves own up to the title unless they were accorded the prefix of 'liberal', e.g. possibly Bishop John V. Taylor of Winchester. There would appear to be disproportionately few evangelical diocesans compared with the number of Anglo-Catholics. However, the evangelical tradition within the Anglican fold is favourably viewed by the critical historian:

There are, of course, many gradations within 'conservative evangelicalism'. The universities and colleges are full of Christian Unions based on a 'personal experience of Jesus Christ', but are also producing many ordained or lay missionaries for Britain and the world. Evangelical preaching and scholarship hold their own bravely; and a church like All Souls, Langham Place, where the work of this school is seen at its best, is rightly a power in the land. The stronger historic evangelicalism becomes, the better for Christendom it will be, for the true evangelical does not lose his sense of the authority of the Church, and does much to help forward the community of all its members.[6]

The same could hardly be said of a liberal theology with its emphasis on the secular. But one could say that the strength of Evangelical Anglicans arises in the parishes and from the Biblical ministry of their pulpits generated at source by the evangelical theological colleges. These colleges would nowadays reveal a wide and healthy spectrum of social and educational background, from comprehensive, through grammar schools to independent public schools. Inevitably, with general social change there has been a broadening of the ordinands' school experience which, at one time, was almost exclusively public school and, years ago, Oxbridge in university terms.

In the field of public school education, Evangelicals are rightly proud of the achievement represented by Monkton Combe School, Bath, and St Lawrence College, Ramsgate, both mainly boys' schools. Monkton was founded in 1868 by the then vicar of the parish, the Rev. F. Pocock who, after seven years, was looking for his successor, 'an Evangelist who was also a schoolmaster'. By 1903, the school was a member of the Headmasters Conference and developing a strong missionary connection. In due course, the school also became renowned for its rowing tradition. Although Monkton is an avowed Anglican school, Christian parents of all persuasions within the evangelical fold support the school, so much so that a Parents Prayer Union was founded. Derek Wigram, headmaster from 1946 to 1968, succinctly expressed the views of a school such as Monkton Combe in an article in the *Record* (Church of England Newspaper) in 1947:

If the public schools contain Christian headmasters and staff, their opportunities are very great. As boarding schools they are communities which contain the whole life of the boy for a large part of the year. They are not only working but also worshipping and leisure-spending communities. They are school and church and home in one . . . The Christian faith can be worked out in practical living with more experienced Christians always at hand to help.[7]

St Lawrence College, Ramsgate, was founded in 1879 with a strong evangelical tradition and having the same kind of history as Monkton Combe. For many years it produced as many hockey blues as any other school in the country and it can number among its old boys such well known Evangelical Anglicans as the Bishop of Winchester (John Taylor), Professor Sir Norman Anderson, formerly lay chairman of General Synod, and Robert Drayson, an outstanding headmaster. The present chairman of governors is Sir Kirby Laing of Laing building fame.

Other boys' public schools set out with firm evangelical hopes, such as Trent College at Long Eaton, Nottingham and Weymouth College. The former, however, has not for many years had anything like an evangelical flavour and the latter collapsed during the economic depression of the 1930s, which, in varying degrees, hit all fee-paying schools, even Harrow.

In the field of specifically girls' education, the name of Wadhurst College, Kent, comes readily to mind as having about the same evangelical standing as Monkton Combe and St Lawrence but alongside Wadhurst one should place Clarendon School, Bedford, which, however, is perhaps more Brethren than Anglican in flavour.

Within the Martyrs Memorial Trust (Allied Schools) are girls public schools, Felixstowe College, Harrogate College and Westonbirt School, and also, among the boys' public schools, Wrekin College, Stowe and Canford. These schools owe their origins to a remarkable Protestant clergyman, who could hardly be described as an Evangelical, the Rev. P. E. Warrington, again a vicar at Monkton Combe. In 1923, he achieved the considerable feat of founding both Canford and Stowe. He appeared to have combined the role of Protestant zealot with financial juggler and gathered to his control not only boarding schools but church livings here and there. Stowe was perhaps his outstanding achievement, for there, in a corner of Buckinghamshire, he transformed a magnificent country mansion, with 280 acres of grounds, into a new and immediately acclaimed, thriving boys' public school. Warrington was fortunate in obtaining, as the school's first headmaster, a brilliant personality in the person of J. F. Roxburgh, who brought unusual gifts which gave Stowe an immediate place in the field of private education. Noel Annan, writing of Stowe, said:

The chairman of the first Council to govern Stowe was Lord Gisborough. But Gisborough was a figurehead – his talents did not permit him to be anything else. The prime mover was the Reverend Percy Warrington, Vicar of Monkton Combe, near Bath, whom journalists were later to call 'the financier in the surplice'. Stowe was not the first school he had bought. In 1922 he met Mr (later Sir) John Bayley and purchased from him a school in

Wellington, Shropshire, which he renamed Wrekin College. Wrekin College Company immediately entered upon a contract to purchase Stowe House with Wrekin College as guarantor and security. No sooner was this done than the Company bought Canford, Lord Wimborne's home in Dorset, Wrekin and Stowe now guaranteeing the new foundation.[8]

In all, fourteen schools were embraced in the financial complex which itself was allied to the Martyrs Memorial and Church of England Trust, now administered by the Church Pastoral Aid Society. Roxburgh, coming from a leading Anglo-Catholic school in the Woodard Foundation, Lancing College, and although himself far from being a High-Churchman, was not an Evangelical. However, like Warrington, he appears to have been simple and Protestant in his ideas of churchmanship but there the similarity between the two characters ended, for, although each admired the other's ability, they constantly quarrelled over financial and administrative matters.

Warrington saw his enterprises as the vanguard against 'the insidious wiles of Rome and the even more treacherous machinations of the Anglo-Catholics'. However, in 1932, the financial storm which had threatened for so long broke and the Legal and General Assurance Society, to their eternal credit, came to the rescue with a loan at a low, fixed rate of interest, insisting that their own executives join the board of Stowe, Martyrs Memorial Trust retaining two seats on the governing body, thus maintaining an evangelical influence: 'Roxburgh grew up at a time when church-going was declining yet when religious controversy remained exceedingly pungent. In the Church of England Evangelicalism had lost ground but its revivals and missions still generated enthusiasm; and on the other wing the extreme Anglo-Catholics were at their most provocative in mocking Protestantism.'[9]

Whilst Warrington persisted with his visionary gleam of sound Protestant education, Roxburgh stood aside from all religious controversy. Theology meant little to him. His faith was simple: 'Religion in his eyes, therefore, sprang from two simple needs: the need to love other people and the need to ask God for help to do so.'

An extract from the Articles of Association of the Allied Schools Group indicates the evangelical nature of the foundation:

Religious Principles

In all schools for the time being owned by the Company, notwithstanding that the schools and all their benefits (including scholarships, exhibitions and other awards) shall be open to children of all creeds:

(a) instruction shall be given in the doctrines and duties of Christianity in accordance with the Protestant and Evangelical principles of the Church of England.

(b) all principals, headmasters and headmistresses of such schools shall be members of the Church of England or of the Church of Wales or of the established Church of Scotland or of some other church for the time being in communion with the Church of England, or such practising Christian as shall be in accord with the Protestant and Evangelical principles of the Church of England.

At least two governors of each of the Allied Schools are still nominated by the Martyrs Memorial Trust and, in recent times, significantly, Stowe School had an outstanding headmaster in Robert Drayson, already mentioned, who considerably increased the educational standard of the school, whilst being himself a well balanced Evangelical. He has been lay chaplain to the Bishop of Norwich.

There are now only eight Allied Schools and it was reported in the *Daily Telegraph* (18 April 1980) that the loan of one million pounds, arranged at a very low rate of interest with the Legal and General Assurance Company forty years ago, has now been repaid. A previous chief executive of this Company, G. W. Bridge, an oratorical after-dinner speaker and a strong Christian, for many years took a deep interest in the affairs of the schools.

Not surprisingly, it is difficult, if not impossible, to evaluate the impact, in Christian terms, of schools in the Allied Group. Like any educational establishment, their standards can never rise above those of the teaching staff, set, in the main, by the headmaster or headmistress. It would be easier to detect the evangelical influence of Monkton Combe and St Lawrence but insofar as all schools, or almost all, would have Evangelicals on the teaching staff, evangelical influence would, in simplistic terms, be in direct proportion to the number and quality of staff members. And to take a case in point, a school like Monkton would expect to have a higher percentage of committed Evangelicals on the staff than, say, Sedbergh or Bedford and rather more than, say, Stowe, even in Drayson's day.

Evangelical Anglicans for many years appeared to neglect the more down-town parishes, such as those often favoured by Anglo-Catholics but there is evidence that the situation is being rectified and opportunities are being taken up to bridge the gap between the Anglican Church and working class people. In the East End of London, for example, Prebendary John Pearce, the Revs. Peter Ronayne (since moved), Chris Idle and Eddy Stride have made an outstanding contribution to parochial life by carrying the evangelical faith to East-Enders. In this regard, one must also record the insistent emphasis in recent years by the Bishop of Liverpool, David Sheppard, in *Built as a City, God and the Urban World To-day* (Hodder and Stoughton, 1974), on the problems of church witness and growth in a city such as Liverpool, probably the most evangelical diocese, where he has been prominent with the Roman Catholic Archbishop Derek Worlock in pleading for a fairer society. He actually wrote the book as Bishop of Woolwich and recalled that 'One Church leader used to say that we should put our resources where there was response. That meant Woodford and Buckhurst Hill and not West Ham.' West Ham is, in fact, exactly the type of East London parish where men like John Pearce are working. The Bishop of Liverpool drew heavily on his earlier experience as Warden of the Mayflower Centre, Canning Town (1958–69) and also refers to many parishes in south London. The book is a major work covering nearly 400 pages, is wide ranging over every aspect of city life and identifies the Church's task as one of involvement at every level. Experience has, however, shown that generally the areas of growth in the Church as a whole have been in separate ethnic groups within an urban situation rather than in churches endeavouring to cater for multi-racial Christians. Bishop David Sheppard followed his book with *Bias To The Poor* (Hodder, 1983) – a further examination of the problems and potentialities of fully involving the urban poor with the blessings of the gospel.

Another area of evangelical growth has been in the Pathfinder Movement sponsored from 1975 by the Church Pastoral Aid Society but originally by the Church Society. By 1980, there were over 1,170 Pathfinder groups, all attached to Anglican parishes. Ten years previously, there were only 800 units and a considerably smaller membership so that, in a decade of diminishing numbers in almost all other youth movements and parochial life, such development must be judged as spectacular. Some independent youth groups, however, joined the Pathfinder Movement for the reason that the teaching material produced was a good deal better than anything else available. Pathfinders began in 1935 as a private venture in Emmanuel Church, Tolworth, and was the brain-child of Canon Herbert Taylor who, on moving to Christ Church, Orpington, formed another group. In 1953, Pathfinders became a national youth movement, very similar in style to Crusaders, with Sunday Bible Class and Summer Camps. The old style Sunday School structure has been abandoned by churches having Pathfinders (aged 11–14), where three other groupings are separately catered for – Climbers (aged 4–6), Explorers (7–10), and then, beyond Pathfinders, for the 14–20 age group, the Church Youth Fellowship Association (C.Y.F.A.). This range of specialist activities naturally requires dedicated leadership and it is the duty of each incumbent gently to supervise the appointment and overall efficiency of the group leaders. Children are thus passed from one organisation to another with the minimum loss of interest and are, it is expected, gradually drawn into the full life of the local church. Often, these organisations will share, at least once a month, the first part of the morning worship. A full range of teaching material for the different ages is provided by the headquarters of C.P.A.S.

Unquestionably, Pathfinders has been a notable success story in recent times and demonstrates the advantage, which Crusaders do not have, of working within the local church structure. Both movements draw from the same strata of society but Crusaders, being interdenominational, has a much more difficult task in reaching, holding and eventually passing on boys and girls to local churches. Both organisations are strongly Evangelical and agree that, however successful a local Pathfinder group may be, there are always plenty of children besides for Crusaders to reach. The growth of Pathfinders and the static position of Crusaders probably means that, proportionately, there are now fewer Evangelical Anglican leaders in Crusaders as the other denominations tend not to have similar national youth movements to attract leadership from within their churches. However, although the number of Crusader units is a good deal fewer than those of Pathfinders, their camps, numbering about eighty, are about 50 per cent greater than the number run under the banner of Pathfinders.

Apart from the thriving youth work, C.P.A.S. is heavily involved with patronage trusts for Anglican livings and also in encouraging candidates to apply for training for ordination. Not only so, C.P.A.S. is involved in very many supporting roles – financial, Evangelistic and pastoral. All in all, one might say that the Society is the heart of the Evangelical Anglican anatomy with Church Society seeing itself as purifying the blood stream. This latter service is conducted partly through the Fellowship of Diocesan Evangelical Unions and by the Evangelical Group in General Synod, both of which are serviced by Church Society. Whereas C.P.A.S. is, as its name implies, pastoral and support-ive (also evangelistic), Church Society provides the doctrinal and theological emphasis in Reformed, Protestant and Evangelical truth. And, providing the 'think-tank' for Evangelical Anglican-ism is the Church of England Evangelical Council, originally chaired by the Rev. John Stott,. It is mainly a consultative body but, with its gathering momentum, has very close relationships both with the Diocesan Evangelical Unions and The Evangelical Group in General Synod.

Arising out of the work of the Church of England Evangelical Council, which includes representatives of all the evangelical societies, elected diocesan council members, as well as represen-tatives of the theological colleges, came the Annual Evangelical Assembly, which is outside the chronological range of this book but which first took place in 1983.Out of the Assembly came a reconstituted C.E.E.C. as its standing committee.

It is important to include in the anatomy of Evangelicalism reference to Lee Abbey, 'the home of a Christian community' at Lynton, Devon. The Rev. John Perry is currently warden, they serve the whole Church of England and welcome 6,500 guests a year. Lee Abbey is a retreat of peace and healing where the widest spectrum of Evangelicals has been at home and it would be fair to say that its present popularity owes much to the work of Canon Geoffrey Rogers who was warden from 1950 to 1964. There are those who, wishing to be very precise, would describe the work of Lee Abbey as liberal Evangelicalism at its best.

To add to the picture mention must be made of two important evangelical societies, the Eclectics in particular and the Senior Evangelical Anglican Clergy. Eclectics was, in fact, founded by John Newton, the famous hymnwriter and ex-slave trader of the eighteenth century, a leading Evangelical Anglican of the great Revival. However, the society lapsed until it was revived in the mid-fifties by John Stott who saw an opportunity to bring together a younger, somewhat restive generation of clergy for uninhibited study, fellowship and encouragement, with the object of spiritual, doctrinal and intellectual stimulus. Evangelicals had not, up to that time, been particularly noted for their scholarship and in-depth study, but Eclectics took off in a remarkable way and many clergy under forty (the age limit) have been inspired and motivated by the movement which, while beginning in London, spread to a regional basis. A whole generation of Evangelical Anglican clergy was able to 'let their hair down' on any matter concerning their faith, particularly at their annual three-day conference. It was a remarkable move forward, the Eclectics reaching a membership, in 1983, of about 450.

As Eclectics reached their retirement age of forty, they not unnaturally felt a need for a replacement forum and in 1974, the Rev. Gavin Reid and Rev. Derek Wooldridge formed up under the leadership of Michael Baughen, now Bishop of Chester, with Canon Michael Botting, as secretary, to create the Senior Evangelical Anglican Clergy Conference. Since then they have filled the Swanwick Conference Centre every year and have included as their speakers interesting people of some different dispositions, notably the Bishop of London, Graham Leonard.

One is, I think, entitled to believe that the various evangelical societies and groupings within Anglicanism perform a very useful function. However, the strength of Evangelicalism is in the parishes, deriving from ministry of word, sacrament and pastoral care, which themselves must originate from the theological colleges. The anatomy is organic, partly unseen and depends, for its full functioning, on the continual inbreathing of the Spirit of God.

9

The Fundamentalist Issue

A MONG THE OPPONENTS of Evangelicals are those who insist on giving them the label 'Fundamentalist'. In some quarters it has become a kind of theological swear-word and, probably, the issues of Fundamentalism in general reached boiling point soon after the Billy Graham Crusades in 1954 and 1955. In a way, it was natural that a reaction should set in and there were those only too eager to explain away the results of Evangelism on a big scale and to point up its dangers.

However, there can be little doubt that the work of Billy Graham had lasting effects throughout Anglicanism, its benefits by far outweighing any attendant disadvantages. For one thing, very many men who were deeply moved at Harringay, Wembley and elsewhere went on to ordination. Autobiographical reference can be eloquent, for example, Lord Home:

Another who, many years later, influenced my thinking, was Billy Graham, the American evangelist. Like Dr Alington, he spread the joy and hope in Christianity. I cannot say that I was particularly attracted by the spectacular stage-management of his Christian circus, but he got results.

I asked Dr Ramsey, the Archbishop of Canterbury, how he felt about the techniques employed, and he replied that all he could say was that after each of Dr Graham's campaigns in Britain there was a significant number of individuals who joined the Anglican ministry.[1]

There was, indeed, a rise in the number of ordinands from the mid-fifties and into the sixties and this was partly due to the Billy Graham Crusades. He insisted on handing back (or handing on) converts to local churches and this proved a considerable safeguard against a danger of 'lone Christians' of which some warned. However, there were harsh criticisms from some quarters: 'In the history of Christianity, Evangelicals more than most have suffered from a tyranny imposed by evangelists anxious and determined to force their own will upon, and reproduce their own experiences within, their converts. This is not the way of Christ.'[2]

112

The Fundamentalist issue

As to his theology, Billy Graham himself was always being dubbed a Fundamentalist, largely because he came from that part of the United States where the fundamentalist standpoint predominated among the free church denominations but, without wishing to split hairs, it seems that his world-wide experiences and interrogation by the media everywhere tend to reveal an attitude to the Bible which is conservative rather than fundamentalist. In this, Billy Graham would align himself with John Stott and Jim Packer, two of the leading advocates in the past twenty years of a more gracious and scholarly approach to any controversy centred on the Bible. However, some would go so far as to consider the line of demarcation hardly discernible; for example, James Barr:

As a practical course of procedure within this book, I shall therefore continue to use the term 'fundamentalist' for a certain basic personal religious and existential attitude, which will be described. This attitude I consider to be a pathological condition of Christianity, and one which, when it appears, commonly appears within, and overlaps with, the ecclesiastical grouping known as 'conservative evangelical'. I do not say therefore that all conservative evangelicals are also fundamentalists; but the overlap is very great.[3]

It is the more scholarly approach which tends to keep the conservative Evangelical humble and, in general, gracious in controversy whereas the Fundamentalist tends to go like a bull at a gate against any opposition and without much reliable scholarship to back him up. However, even so, there are other weighty considerations, as J. E. Fison pointed out:

In retrospect it seems to me that on the more specifically theological and especially on the biblical issues raised by the liberal theology of the so-called higher criticism, there was undoubtedly a long period, lasting from before the turn of the century and persisting in many quarters even today, during which Evangelicals either wilfully or unwittingly refused to face facts and preferred to rely on unqualified or out-of-date authorities. But even if this be so, no obscurantism must blind us to the real source of spiritual strength and vitality which this inter-denominational evangelicalism has undoubtedly evidenced. The fact is that over against much in the prevailing trends of liberalism, it did stand for the supernatural and it undoubtedly stood for the supernatural made available to men only at the foot of the Cross and also (when it was true to its own deepest insights) only by the power of the Holy Spirit.[4]

It was only as Evangelical Anglicans sought to break out of their enclaves and capture new strongholds for the gospel of justification by faith that they felt the need for the back-up or foundation of scholarship but, by the Grace of God, these Evangelicals have lost neither their sense of the supernatural nor their simple-hearted joy in the salvation found in Jesus Christ. J. E. Fison contended that 'It is this buoyant, spontaneous assurance which the evangelical regards as central to his outlook and which he often feels is lacking in Anglo-Catholicism'.

One area in which Fundamentalists and Evangelicals have been placed together by their critics, is literature and this strikes at the fruit of their scholarship:

It is indisputable that in recent decades scholarship has become more and more important for conservative evangelicals. At one time many of them might have been content to dismiss scholarship as a quite unimportant factor in the understanding of the Bible: after all, had not the apostle Paul declared that not many wise men after the flesh are called? Thus at one time one might have been happy to be a quite unlearned believer with no knowledge of any book other than the English Bible but today there is visible a deep anxiety to have learning on one's side. Valiant efforts are being made to improve the standard of conservative publications.[5]

James Barr instances *The New Bible Dictionary* which was published by the I.V.F. in 1962 and *The New Bible Commentary* which they brought out in 1953. He adds: 'The production of this better literature in itself indicates that an increasing number of conservative evangelicals are developing scholarly interests and are prepared to write articles and books which aspire to a scholarly level.'[6] Barr goes so far as to regard as 'dubious' the two volumes he mentions and contends that, 'Conservative evangelical literature about the Bible is not just scholarly literature, it is scholarly literature prepared, published and diffused with a particular purpose in mind: to provide literature that the evangelical student or reader can *trust*.'[7] He continues:

Conservative books published in this way will often cite and describe non-conservative scholarly opinions, but this will always be done within the framework and under the scheme of presentation set up by the more or less conservative author. The conservative student will no doubt read books representing other schools of opinion, but he will return again and again to the kind of book he can trust because he knows that its soundness is assured.[8]

James Barr has, in fact, little good to say about either Fundamentalists or conservative Evangelicals but his book received the following trenchant review from a non-Evangelical source:

But in this book of some 380 pages, Professor Barr never discusses the teaching of Mr Stott, the most influential conservative evangelical in the Church

114

of England. He lists only two of Mr Stott's books, both on evangelism, one from 1949 and another from 1962. But more important: he does little to prepare his readers for the fact that Mr Stott has, like the rest of us, gradually changed his mind or at least his emphasis.[9]

The fact of the matter is that Professor Barr's comments, whilst once having some substance, are now rather dated and we may turn to a younger evangelical theologian for another considered criticism of the book:

In summary, then, Professor Barr's analogies and critique of the fundamentalist cast of mind is frequently compelling though sometimes misled and often overstated, and over one particular theological issue (the doctrine of inspiration/infallibility itself) unsatisfactory. But he is mistaken in believing that this cast of mind, with its hostility to modern theology and biblical study and its exclusivism, is normative, or probably even dominant (though it is certainly present) among those who subscribe to the U.C.C.F. basis of faith, or specifically among theologians and biblical scholars who identify themselves with U.C.C.F.[10]

It ought to be added that a relatively new evangelical publisher – Lion – has brought to the market already much popular scholarly work, which gives the sense of being written, not for consumption within a party but with the authority of truth itself, based on sound scholarship. Good examples of their work are the *Lion Handbook of the Bible* (1973), and the *Lion Encyclopaedia of the Bible* (1978).

Looking at evangelical history it does seem that the critics came out heavily against Evangelicals once the Billy Graham euphoria was over but the campaigns had at least brought the Anglicans into closer general relationships with their free church Evangelical brethren and there came about a wave of enthusiasm for co-operation in evangelism at the local level. Evangelical Anglicans, as a result of the campaigns were, temporarily at least, on the increase and they were gradually learning the advantages of working together wherever possible. Too often Evangelicals had found reasons for 'getting out' rather than remaining in a local situation, although they would have to wait until the famous conference at Keele in 1967 before they came thoroughly to accept and appreciate their non-Evangelical brethren within Anglicanism and therefore to become fully committed to the Anglican Church:

Perhaps no single text taken out of the context of a living positive relationship of holiness unto God has done more harm to religion – certainly to evangelical religion since the beginning of its gradual decline in 1870 – than the Old Testament quotation by St Paul, in 2 Corinthians 6.17, 'Come ye out from among them and be ye separate' saith the Lord, 'and touch no unclean thing' . . . Instead of placing it in its true setting in a positive and triumphant context, it has been the defeatist justification of strategic withdrawal after withdrawal. And no amount of special pleading in communiques either military or ecclesiastical can go on concealing the real rout that such phraseology camouflages.[11]

After the magnificent co-operation at all levels represented by the Billy Graham campaigns there was abroad a distinct mood of optimism for proclaiming the gospel in the local churches and Christians were saying that never again would they settle back into their easy-going isolationism where they thought only in terms of small enterprises and slender returns.

The mood of being more adventurous, among Evangelicals, was expressed somewhat guardedly by the Rev. J. Stafford Wright, then principal of Tyndale Hall, Bristol:

Conservative Evangelicals share in the growing desire to understand the differing viewpoints within the Church. Coupled with this, many are anxious to co-operate more fully than in the past. This, of course, is a general statement; there are as many churches and individuals of the conservative tradition who will not go as far as I would; there are others who would go further.[12]

Evangelicals have not always been blessed with an adequacy of statesmanlike advocates. Fighters they have had in plenty but not many diplomats. But John Stott has always combined a reasoned advocacy in debate with a very firm adherence to conservative evangelical truth and, unusually, he has also combined the gift of preaching with that of writing. Almost unrecorded at the time was his prestigious start as an author when, in 1954, his first book was chosen as the Lent Book for the diocese of London, commended in a foreword by the bishop and, what is more, published by a front-line secular publisher, *Men with a Message* (Longmans, 1954). In the introduction, the author states that the book 'is an attempt to introduce the New Testament, its authors and their writings, to the man in the pew'.

Another Evangelical of great standing but mainly in the missionary field was Canon Max Warren, from 1942 until 1963 Secretary of the Church Missionary Society. A missionary before his ordination, he always evinced statesmanlike qualities, becoming in later life a Canon at Westminster, which gave him a degree of freedom to be of service to the Church at large. Some would describe him as the archetypal liberal Evangelical – charming, moderate and understanding. Max Warren was Vicar of Holy Trinity, Cambridge, from 1936 to 1942, being properly conscious of following in the steps there of the great Charles Simeon. Then, as always, he combined evangelical strength with diplomacy, was never just a party man and saw issues with unprejudiced eyes. Canon F. W. Dillistone, in the biography of Max Warren, *Into all the World* (Hodder and Stoughton, 1980) wrote (p. 6), 'I regard him as the greatest all-round Christian leader of my own generation.'

Max Warren himself refused to accept any qualifying adjective to the name Evangelical – neither liberal nor conservative. He took a central position but never a simplistic one:

I was deeply convinced that an Evangelicalism which stressed reverence and care in the conduct of corporate worship, and was not afraid of beauty and symbolism, and which knew how to combine these with the word of interpretation, had a great contribution to give everywhere, not least overseas. To this end I did all I could to encourage a deeper understanding of Holy Communion, gratefully introducing the Clare College 'use' as pioneered by John Robinson, as well as interpreting the inner dynamic of sacramental worship as I understood it.[13]

Max Warren was thinking, in the main, of missionaries on active service but, in every way, he was a man of sober judgments and broad sympathies:

Evangelical religion is, of course, much more than this. It is the whole Christian faith held in a particular balance. There is no question of claiming a monopoly. The Evangelical is no more Christian than others who, in understanding and practice, have worked out a different balance, another proportion of Faith.[14]

This kind of statement would not be popular with all Evangelicals, certainly not with the hard-liners represented by the average pre-Keele incumbent. Max Warren enlarged on his point:

The insistence upon the diversity of balance in which the Faith is held is, so I judge, a matter of very great importance indeed. To ignore the validity of different understandings of the mystery of our religion, or the equal authenticity of the experiences which result from such different understandings, is a disastrous obstacle to true Christian unity. Failure frankly to thrash out the theological significance of our differences is one reason for the paralysis which today threatens the whole movement towards Christian unity. An equal threat to any discovery of true unity is to pretend that differences do not matter whereas the spiritual challenge is positively to enjoy them.[15]

117

The currents of evangelical scholarship were beginning to be discernible in the early forties and pioneer work was done by the Evangelical Fellowship for Theological Literature, formed in 1942, with a maximum membership of 200. Max Warren was a founder member, later to be joined in the lead by John V. Taylor, who became Bishop of Winchester. The Fellowship published several theological works, notably in the fifties and sixties and would admit to neither conservative nor liberal prefix. The Church Missionary Society had been feeling that they needed to be undergirded with theological strength, for, following the upsurge of biblical theology, liberal theology as a whole was in a decline. Inevitably the more conservative members of E.F.T.L. preferred the work of the Tyndale Fellowship and in 1972 E.F.T.L. ceased to exist. The first two secretaries of E.F.T.L. were Canons Gordon Hewitt and Michael Hennell.

Max Warren was greatly in demand on all sides, to sit on committees or commissions, to write prayers for some special occasion. He said that he thought the Archbishop of Canterbury gave him credit for being able to contribute on more subjects than he really felt able but that was the measure of esteem in which Canon Max Warren was held. Had he not been devoted to missionary work he would, one may judge, have made a worthy evangelical bishop – in the succession of Ryle, Moule, Knox and Chavasse.

With the upsurge of evangelical witness of which the Billy Graham crusades represented something of a climax, it was fortuitous that men like Max Warren and John Stott were able to 'hold the line' for Evangelicalism and, when it came to the inevitable fundamentalist controversy, which followed as a reaction to Evangelical advance, again it was fortunate that men like John Stott and Jim Packer were ready and able to answer any charges. The debate began with correspondence in *The Times* from 15 August 1955 and centred on the meaning of the word 'Fundamentalist', the history of Fundamentalism having been written, as it was pointed out, several years before (in 1931) and published in the United States as *The History of Fundamentalism* by S. G. Cole. It appears that the word in question first became current with a series of twelve paper-covered books published between 1909 and 1912 by two wealthy Californians, the brothers Lyman and Milton Stewart. Their purpose was to define historic orthodoxy.

In 1920, the word 'Fundamentalist' was used in a New York

newspaper (unknown) to describe the delegates to a northern Baptist convention who wished 'to re-instate, re-affirm and re-emphasise the fundamentals of our New Testament faith' and since that date 'Fundamentalism' has become linked with certain extremes and extravagances, particularly in the United States, which brought the term into disrepute and made it, in some circles, almost synonymous with Obscurantism.

John Stott, in an article in *Crusade* in 1956, which they later published as a booklet, dealt with some of the 'extremes and extravagances', viz. 'a total rejection of all *Biblical criticism*', an 'excessively literalist interpretation of the Bible' and view of 'the nature of Biblical inspiration'. The author then went on to define the more traditional and conservative attitudes to Scripture which, it was true to say, few of the opponents of so-called Fundamentalism really appreciated. This part of the booklet concluded with a statement of disarming simplicity – John Stott at his most persuasive and like C. S. Lewis in style:

A man who loves his wife will love her letters and her photographs because they speak to him of her. So if we love the Lord Jesus we shall love the Bible because it speaks of Him. The husband is not so stupid as to prefer his wife's letters to her voice, or her photograph to herself. He simply loves them because of her. So too we love the Bible because of Christ. It is his portrait. It is His love letter.

Christ is thus the Key to the Scriptures. It is He who sets His seal on them, and it is to Him that they bear witness.

The booklet dealt, in part two, with the other main criticism voiced by opponents, the charge of 'emotionalism'. The place of the mind, the emotions and the will in personal conversion are all dealt with and reference is made to the essential doctrines present in Evangelism. Finally, the need for a decision and the possibility of sudden conversion are covered.

It was as well that this forty-one page booklet reached the evangelical public in 1956 for, in June 1957, something of a bomb burst on them with the publication of a book by Gabriel Hebert attacking conservative Evangelicals for their fundamentalist views – another counterblast to the Billy Graham missions. Early on, the author raised a wider issue which, in the eighties, appears very dated:

Here is I.V.F., with its splendid witness to the authority of the Gospel of God over men's personal lives and the saving of their individual souls. Here it stands in the line of the biblical and Christian tradition. But what has it to say

119

about God's world, and the problems of our social life? For it is not sufficient to say that if only individuals are converted and give their hearts to God all will be well; it is still necessary for them to know how to live their lives after they are converted, amid all the problems of business, commerce and social relations.

And here is S.C.M., bravely setting out to tackle the whole problem of Christian living, those of social life, and of Biblical criticism, and of the unity of all Christians, and all the rest, and these problems are so pressing and so complicated that, however much one tries to find the Christian way, one is in danger of becoming immersed in the discussion of problems and yet more problems, and losing sight of the one thing needful – the knowledge of God Himself.

S.C.M. and I.V.F. find it difficult to work together; they pursue separate paths, not helping one another. The one is seeking the salvation of the whole man, and of the social life in which he is immersed; the other, the entire conversion of the individual to God. Can they not come together, for the sake of what each has to give to the other, to God's glory.[16]

Gabriel Hebert bases his attack on Fundamentalism mainly on the conservative Evangelical attitude to inspiration and biblical interpretation and he also hit hard at 'the religion of experience'. But he is wise enough to see the sincerity of the conversion experience:

Here is part of one of the letters from *The Times* correspondence (22 Aug. 1955): 'I am a university graduate, and a comparatively successful business man of thirty-one. I lived with no church, Bible, or other religious background until last year and in spite of having many friends, good health, worldly goods, and no particular worries, I was frustrated, dissatisfied, and unhappy with life . . . At Harringay on the 3rd May 1954 I heard the New Testament gospel for the first time in my life. Since then my life has been completely changed – pride, snobbery, frustration, anxiety, and a meaningless existence have been replaced by love, joy and an abundant and purposeful life. What I could not do, Christ has done . . . ' Reading through that correspondence, one longs that many of the critics of Fundamentalism might know what the Fundamentalists have known'.[17]

Three days after the letter in *The Times* quoted above appeared, John Stott entered the correspondence by contending that the word 'Fundamentalism' had become 'almost a symbol for Obscurantism, and is generally used as a term of opprobrium. It appears to describe the bigoted rejection of all biblical criticism, a mechanical view of inspiration and an excessively literalist interpretation of Scripture'. He said he would prefer to be called a 'conservative Evangelical'. 'Conservative Evangelical' still remains an acceptable label, if label there must be, for those who continue to believe in the need for personal salvation through faith in the substitutionary death of Jesus Christ on the cross, also in the divine inspiration and essential reliability of the Scriptures insisting on the Reformed truth that the teaching of the church and human reasoning must always be tested against the normative witness of Scripture. Evangelicals remember that Luther sat under Scripture and allowed himself to be judged by it whereas his opponent Erasmus stood above Scripture and judged it. This is the real difference between Evangelicals and so many others. In due course the term 'Fundamentalist' came to have rather loaded overtones: 'In later years the term "fundamentalism" came to denote an unduly defensive and obscurantist attitude which was anti-scholarly, anti-intellectual and anti-cultural. For this reason many conservative theologians who might be regarded as heirs of the original fundamentalists disown this label today.'[18]

The anti-intellectual attitude among earlier Evangelicals had persisted for many years and proved a great stumbling block to progress. It lasted for about eighty years until after the end of the Second World War and contributed an 'anti' complex. 'They continued their good works but were thrown on the defensive intellectually, becoming anti-Rome, anti-ritual, anti-biblical criticism, anti-Darwin and anti-worldliness.'[19]

Reviewing Gabriel Hebert's work in the *Church of England Newspaper*, Hugh Montefiore, now Bishop of Birmingham, wrote that 'whatever else Billy Graham's campaign achieved in this country there can be no doubt that it focussed attention on the issue of "Fundamentalism" '. To be fair to Herbert, although he believed that Fundamentalism, in its worst aspects, was 'a grave menace to the church', he saw the good points of Evangelicalism and he hoped to find, through his controversy, the ground for true unity – the unity he once hoped for in Parish Communion.

The year following the appearance of Hebert's book, the evangelical riposte appeared on the scene. Dr Packer's work, *Fundamentalism and the Word of God* (I.V.F., 1958), gave Evangelical Anglicans the chance to reassess their position in the light of evangelism's success under Billy Graham and under the impact of the criticism which almost inevitably followed. He said: 'The fact is that here we are faced in principle with a choice between historic Evangelicalism and modern Subjectivism:

between a Christianity that is consistent with itself and one that is not; in effect, between one that is wholly God-given and one that is partly man-made.'

Dr Packer admitted that Evangelicals had not always submitted to the full authority of Scripture as much as they thought they had. (Doubtless partly a reference to the need for faithful scholarship and a continuing Reformation.) He went on to underline that the real controversy was over the authority of Christ and of Scripture; the relation between the Bible and reason. However, Packer readily admitted that there was room, in an evangelical outlook, for human reason, intelligence and criticism:

We would not be misunderstood. We have nothing to say in defence of the real obscurantism which would ignore altogether the questions raised by modern critical enquiry. We deplore the idea that Evangelicals ought to have, or look for, ready-made 'party-line' answers to all these problems. On many questions of biblical history and exposition there is room for real and legitimate difference of opinion, and no doubt always will be. All that we insist on is that no critical discussion is sound or legitimate that is not based on the Bible's own view of itself. We entirely agree with Hebert that in Bible study 'we are required to be at once humble and docile, and alert and critical'.[20]

With the rebirth of Biblical theology and the decay of the old liberalism evangelical scholarship had come to life but it was due in large measure to the work of the Inter-Varsity Fellowship and the Evangelical Fellowship for Theological Literature, although many would not mention these in the same breath. Men like Jim Packer, Derek Kidner, G. W. Bromiley and, in Australia, Leon Morris were later joined by such men as Michael Green and John B. Taylor (becoming Bishop of St Albans) but, always, Evangelical Anglicans leant, to some extent, on non-Anglican scholars, with whom they had very much in common, for example, of the Christian Brethren, Professor F. F. Bruce and the Baptist Dr G. R. Beasley Murray. Such men were united with their Anglican brethren in the publishing programme of I.V.F. (U.C.C.F.).

10
The Hard Facts of Evangelicals and Unity

THE PROBLEMS OF UNITY sufficiently exercised the mind of Geoffrey Fisher, the Archbishop of Canterbury, that he asked both Catholics and Evangelicals to produce documents, declaring their standpoints, hopefully with the result that common ground might be established and differences, if possible, resolved. After the publication of *Catholicity* (London, 1947) came the evangelical response *The Fulness of Christ* (S.P.C.K., 1950), with a foreword by the archbishop. With the perspectives of evangelical history it is interesting to note that the writers included the principals of four theological colleges, Ridley Hall, London College of Divinity which became St John's, Nottingham (Donald Coggan), Wycliffe Hall and St John's, Durham, also theologians Henry Chadwick and Geoffrey Lampe plus Max Warren. The chairman was the Archdeacon of Sheffield, D. E. W. Harrison and all were members of the Evangelical Fellowship for Theological Literature (1942–72).

The book referred to the 'conflict left by the Reformation', and to that time when 'the champions of the old order would have nothing to do with the new insights'. *The Fulness of Christ* made clear statements of the evangelical doctrines of grace and faith, justification and sanctification – it was an exemplary, confessional work. 'The weight of historic precedent is authoritative', the book declared 'but it is not conclusive: the final criterion is the Word of God.' Along the path to unity hopes were raised of resolving the conflict between Evangelicals and Catholics but there were no obvious long-term results.

Evangelical Anglicans have even been somewhat ambivalent in relation to unity with fellow evangelicals, let alone with others of different persuasions. On the one hand, they thrive in the atmosphere of the Keswick Convention, where the different denominations are all represented but, on the other hand, they often find it difficult actually to work with other branches of the Christian Church in evangelistic work (where they should feel, intrinsically, on 'their own ground'). Still more difficult have

Evangelicals in Anglicanism found it to consider effectively a move towards unification and fellowship with other Churches. There has been individual love and co-operation at a spiritual level but sadly wanting is the drawing together of broadly evangelical denominations in a united Church.

However, a notable exception was evidenced in the Church of South India which came into being in September 1947 and represented the coming together of the Anglican Church of India, Burma and Ceylon with the Methodists in the South India Province and the Presbyterian, Congregational and Dutch Reformed elements. The new Church splendidly preserved the congregational, presbyterian and episcopal elements of all the churches and agreed gradually to take episcopacy into its system. However, some 40,000 Anglicans refused to join the Church and the new union was given a kind of provisional approval in 1955 by the Convocations of Canterbury and York declaring a state of 'limited inter-communion'. It must be admitted that Evangelicals of all the participating denominations were not specially enthusiastic but Bishop Stephen Neill, missionary statesman and writer, led the way in showing keenness.

The idea of unity was in the air when, in 1955, the Methodist Conference accepted the invitation from the Church of England to commence talks to explore the possibility of union and formal conversations duly commenced. The Committee was chaired by Dr H. J. Carpenter, Bishop of Oxford, and the leading evangelical on his side was Dr C. A. Martin, Bishop of Liverpool. On the Methodist bench, evangelical leaders were Dr W. E. Sangster of Central Hall, Westminster, and the Rev. T. D. Meadley, Principal of Cliff College, Sheffield. Dr Leslie Weatherhead also represented the Methodists. Clearly, enormously important issues had to be faced, notably episcopacy and the priesthood, to say nothing of the nature of the sacraments, but it was certainly a day of high hopes for unity and Evangelicalism when the two Churches agreed to explore together the possibility of growing into union. Re-reading the report of this Committee, *Conversations between the Church of England and the Methodist Church* (C.I.O., 1963), is encouraging compared with the minutiae of debate on more recent liturgical problems and, in view of the very considerable give and take agreed upon, it is exceedingly disappointing to realise that Anglican and Methodist Churches largely still go their own separate ways. At least the two sides set out with an expectation of achieving something acceptable to each of the two Churches and one cannot resist the thought that, brooding over their deliberations, was the spirit of John Wesley himself who had, to his dying day, seen himself as a member of the Church of England and who was, one could say, the archetypal Evangelical Anglican. The coming back again into the Anglican fold of the newer, breakaway evangelical Church seemed, at least to all but the Anglo-Catholics, a very natural development – in principle at least. There was also a feeling, in the deliberations, that they provided an ideal opportunity for re-examining primitive Christianity and for re-emphasising the nature of the Christian Gospel of salvation, by grace, through faith: 'God has blessed his people despite their separation and our varying traditions are rich with his gifts. But what should have been a rich and diverse catholicity has in fact often become merely the compulsive narrowness of a denominational ethos, or a sterile and backward acceptance of an uncriticised inheritance.' (p. 19 of the report.)

Few difficulties were envisaged on questions of Church order, ministry and on acceptance, in due course, of the episcopacy, but the nature of the priesthood required special examination when it was borne in mind that in Methodism the lay preacher sometimes presided at the Lord's Supper, but a refreshingly new view was taken in at least one respect, demonstrating a growing feeling that the whole people of God had a 'priestly' ministry: 'By sharing in his priestly ministry, the church corporately is a royal priesthood, a holy nation. In and under Christ it offers God's pardon and grace to the world, intercedes with God for the world, and offers itself and its worship as a living sacrifice to God.' (p. 23 of the report.)

The Methodists on the committee insisted that any moves towards union should show no repudiation of their spiritual history. Clearly, they were very conscious of their origins, centuries before, in a debilitated and hardly effective Anglican Church with its need for revival of spiritual life in an age of great spiritual decadence. Realising that the episcopate was an inalienable element in the Anglican inheritance, Methodists were not slow to point out that they had their own form of episcopacy in their President and District Chairman. Rather surprisingly to their Anglican brethren, the Methodists felt bound to point out that their adherents would find it difficult to accept fermented wine at the Holy Communion. Not unnaturally, they pointed out that the liturgical vestures of some sections of the Anglican

Church might provide a stumbling block. The report ignored the fact that the Catholic wing of Anglicanism recognised seven sacraments, including such as penance and extreme unction, which would have been 'offensive' to methodism. Therefore, it concentrated on baptism and the Lord's Supper and very considerable agreement was reached on both subjects. Astutely, so as to satisfy all the elements in the debate, baptism was seen as a *sacrament* of cleansing, repentance and regeneration and the quite difficult problem of infant baptism, always the main bone of contention between Anglicans and some free churchmen (Baptists and Brethren) was dealt with in a conciliatory way by stating that 'in infant baptism, the faith exercised is that of the Church, not of the child'. (p. 31.)

So far as the Lord's Supper was concerned, a central truth was clearly enumerated: 'Any view of the Eucharist that implies that the work of Christ was 'unfinished' in the sense that we can add to it by anything we do, or that it needs to be done again, must be repudiated as unscriptural.' (p. 32.)

It was hoped that the plan would go before the Convocations of the Church of England and the Conference of the Methodist Church in 1965 and undoubtedly the highlight of the report was the suggested Service of Reconciliation which had been most carefully and sensitively drawn up to involve bishops, priests, ministers and representative lay members of both Churches. In the declaration of intent there was both an Act of Thanksgiving and of Penitence. At such services, the bishop was to declare: 'We receive you, and those whom you represent, into the fellowship of the Church of England, to share and to work with us in the mission to which God has called us.'

Hands were to be outstretched in a gesture of welcome and not only was there to be a laying-on of hands on all ministers of the Methodist Church but the reception of bishops and priests into the fellowship of their counterparts was to be expressed by an equivalent laying-on of hands *on* the Anglicans. Services of this kind were then to be followed by Holy Communion. It was to be a most imaginative procedure.

It was rightly emphasised in the report that, although the Methodist Church stood in the main stream of evangelical tradition, union would mean that it would be prepared to live with both Anglican Evangelicals and Anglo-Catholics. However, it ought surely to have impressed the Evangelicals within Anglicanism that, although their tradition had endured for four centuries,

126

useful reinforcements could be expected from Methodism. Nevertheless, the report made some concession to the Catholic wing by pointing out that Evangelicals and Catholics were *not* mutually exclusive in the Church of Jesus Christ. Of course, there were parts of Anglicanism which Methodists found it difficult to swallow and the 'loaded' words epitomising the problems were, for instance, 'priest', 'priesthood', 'confession' and 'absolution'. However, these difficulties were not emphasised and confidence was expressed that union would be achieved in two phases; 'Full Communion', whilst the two Churches retained their separateness, followed by 'Organic Union' at a later stage. One substantial concession made to the Anglicans was Methodists agreeing that lay administration of the Holy Communion should cease.

Sadly, the report had to include a 'Dissentient View', signed by four of the Methodist members of the committee, including the Principal of Cliff College. Reading their lines of dissidence and also reading between the lines it is clear that objection was being made to the implication that Methodist ministers were to be 're-ordained' and that historic episcopacy included 'apostolic succession', something which, in Wesley's view, was far from proven by Scripture. The four were also unhappy to abandon the right of the non-ordained to preside at communion, in cases of local need. The minority view saw Methodism as keeping bright the lantern of evangelical faith in the universal and authentic (Catholic) Church and they feared they might be leaving an evangelical body to join a 'mixed multitude'.

Exactly as arranged the propositions were put before the Methodist Conference at Plymouth in 1965, it having been agreed that a 75 per cent majority was required before any progress could be made. In fact, the voting was 78 per cent in favour of the scheme so it was then up to the Anglicans to approve or otherwise. The matter dragged on through Convocation; in 1969 the scheme failed to get the overall majority required and in 1972 a further vote was taken but this time, slightly fewer, only 68 per cent of Anglican members approved of the proposals. One might have thought that the Service of Reconciliation, which was a masterpiece of studied ambiguities, would have appealed to the whole Anglican spectrum but it was not to be and the Church witnessed the strange phenomenon, as it was then, of Catholics and Evangelicals voting against a scheme but for opposing reasons. The Anglo-Catholics took exception to the formal 're-ordination' of Methodist ministers on the grounds that it inclined to ignore the doctrine of apostolic succession and the Evangelicals implied that they accepted the Methodists as already being in valid orders. There was a strange irony about all this, particularly when it is remembered, not only that Methodism grew out of Anglicanism but that, of all the free church denominations, Methodism had most in common with the Anglican Church. The Methodists had their own form of episcopacy, they more or less agreed about the sacraments and their form of Sunday worship had strong similarity to Anglican mattins or evensong. With the Congregational and Presbyterian churches there were pronounced differences in Church government and, with the Baptists, the seemingly insuperable extra problems of baptism, so the Methodists, of all Christian people, ought to have been able to 'put it together' with the Church from which they had been hewn and, all honour to them, they were able to agree, but not so with the Anglicans, whose very comprehensiveness proved the real obstacle to accepting Methodism. Ironically enough, in the very year (1972) that the scheme was finally rejected and that in spite of impassioned pleading on its behalf by the Archbishop of Canterbury, Dr Ramsey, the Congregational and Presbyterian Churches agreed to come together to form the United Reformed Church.

Among Evangelical Anglicans, there must have been some who found the thought of outward, constitutional union with Methodists something of a luxury, as they already possessed, in their judgment, through the Keswick kind of spirit, invisible spiritual unity, the only unity worth seeking, some might have said. 'Many Evangelicals also say that the true Church has that unity which God wills', wrote John Lawrence in *The Hard Facts of Unity* (S.C.M., 1961, p. 9).

However, by far the majority of Christians were and are impatient over the quest for unity and there came over the Anglican Church as a whole a certain disillusionment, forcibly expressed by a young intellectual, the Rev. Nick Earle.[1] Writing of the weakness of all schism, he declared:

Another name for this weakness is Sectarianism; and from the moment that two rival organisations claiming the name of Christ appeared in the world the church appeared to the outsider as a sectarian body. It is an appearance which a thousand years of history have made no less damaging to the cause of faith.[2]

128

The hard facts of Evangelicals and unity

Analysing the causes of a failure to agree, Nick Earle writes:

Much is made of the fact that the only obstacle to reunion among Protestant Churches in England is disagreement about the doctrine of the ministry. As, for most people, it is the ministry which defines the Church anyway (Congregational Churches consisting of Congregational ministers and their following, Anglican of the Anglican Bishops and their following, etc.) this does not seem to get one very much further forward.[3]

This may appear somewhat simplistic but the fact of the matter has always been the conflict between the 'high' and the 'low' view of the episcopacy, apostolic succession and the priestly order. Evangelicals have tended to play down these points and for many years they took a 'low' view of the Church as such, partly because, at one time, the evangelical revival commenced by the I.V.F. and Crusaders and other similar organisations was inclined to produce its own brand of Keswick 'All one in Christ Jesus' and partly because the Christian Unions and the Crusader units easily developed, where they were really successful, into para-church organisations. The following is an obvious over-statement by John Lawrence in *The Hard Facts of Unity* (S.C.M., 1961) 'the I.V.F. insists on a narrow Evangelicalism which bars access to spiritual treasures that ought to belong to all Christians.'

This is also a hard criticism but, nevertheless, there is a strong element of truth in the implied view that those Evangelical Anglicans who derive their spiritual birthright from organis-ations with little interest in the doctrine of the Church are gener-ally slow to tackle the really difficult problems of Church unity. At one time it seemed to them that there were too many earthy matters which almost defied hope of solution and that it was far better to concentrate on co-operation in Evangelism, Bible Study and conferences. John Lawrence continued:

One side of Protestant Christianity remains outside the modern ecumenical movement. Both sides suffer more than they know through their separation from each other.

Conservative Evangelicals view ecumenism with suspicion, if not hostility, but it may be doubted whether the movement for unity can make much pro-gress until it gets on better terms with the Conservative Evangelicals.

The author enlarges on the weakness, which he observed, in Anglican Evangelicals and their seeming lack of concern for church life:

Conservative Evangelicals have an apostolic fervour and send more missionaries overseas than all the churches belonging to the World Council, but their
work does not always have the lasting consequences which their zeal
promises. They are apt to allow an interest in the moment of conversion to
obscure the need for the converted to be built up in the community of the
faithful. Not infrequently their converts gravitate eventually to more solid
churches.

However, John Lawrence concedes the point that Evangeli-
cals emphasise the most important factors in true Christian unity,
those of faith and love, and he comes to the judgment that 'In
England, if the Conservative Evangelical wing of the Church of
England began to work actively for the visible unity of the
Church, the situation would be transformed in a few years.'

He points out that in the nineteenth century, through the
foundation of the Bible Society, the Y.M.C.A., the Y.W.C.A.
and the World Evangelical Alliance grew the modern desire for
unity but it has to be added that those movements, like the I.V.F.
and Crusaders, had none of the really 'hard bargaining' to do in
the structures and infra-structures of denominationalism. John
Lawrence concluded,

in retrospect, it looks as if the Conservative Evangelical movement in Britain
crossed the ecumenical watershed at Dr Billy Graham's crusade at Harringay in 1954. At that series of meetings, strict Evangelicals discovered that
they could co-operate in evangelism with other Christians without compromising their distinctive beliefs. In other countries the same forces are
operating but they will work out in different ways.

But how hard the path towards unity has become, even after
the experiences of Harringay! Local Councils of Churches work
their way along it with limited success and here and there rather
enfeebled local mergers take place. Denominational enthusiasms are one thing, it seems, but loyalty to a rather nebulous
inter-Church relationship another matter. 'Why not stay at home
and turn on the TV Sunday service?' some will say.

The element of urgency depends upon God, naturally. But, unlike the path
to be followed, it also depends upon man. It may be that the time is *not* ripe,
that the motives of those seeking reunion are not sufficiently free of oppor-
tunism or the fear of consequences to reach the goal of truth. But if it is not
ripe, if the Church of God must continue to be represented by a handful of
squabbling sects mainly, on the historical side, because of the impatience,
the lack of forgiveness, and the lack of willingness to understand among our
forefathers of three or four hundred years back, then at least let us be in no
doubt where the fault lies on the moral side.[4]

The hard facts of Evangelicals and unity

In spite of the problems, which are as much practical as theological, hierarchical rather than congregational, there is common agreement, even among Evangelical Anglicans, on the desiderata of unity: 'We must rather assert that the one Catholic Church includes, despite internal schism and varying degrees of imperfection, all those Communions which acknowledge the Lordship of Christ, accept and use the apostolic Scriptures, Creeds and Sacraments, and recognise the need of a ministry set apart with divine authority.'[5] Somewhat sweepingly, yet with a true diagnosis of the real trouble, the author adds that 'the pietistic concept of the invisible Church, as a substitute for the discipline of living together in a true fellowship which demands real sacrifice and love, has no place in Anglican thought'.

If only the Evangelical Anglicans were able to see a visible unity as a spiritual unity as well, they ought to be able to make their wholehearted contribution towards the union of denominations:

It makes no difference how often we assure the outside world that we love each other; so long as we continue to live in separate houses, to make our own family arrangements, to divorce the *koinonia* of fellowship from the *koinonia* of contribution, to sit at isolated tables, even to meet at five-yearly intervals in solemn conference, our actions will speak louder than our words.[6]

But the real stumbling block to organic and identifiable unity must remain in the field of the apostolic succession, producing the priestly function, the exclusive ability to consecrate the elements and to pronounce the absolution. Its mystique appeals to the Anglo-Catholics ('I am in love with religion' said one), it is played down by Evangelical Anglicans and it is utterly rejected by the free churches. The extreme form of this priestly function for which, Evangelical Anglicans remember, nearly 300 Reformation martyrs died, since they were unwilling to agree to it is the Real Presence brought into the bread and wine by the hands of the consecrating priest.

Another major problem is that existing between the Anglican and Baptist Churches over baptism but many Evangelicals feel that even this problem could be overcome if both baptism by immersion of the adult believer and baptism of infants 'into' the visible church (with parents and godparents making vows) could be made alternatives, although any overall scheme of unity would have to make 're-baptism' out of the question, unless it was conscientiously desired by the individual. However, it must be admitted that these alternatives are not enthusiastically publicised, as yet, by Evangelicals or others. Overriding these identifiable doctrinal problems in the way of unity is the *fact* of 'Rome' against Protestantism and the differences of Church authority represented thereby.

Apostolic succession is, of course, the cornerstone, in Anglican minds, of Absolution and Consecration of the Elements, the words of which only an ordained person may speak. However, there is another view:

When he declares the forgiveness of sinners, whether in public or private ministry, he does so, not by virtue of a mysterious power of absolution conferred on him as an ordained priest, but as the representative spokesman of the church to which has been committed the saving gospel of forgiveness. Absolution is one aspect of the total ministry of the word of reconciliation. It should be observed here that a misunderstanding of John 20.23 has contributed powerfully to the emergence of a false doctrine of apostolic succession; the apostles were not given a special power of absolution to transmit to successors in their office, but were sent by the risen Christ to continue his own ministry of reconciliation.[7]

It is always difficult for Free Churchmen to understand why an Anglican Reader is fully entrusted with the ministry of the Word but is not allowed to pronounce the Absolution and why, generally, he may officiate at a Burial Service but not consecrate the Elements.

At the outset of this chapter much was made of the Anglican–Methodist conversations – a *cause célèbre* for evangelical unity – so it seems appropriate to conclude by referring to the Methodist angle on episcopacy, as seen by an Evangelical Anglican:

In all our discussions about the practicalities of approaches to intercommunion and reunion we Anglicans cause grave difficulties because we are not clear what are the values of the historic episcopate that we are seeking to commend. The symbolic value is clear enough and the opportunity given of fatherly, pastoral care, but so often our apologists go on to speak in terms which suggest that some mystique belongs to the episcopal office as such, ignoring the *episcope* possessed by other officers in the church. It is not without importance that no attempt is made to relate in the report we have been considering the statements about the *episcope* which Methodism has in a corporate form to episcopacy in the Church of England and episcopal ordination.[8]

Years later, the High Anglican view of the episcopate dominated thinking and debates on such subjects as the ordination of women and lay presidency but the *episcope*, as a realised and possessed gift in members of the Church, continued to receive little real attention.

As a footnote to the Anglican–Methodist conversations, it may be noted that, in the sixty years prior to the talks, membership of the Methodist Church declined by about 50 per cent, although the other Free Churches declined in membership by slightly higher percentages.

In the latter part of the seventies, Evangelicals within the Anglican Church became more enthusiastically in favour of positive steps towards unity and certain new measures have worked their way through the synods resulting in covenanting for unity within a specific period, which, however, was not approved. Canon Colin Buchanan, Principal of St John's, Nottingham, a leading liturgical evangelical, has been among the Anglican leaders of this movement.

11

The Honest to God Debate

THE Anglican Church's penchant for producing, at least every few decades, a 'turbulent priest' was illustrated when the then Bishop of Woolwich, John A. T. Robinson, published his attack on Christian orthodoxy which he entitled *Honest to God* (S.C.M., 1963). Formerly a Cambridge don, he was a recognised New Testament scholar and also a liturgical scholar of deep pastoral insight, but his book burst on the Christian world with shattering results, popularising the radical theological discussion of the day. 'The publication of this book was the event which loosed the long pent-up thunders of the gathering storm which exploded in a great and sudden roar, and the echoes of it have gone on reverberating round the hills of the world ever since.'[1]

In one sense, Bishop Robinson was reacting against the success of the great Christian communicators of his times, people like C. S. Lewis, Dorothy Sayers and J. B. Phillips, by asserting that, even with their illuminating help, it was necessary to query the language of the Christian faith, originating with the Apostles. The bishop admitted that his thinking had been coloured by the writings of revolutionary theologians such as Paul Tillich (*The Shaking of the Foundations*),[2] by the questions of Dietrich Bonhoeffer before he was hanged by the S.S. in Hitler's Germany and by Rudolf Bultmann. He questioned the language of Christianity which so often referred to God as being 'up there' or 'out there' and to Jesus Christ as 'ascended to heaven'. He scorned the 'three tier' view of the universe – heaven, earth and hell – adopted by earlier generations. Much more than an up-dating of religious language, the book suggested that the text of the New Testament was couched in 'mythological' terms, that perhaps man had 'come of age', could throw off the language and the moral restraints of his 'childhood', having little or no need for religion as such and so there came about the theme of the 'death of God'. Bishop Robinson regarded the new thinking he advocated as being similar to the discovery that the earth was

134

round, not flat. He compared the proposed new abandonment of orthodox belief with St Paul giving up the Jewish ritual of circumcision. He added:

If Christianity is to survive, let alone to recapture 'secular' man, there is no time to lose in detaching it from the scheme of thought, from this particular theology or *logos* about *theos*, and thinking hard about what we should put in its place. We may not have a name yet with which to replace 'theism'; indeed, it may not prove necessary or possible to dispense with the term. But it is urgent that we should work away at framing a conception of God and the Christian Gospel which does not depend upon that projection.[3]

Denying the transcendence of God, as well as His existence in space or heaven, he advocated 'the Ground of our Being' as the better name for God. As for the activities of God, One who 'inhabits eternity' or 'walks in the garden in the cool of the evening', Bishop Robinson categorised them as 'highly mythological terms'. He implied that the purely secular is the best approach to a knowledge of God and that religion is usually, as in Judaism, a hindrance in that pursuit.

The storm which burst over the Christian Church was one of the most shattering for generations. Some demanded the resignation from his bishopric of John Robinson and even his publisher, the Rev. David Edwards, managing director and editor of the S.C.M. Press, had to admit in the *Church Times*: 'I am well aware that, from the position taken in *Honest to God*, a man might evolve into atheism. But the Bishop is miles away from atheism.'

The book caused many to re-think their faith and possibly to re-state it but it must be freely admitted that theological language was overdue for a 'spring clean'. The point was made by Canon Bryan Green, then Rector of Birmingham, himself once strongly Evangelical: 'I'm delighted with the book, because in my work I'm constantly discussing just this sort of question with many people I meet outside the Christian tradition'.

Bishop Wand had earlier reviewed the book in the *Church Times* making a moderate and calm assessment:

Historians faced with what purports to be an unusually liberal attitude on sex would remember that St Augustine in a particular set of circumstances argued for a charitable judgment many centuries ago. The man in the pew might say that, in spite of the dangers of formalism, a few plain rules and a few liturgical prayers, help to keep him on the upward path (if he may still use the term) when mind and body are alike too weary for independent effort.

Nevertheless, the Bishop's protest is valuable because it will help us to recognise that we have not yet penetrated to the ultimate meaning of God. There is much still to be learnt, and a humble agnosticism is the mark of the greatest Christian thinkers . . . For the man in the street, as well as for the man in the pew, the word 'religion' stands for the best that he knows.[4]

A more trenchant comment was made in a letter to the *Church Times* by Canon Fenton Morley, Vicar of Leeds: 'The book represents a tendency to please the senior common-room agnostic and to spell God with a small g. Dr Robinson's flexible position on morality is fundamentally wrong-headed.'

Inevitably, Bishop Mervyn Stockwood of Southwark, Dr Robinson's diocesan, was heavily involved in the controversy produced by *Honest to God* and was anxious to avoid a split with the Archbishop of Canterbury, Michael Ramsey, who felt bound to address himself to the problem of mounting hostility. It is interesting to note that Bishop Stockwood, who at that time was not very sympathetic to Evangelicals, appointed as his chief adviser over the troubles, Canon Max Warren, a moderate or liberal Evangelical and one respected on all sides.

Max Warren then wrote to the two archbishops, Michael Ramsey and Donald Coggan:

What has so distressed so many in the past weeks of the controversy about the Bishop of Woolwich's book is that so few have sensed his deep missionary concern . . . I know that this missionary concern to confront men with the Christ and so lead them to God is the very heart of his ministry.

So much of the comment on his book, so it seems to me, has picked on sentences which, taken out of context and of the missionary purpose of the book, cannot but be disturbing to many devout souls. Set against that, however, is the fact of which I have myself had ample evidence, from a surprisingly wide selection of people no less devout, that the book has been not only a stimulus to their minds but also a reinforcement of their faith.[5]

Max Warren, as one would expect, showed the moderation and tolerance of a gentle Evangelical but his views were hardly typical and summarising more general evangelical reaction to *Honest to God*, Dr J. I. Packer wrote: 'And now there lies before us another episcopal essay in iconoclasm this time from the Bishop of Woolwich, under the title – catchy, disarming, cocky, testy, priggish, take it how you will – *Honest to God*.'[6]

Dr Packer, whilst readily agreeing that fresh appraisals are always needed in an era of cultural change, found that Dr Robinson was offering, for the most part, second-hand views – those of the German theologians – and this is how Dr Packer summarised the work: '*Honest to God* is confessedly a tentative book. Indeed, for one of such an original mind as Dr Robinson, its ideas are surprisingly second-hand; it is just a plateful of washed-up Tillich fried in Bultmann and garnished with Bonhoeffer.'[7]

From an evangelical point of view, it was important that a theological reply to Dr Robinson's startling suggestions should have been given without delay and Dr Packer provided just that. He pointed out that all that is distinctive in the Christian faith had been elbowed out of the mind of Dr Robinson, including the divinity, virgin birth, atonement and resurrection of the Lord Jesus Christ. The Christian life was to be reduced merely to loving and evil to just a failure to love. *Honest to God*, significantly, came to a society which had become affluent after the seven years of the Macmillan government with his own phrase 'You've never had it so good'. The book's publication also came to 'the permissive society', with the gradual collapse of conventional Christian morality, open discussion of homosexuality and an alarming increase in juvenile crime. The flames of humanism were fuelled by *Honest to God*. Was there a positive connexion between Bishop Robinson's apparently attempted overthrow of conventional Christianity and the contemporary discarding of orthodox morality? That there is a relationship few would deny but it is at least interesting to note that the printing of many impressions of the book coincided with the then concurrent exposure of John Profumo, Secretary of State for War, in June 1963, for lying to his colleagues and to Parliament about his association with a coterie of dubious characters. And *Lady Chatterley's Lover* had been reprieved in 1960, with Bishop Robinson as one of its passionate advocates.

Although Dr Robinson made many people re-think their Christianity, he was thoroughly destructive in his attack on Christian doctrine. He ridiculed, he guyed orthodoxy and he sought to undermine the faith of the faithful. But like Dr Barnes, Bishop of Birmingham, thirty years before, he overplayed his hand and his book was soon, if not forgotten, almost discarded. But his influence on the Christian Church at the time was undoubted for by his clever assertions he unsettled many. He would reduce the Son of God, the Saviour of the world, simply to 'the Man for others'. In his pursuit of what he describes as 'Worldly Holiness', the bishop urged a 'non-religious' understanding of Prayer and when it came to ethics, whilst he welcomed the revolution of 'The New Morality', he appeared to lament the passing of sound doctrine and morals: 'There are plenty of voices within the Church greeting it with vociferous dismay. The religious sanctions are losing their strength, the moral landmarks are disappearing beneath the flood, the nation is in danger. This is the end-term of the apostasy from Christianity: the fathers rejected the doctrine, the children have abandoned the morals.'[8]

Dr Robinson insisted that the 'new morality' was merely the insistence on love, absolute love, as he saw it, without the absolutes of Christianity. He looked for a religionless metamorphosis of some kind of Christian belief and practice; he allied himself with Julian Huxley as well as with the German theologians. Small wonder that, in the preface to his book, *Keep Yourselves from Idols* (Church Book Room Press, 1963), Dr Packer reminds us that a bishop, consecrated to uphold the doctrines of the Scriptures and of the Thirty-nine Articles, is not expected to air his disbelief in public or appear 'to be driving a coach and four through the plain and acknowledged sense of scripture, the teaching of the Thirty-nine Articles and the beliefs of the mass of English churchmen'. However, Dr Packer admitted that Dr Robinson had very worthy intentions in his writing and that there were sad deficiencies in orthodoxy which needed correction, but he thought that

the saddest thing about *Honest to God* is that it was written with genuine pastoral and evangelistic intent, to meet genuine pastoral and evangelistic needs. The bishop is rightly unhappy about the arrogant and unsympathetic theological formalism with which the orthodox are inclined to rough-house doubters and questioners ('God is in heaven, and you can't catch him – now open your mouth and swallow the creed!').

Clearly, Jim Packer's admission reflected some of the hectoring, high-pressure tactics of certain elements in Evangelicalism which, fortunately, found less and less place in Anglicanism but it also reflected an evangelical willingness to recognise good motives. Perhaps the most important point made by Dr Packer on the deficiency of Dr Robinson's particular understanding of love as the expression of the Christian faith is made thus:

But I could never learn what love is from contemplating the non-personal, non-redeeming 'God' of Tillichite theology. Nor could I learn it from Dr Robinson's Jesus, who, it seems, neither came down from heaven nor put away anyone's sins by his death. Dr Robinson talks glowingly about love being perfectly revealed in Jesus, but it is not clear what that can mean when the biblical meaning of the cross is denied.

The former Bishop of Woolwich went further than all the old modernists in his destruction of scriptural authority and in *Keep Yourselves from Idols*, Dr Packer highlights this fundamental deviation:

> The source from which the bishop's mishandling of Scripture, his eroding of the substance of the faith, and his disastrous pastoral and evangelistic suggestions, all spring, is in his mistaken view of the relations between the Bible, that of which it speaks, and the world which it addresses. This is the real root of all the trouble.

And, arrestingly, he points out the deficiency of the new gospel, 'which is no gospel' of Dr John Robinson: 'To accept the anti-theistic presuppositions of humanism, and then to disembowel the Christian story in order to be able to tell it to humanists more arrestingly, is evangelistic *hara-kiri*, and the poorest ambassadorship for Christ.'

Undoubtedly, *Honest to God*, written in some haste and during a period of recovery from an illness, created enormous interest throughout the Christian world. The book became a bestseller, compulsory reading for all Christians and fuel for the flames of any theological controversy. At least, it made all Christians with any desire intellectually to appreciate their faith and to love God with their minds, re-examine what they meant by *where* God is and what they implied by using some of the well-known phrases of the faith. Dr Robinson frequently affirmed during the controversy, that he accepted the Catholic Faith and wished to commend it to all those as yet unable to accept 'the Living Christ as their Saviour and Lord'.

An interesting sidelight on Bishop Robinson's book is that he quoted extensively from the New Testament of the New English Bible, published in 1961. This has never been a very popular version with Evangelicals, who up to that time, following John Stott and others, stood by the Revised Standard Version for general accuracy of translation. However, at a large meeting at the Albert Hall in 1961, to celebrate the 350th anniversary of the publication of the Authorised Version of the Bible, otherwise known as the King James version, Dr Martyn Lloyd-Jones of the Westminster Congregational Chapel, a champion of Protestant Evangelicalism, said that 'to hear people talk one might think that N.E.B. stood for 'New Evangelical Bible'!

It was not only Evangelicals who rose to do battle with the Bishop of Woolwich and his Teutonic mentors – the Anglican Church as a whole was thoroughly offended. One of those who wrote at some length was the Rev. O. Fielding Clarke, a theologian of not strictly evangelical persuasion, who had been chaplain of Worcester College, Oxford, before turning to parochial life. His book *For Christ's Sake* was a reply to *Honest to God* and he attacked in no uncertain terms:

But one cannot have one's cake and eat it. Either one is 'an ordinary churchman' and not 'a professional theologian' or one is bishop and pastor, in this case with more than ordinary attainments as a theologian. If one is the latter it is one's duty to think *before* speaking and, if one cannot make up one's mind, at least to refrain from expressing the confusion of one's thought in a five shilling paper-back for our means of mass communication to din into the ears of the unfortunate half-educated – the last people on earth to be helped by such incoherences.[9]

The author deals, as Dr Packer does, with each of Dr Robinson's proposals and he summarises their defections: 'This is one more reason why *Honest to God* is such a deplorable piece of work. It laments the self-absorption of the church only to provide her with more fodder for ingrowing speculation, instead of holding up the already given light of Christ, the Image of God, to a distracted, floundering civilisation.'[10] And he concludes his book with a stirring call:

Yes, Dr Robinson! For Christ's sake let the Church look outwards, but also, for Christ's sake, let it hold up Christ, the given Image of the Invisible God, crucified, risen and to come again in glory. Let the Church hold up Christ as the beacon-light to man himself who is crucified by the greed, stupidity and pride of his fellow man. Let the Church so hold up Christ that men thirsting for justice, peace and abundant life at *all* levels may find in Him their satisfaction.[11]

So the Bishop of Woolwich threw a theological bomb into the Anglican Church which shook the edifice to its foundations. Some good came of it in that the faithful had to re-examine themselves and the rationale of their cherished beliefs but the humanists and agnostics were delighted to have a bishop on their side or so it seemed to them. Evangelical Anglicans, almost to a man, rose up and condemned the iconoclasm of the book and reasserted the fundamentals of the faith. They had always held strictly to the Thirty-nine Articles, for so long under attack by Dr Robinson and many others, such as his bishop, Mervyn

Stockwood, who were for their revision or rejection. No one has done more, over the years, to hold the scholarly and doctrinal line for evangelicals than Dr Jim Packer and, apart from his immediate riposte, in 1963, to *Honest to God*, he contributed very effectively to the doctrinal stability of Evangelical Anglicans by other writing. His pamphlet, *The Thirty-nine Articles* (Church Pastoral Aid Society, 1961), was most timely. He had in mind the changing liturgy which was suggested by the Lambeth Conference of 1958 and he feared that the Church would seek to base its doctrine on the Prayer Book by itself rather than on the Articles. But as Dr Packer pointed out: 'When Parliament ratified our present Articles in 1571, clerical subscription was made obligatory. It is so still', but he admits, 'In fact, the only people since the seventeenth century who have been really enthusiastic about the Articles have been the Evangelicals.'

The erosion of doctrine, with many theologians a long process, and culminating in Dr Robinson's diatribe was, basically, a shift from the moorings of the Articles which themselves underlined the sufficiency and supremacy of Scripture as well as the subordination of the Church to that rule. Furthermore, the great evangelical doctrine of justification by faith, through the grace of God as revealed in Jesus Christ, was, as Dr Packer said, unequivocally enshrined in the Articles: 'The Thirty-Nine Articles, as we have seen, exist to guard the gospel for the Church of England: to keep the clergy preaching it, and the whole Church facing it. For the gospel, the good news of God's remedy for sin, is the food on which the Church must live.'

Objection to the Articles by the High-Churchman stems mainly from the fact that he sees the language of the Reformation in need of up-dating, since theology and knowledge of man has moved on since then. He would say that the Oxford Movement established insights which are not reflected in the Articles. Among some Anglo-Catholic clergy aversion to the Articles is due to the fact they condemn, *inter alia*, the 'sacrifice of masses', the false doctrine abandoned by the Reformers. Certain High Anglicans wish to see in the Lord's Supper another offering of the sacrifice of Christ and, all of them, at least the Real Presence. Evangelicals constantly remind their more Catholic brethren of their mutual subscription and assent to the Articles of Religion.

Evangelical Anglicans should, however, appreciate that the Anglo-Catholic, in his search for revealed truth, wishes to go back historically beyond the time of the Articles to the classical literature of the early fathers, such as Augustine, Cyprian, Ignatius, ('the bread that is the flesh of Jesus Christ, this flesh which has suffered for our sins'), Irenaeus and the Greek Fathers.

Radical clergy wish to revise the Articles because, like Dr Robinson, they wish to move away from Cranmer's unambiguous Protestantism, the orthodox doctrine of the Christian faith. Dr Packer concludes his booklet:

Theologically, the Church of England is adrift today. She is rocked by the storms of doctrinal confusion; and the currents of theological agnosticism and indifference to truth – the fag-end of Latitudinarianism – threaten to carry her away. She knows, in a general sense, that she is out of her proper course. She half-desires to get back to the Bible; but she does not see how. She suspects at times that she ought to be preaching a clearer gospel; but she cannot for the moment do anything about it, because she is not clear herself as to what the gospel is. She has, it seems, forgotten that the Articles, to which she is officially committed – the chart by which she has so long neglected to steer – contain the answer to both her problems. Yet it is so. And it needs to be said quite categorically that the Church of England has no hope whatever of recapturing our country for Christ till the theology of the Articles possesses her mind once more, and the gospel of the Articles is preached once more from her pulpits.

Another evangelical theologian in the Anglican Church who contributed materially in his day to the stability of doctrine was the Rev. Alan Stibbs, Vice-Principal of Oak Hill Theological College. He was a lucid expositor of the Word both as a lecturer and as a writer and one of his best works was *Sacrament, Sacrifice and Eucharist*. The long-running battle with the sacerdotalists and the sacramentalists, also the changes in liturgy which were now being contemplated, caused this much-loved Anglican theologian to write clarifying the issue on the sacrament over which so much controversy had ranged:

Here is the old difference in faith and practice: either the deliberate use of the consecrated elements in the Lord's Supper to make an offering to God, propitiatory in character and intention; or the complete disowning of any such idea or God-ward movement, and the exclusive concentration in the sacrament proper on a movement manwards, by which Christ's death for us is vividly brought to mind, and its enduring benefits symbolically offered for actual appropriation by the believing recipient.[12]

The great error seen by evangelical eyes was that the Trac-tarian or Anglo-Catholic views the consecrated bread and wine as an offering to God, as a re-enactment of sacrifice, the Sacrifice of Christ's Body and Blood. The once-for-all nature of His redeeming death tends to be made by the Anglo-Catholic into a continuing offering to God, in an intercessory way, of the great sacrifice. Evangelicals contend that the only offering to God at the service of Holy Communion is that of themselves as a living sacrifice of gratitude and service. They seek to safeguard the sacrament as bearing witness to the unique and unrepeatable fact of the Lord Christ giving himself once in time as a 'full, perfect and sufficient sacrifice, oblation and satisfaction, for the sins of the whole world'. Evangelicals have sometimes been accused of being 'anti-sacramentalist' in outlook, so far as Holy Communion is concerned and some have undoubtedly given this impression. It is due to an insistence on the primacy of the ministry of the Word of God and an over-reaction against the sacramental emphasis. However, the charismatic movement, bringing together different emphases, has helped to correct the balance.

Evangelical Anglicans have always held strongly to the aspect of the Lord's Supper as the memorial of His death for His people. It is, they contend, a reminder by God to us of His saving work, as Christians plead the efficacy of 'Beneath the cross of Jesus, I fain would take my stand'. Salvation and its sacrament are about God's movement manward, reminding us constantly of Christ offering Himself for us and to us. The Altar is His cross. The Holy Communion is a supper, not a sacrifice: 'We love Him, because He first loved us'. But Evangelicals experience not only remembrance but participation as they receive Christ, symbolically present in the elements, for literally and physically He is now at the right hand of God. But the Lord is still present among His people, in the heart and life of those partaking in His supper, where, through repentance and by faith, they receive Him.

The title of Eucharist comes to us as meaning the service of supreme 'thanksgiving', also perhaps recalling our Lord's words of thanksgiving at the institution of His Supper. However, the term 'eucharistic sacrifice' is not one which Evangelicals can accept and they may feel that even to refer to the Lord's Supper or Holy Communion (the Prayer Book titles) as the Eucharist might detract from the main emphasis of the service.

Similarly in participating in this sacrament we ought to speak not of going to the altar, as though the primary interest is our offering to God, but rather of

143

going to the Lord's table, because the primary and distinctive action in this service is his giving to us, and our chief cause for wonder and thanksgiving is that we are invited to be His guests.[13]

As the word Eucharist becomes very generally used by the Anglican Church, evangelicals feel, as they always have, that its meaning needs continual clarification and that, still, there are better, more descriptive, names to give to the feast. After all, they might argue, 'The Lord's Supper' is exactly descriptive and 'Holy Communion' gets to the heart of the matter whereas the Greek word, *Eucharisteo*, means to give thanks, as St Paul did for the bread which he persuaded his fellow travellers to eat before they were shipwrecked:

The danger of some tendencies, described by some as 'the Liturgical Movement' is lest the offering to God of a weekly or even daily liturgy take the place of, or at least take priority over, the offering to God of the obedience of our daily lives. Yet the latter is the true and the best eucharistic sacrifice.[14]

The Rev. Alan Stibbs, a thorough-going Anglican but always one for drawing all Evangelicals together whenever possible, concluded his excellent book by hoping that the 300th anniversary of the Book of Common Prayer, in 1962, would witness a bringing into the centre of the congregation the whole of the service by removing the Lord's Table from the 'mysterious' east and into the body of the church. Furthermore, he reminded us that it was Cranmer's intention that preaching of the Word should always precede the taking of the Communion. He pointed out the sadness and, indeed, the unbalanced 'diet' of the large Easter and Christmas congregations generally being denied the ministry of the Word.

And so, in 1961, the scene had been set for the long process of revision of the services of the Anglican Church. It was to take many years before, finally in 1980, the Alternative Service Book was to see the light of day, but in the intervening years Christian doctrine was to come under the theological microscope as it passed through the Synods of the Church of England. Not surprisingly, the main areas of controversy were in the proposed alternative services of Holy Communion, where evangelical doctrine was to be contested, every inch of the way. However, it was intended that the new services would be more intelligible to the young and even persuade waverers back into the Anglican fold. At least they represented a positive attempt to counteract the rising tide of humanism and radical theology. *Honest to God* may

The Honest to God debate

have come to some as a shattering blow but the Church was making efforts of unprecedented magnitude to refurbish the fabric of worship.

Perhaps the conflict helped to clarify the mind, for instance, of the Bishop of Southwark, Mervyn Stockwood who wrote:

Fortunately, out of the conflict emerged a new school of Evangelicals which, while continuing to make a distinctive contribution was open-minded and flexible. By the time I had left the diocese I had appointed men from this new school to some of the most responsible positions. What is more, the quality of its ordinands was as impressive as those who came from other traditions, perhaps more so.[15]

The year 1964 saw the publication of the *Paul Report*, the result of a two-year study by Leslie Paul covering the deployment and payment of clergy. It came as a shock to the Church to realise that, whereas only 17 per cent of the clergy ministered to 34 per cent of the population in inner-city areas, 38 per cent ministered to 10.5 per cent in rural areas. This was at a time when, incidentally, ordinations were increasing slightly.

Leslie Paul, a widely experienced journalist and tutor, was for two years employed as Research Director by the Central Advisory Council for the Ministry in order to carry out his enquiry for Church Assembly. He followed this with numerous academic posts, in the U.K. and abroad and was a distinguished Christian philosopher with deep insights. The Anglican Church was fortunate in having a man of such ability to demonstrate beyond contradiction that the more thickly populated the part of the country the lower the percentage of churchgoers and, of course, of ordinands. He contended that 'the clergy were walking away from the people' and only the subsequent Sheffield Scheme came to fruition to remedy the maldistribution of clergy so far as the Northern Province was concerned. But, after twenty years, Leslie Paul's main point is still being argued while another Report (by Canon John Tiller) on the shape of the Church's ministry takes the stage.

145

12
Liturgical Debates

THINGS GENERALLY MOVE move rather ponderously in the Anglican Church and never more so than in matters of liturgy, for the long process of revision, virtually initiated in 1904 by the appointment of the 'Royal Commission on Ecclesiastical Discipline', with the joint objectives of satisfying and yet controlling the Anglo-Catholic tradition, did not reach fulfilment until the *Alternative Service Book* was finally published in 1980. The 1927 and 1928 attempts at Prayer Book revision, after being accepted by the Church, were defeated by the will of the people voiced in Parliament but it was to take another thirty-seven years before further attempts at the production of a new Book were initiated in the *Prayer Book Measure* of 1965.

A Liturgical Commission had been established in 1955 and for fifteen years following the Measure of 1965, the Convocations and the House of Laity, then the General Synod, from its formation in 1970, were occupied with a long programme of liturgical business.

It is important to emphasise that only an *alternative* book of liturgy was being provided and that the Book of Common Prayer, 1662, retained its authority as a doctrinal standard. Similarly the Thirty-nine Articles, although not included in the A.S.B., were retained by the Church. It was insisted by the Church that the new services did not in the least alter the doctrinal position of the Church founded, as ever, on Holy Scripture.

From the start, many Evangelical Anglicans were suspicious of a revised liturgy, feeling that the safeguards to the Reformed Faith represented by the Book of Common Prayer, including the Articles, might be whittled away. Therefore, very much public and private debate ensued, phrases and words were argued over until the A.S.B. of 1980 was achieved, finding general acceptance in the Anglican Church.

There are several important things to be said about liturgy and

146

Evangelical Anglicans. The first is that, although they were by no means averse to change, in fact they pioneered change in certain fields, notably hymnody, dance and drama, they were very reluctant to let go the Evangelicalism enshrined in the B.C.P. They rejoiced that Cranmer's work was 'Calvary centred' and they saw it as a masterpiece of the Reformation. They loved, as did many other Anglicans, Cranmer's majestic phrases, the incomparable *Prayer of Humble Access* and his doublets, e.g. 'author of peace and lover of concord'. With other Anglicans too, many of them were steeped in the phraseology of the B.C.P., as they were in that of the Authorised Version and were reluctant, initially, to see any good in the abandonment, as they saw it, of the glorious language of the seventeenth century in favour of the idioms of the twentieth. The older generation of Anglicans, Evangelical and otherwise, knew the old services by heart, their style being deeply ingrained in Anglican consciousness, so these church-goers were horrified at the thought of losing even a proportion of '1662'.

However, the process of revision was set in motion and whereas an earlier generation of Evangelicals might have fought it tooth and nail, a new, more overtly scholarly and wishing-to-be-involved generation of Evangelical Anglicans fortunately decided to enter the thick of the debate. Examples of this commitment were to be found in Canon Colin Buchanan and the Rev. Roger Beckwith, both intellectuals and academics but representing, perhaps, slightly different viewpoints – certainly different styles – within the evangelical tradition.

A start was made on revision with the appearance in 1965 of the first series of alternative services, which approximated very closely to the rejected 1928 book. It may well be wondered why, apparently, the climate had so changed as to make such a re-evaluation possible and there are two main reasons. First, that the age of ecumenism had perhaps caused a greater understanding of theological differences and secondly that the Liturgical Movement within the Anglican Church had caused a greater awareness of possibilities for change.

Series 2 services appeared in 1967 and represented a kind of bridge between the old and the new, retainint the 'thee' and the 'thou' but introducing the Peace as a revolutionary idea in corporate worship. Then, in 1973, came Series 3, to which there was some initial resistance so, in 1976, Series 1 and 2 appeared in a combined revised form (now incorporated in A.S.B. as Rite B):

147

From controversy to co-existence

The aim of the *First Series* is clearly to legalise all the common, current liturgical practices in the Church of England, with the notable exceptions of reservation of the sacrament and auricular confession.

The Alternative Services: Second Series contains the new material compiled by the Liturgical Commission including a Draft Order for Holy Communion, the most interesting and radical feature of the book, intended to provide the Church with some indication of a future of Anglican eucharistic pattern.[1]

But many Evangelicals could sense the dangers of the liturgical reappraisal and not surprisingly they re-emphasised the need to retain the Articles as a safeguard.

It is clear that the Church of England has entered a period of intensive liturgical experiment and innovation; and clear, too, that the motive behind this is not simply the desire for services that will be more intelligible and meaningful today than those which we already have, but also the wish to get into closer step with the rest of the Anglican Communion.

Then, in the second place, one subordinate purpose of the present revision programme is to satisfy the Anglo-Catholics, who have long been vigorous and vocal in complaint because so much of what they think a liturgy should contain is absent from the Prayer Book of 1662.

And, in the third place, the present-day Anglican tradition of liturgical scholarship is notoriously lacking in sympathy with the Protestant theology of the Articles.[2]

Foremost among evangelical theologians and scholars in contention at this time were Colin Buchanan, a member of the Archbishops' Liturgical Commission from 1964 and then on the staff (currently Principal) at St John's College, Nottingham: the Rev. Roger Beckwith, then Librarian of Latimer House, Oxford, and Gervase Duffield, previously editor of *The Churchman* and a thoughtful, vociferous member of Church Assembly.

Evangelicals, always the champions of lay involvement and of the priesthood of all believers, were delighted with the new Congregational involvement and, having a greater awareness of their Free Church brethren, they took some pride in the fact that the liturgy of the new services asserted the fact that congregations in Anglican churches took more part in their services than members of almost any other denomination. Further, Evangelicals welcomed the increased corporateness of the proposals shown in the various responses and they most assuredly liked the idea of a President instead of a Priest, a change which, not surprisingly, caused such a storm of protest from traditional quarters when it appeared in Series 3 in 1973. Was the idea of the 'priesthood', so dear to Anglo-Catholic hearts, about to change? Evangelicals had always pointed out that 'priest' was not really a New Testament word for applying to the Christian ministry, although they conceded, very readily, that 'priest' is derived from 'presbyter'. Incidentally, it was perhaps unfortunate that the launching of the word 'President' on Anglican minds coincided with the presidential scandal of Watergate!

Evangelicals had also to concede that, although the 1662 service of Holy Communion splendidly safeguarded the doctrine of the atonement, it did not do justice to the other central doctrines of the resurrection and the ascension, also the second Advent. On the other hand there was a constant fear among the evangelical constituency that the 'one perfect and sufficient sacrifice' of Cranmer would somehow be diluted by those who saw some other kind of sacrifice in the Eucharist. Furthermore, Evangelicals and others were concerned that the 'offering' of the bread and wine in consecration were only seen in that way and that the only other sacrifice was of ourselves. The proposed New Communion Service was the subject of the dissentient voice of Colin Buchanan on two counts:

In joining with the Commission in generally commending this Report, I reluctantly dissent from the last paragraph but one of section 24. Inquiry has shown that the phrase 'we offer unto thee this bread and this cup' in this paragraph is unacceptable to many Anglicans. I could not use it myself.

I also dissent from the proposed optional petition for the dead in section 14 for doctrinal reasons.[3]

Enlarging on his first dissident note, he argues that the 'offering' of the bread and wine to God is something of an intrusion:

Today, to the question 'What do we need, and what do we *not* need, to say in a eucharistic liturgy?' the answer that many of them will give is 'We *do* need to give thanks over the bread and the cup, but we do *not* need to make specific verbal reference to offering the elements to God in that thanksgiving.'[4]

As this wording was debated in Church Assembly, there was a certain amount of give and take between the Anglo-Catholic and evangelical wings of the church. Miss V. J. Pitt of Southwark diocese said:

I firmly believe in the eucharistic sacrifice, though I do not mean what my Evangelical friends sometimes think I mean. I do not think there is any formula which could exclude that understanding of the Eucharist, and this goes as far as it possibly can without offending our Evangelical brethren to meet the particular difficulty of saying what you are doing.[5]

On the subject of Prayers for the Dead, Colin Buchanan, not surprisingly, objected because they were 'explicitly condemned by the Thirty-nine Articles' and 'the New Testament contains no prayers for the dead'.[6]

Here again, Church Assembly debated much on the subject and a way was sought of remembering the faithful departed with thanksgiving without suggesting that their lot could be or needed to be influenced by prayer. Lady Alethea Eliot of the Worcester diocese had this to say:

Those who opposed this service spoke as if the prayers were imploring God to change his mind about those who had died; as if, in a way, the whole of the Dream of Gerontius, purgatory and all, was being introduced into the service for Burial of the Dead, instead of, as it was, the commending of those who had died to God's loving care.[7]

A thoroughly desirable new concept was found in the substitution in the A.S.B. of 'keep you to everlasting life' by 'keep you in life eternal' for Evangelicals had always stressed that eternal life was to be possessed here and now and that it continued in that same quality after death. But almost nothing caused so much bother as the re-casting of the Lord's Prayer. The introduction with Series 3 in 1973, of the 'You' form of addressing God did not, in general, offend evangelical minds but it was something of a stumbling block to the older generation and those of more modern outlook could rejoice in the change from 'thy creatures of bread and wine' to 'these gifts of your creation'. Evangelicals also welcomed the new emphasis on the two meanings of the Bread, as symbolising both Our Lord's Body and the Body of believers.

The Holy Communion 'Alternative Services Series 1 and 2 Revised' (introduced as a concession to those who never moved to Series 3) found general acceptance as the Church of England moved, slowly and steadily, away from Mattins or Morning Prayer, as its main service, to Family Communion or Parish Communion, sometimes starting as early as 9 a.m. and in some parishes followed by the Parish Breakfast which some likened to the *Agape* or Love Feast of New Testament times. As the whole family was able to come together to the Family Communion and non-communicating children were encouraged to join their parents at the communion rail, kneeling for a blessing, the service became much more central and generally more attractive, at the same time. Furthermore, the new service introduced the preaching or ministry of the Word as an integral part so, one way and another, Evangelical Anglicans were being persuaded that here was an opportunity not to be missed. The marriage of word and sacrament makes very considerable appeal to a broad spectrum of churchmanship. Another development was that a much wider and deeper meaning was found by many evangelicals in the Lord's Supper. The Rev. Alan Stibbs was seen to move 'beyond memorialism'[8] in his book, already referred to, *Sacrament, Sacrifice and Eucharist*.

The wider context of the Holy Communion, its sociological and doctrinal possibilities, are summed up:

> For the Eucharist is not only the supreme Christian act. It is also a rite which has a strong sociological significance, which ties it into the prevailing thought and aspiration of the world. Beyond this, it happens to be the most nearly universal of all Christian acts of worship which, in spite of all the quarrels once surrounding it, today causes almost no strife. Here the radical and the Conservative are one, however much they differ over the creeds and the scriptures. The eucharist is at once peaceable and sociologically evangelistic, and the more the Church teaches about it and lays stress on it, the fairer its future seems likely to be.[9]

There had previously been a tendency for evangelical churches to minimise, by implication, the value of the service of Holy Communion simply because they saw themselves set in the parish for the preaching of the gospel and for this they felt it necessary to steer clear of too great a sacramental emphasis. 'No gospel like this feast' was sung only by the Christian Brethren!

> The modern Evangelical, because the modernization of the Prayer Book has been delayed for centuries, and because his great concern is to reach the modern unchurched masses with the gospel, not because he is opposed to liturgical worship or to the teachings embodied in Cranmer's liturgy (quite the contrary), is sometimes tempted to throw off restraint and act like a non-conformist.[10]

It should be remembered that 'new services' are sometimes required to meet new needs as when the service of adult baptism was added to the Prayer Book to provide for those who, during the disturbed times of Cromwell's day, had been prevented from being baptised in infancy. Could it now be argued that the magnificent language of Cranmer was a bar to modern man understanding the services of the Christian Church? New versions of

151

the Bible had been in vogue for many years, so why not a revised version of the Prayer Book? G. E. Duffield comments:

It is important to locate the problem correctly. It is not simply a question of getting rid of all the theological and technical terms which sound rather mysterious to twentieth century man nurtured in his scientific culture. It is easy to complain that people do not understand what we Christians mean by justification, sanctification, regeneration and other similar terms. Of course they do not understand. If they want to understand the Christian faith they will have to learn it.[11]

The author wisely points out that to learn any science one has to assimilate the appropriate scientific terms but neither Christians nor scientists should overdo their use of technical terms in the interests of communication:

When people complain that the Prayer Book is unintelligible and keeps men away from church, we need to enquire whether the Bible is similarly unintelligible. The problem must be properly analysed: is it one of linguistics and intellect or is it one of the spirit, heart and will? If we do not analyse aright, we shall be in danger of emasculating the rich teaching value of our present Prayer Book. And if homely phraseology would solve all the problems, one would have expected the Free Churches to have attracted all the lapsed churchgoers; but the situation in England seems to be that they are worse off than the Anglicans with their allegedly unintelligible liturgy! The problem surely cannot be one of language alone.[12]

This was a very interesting point which became clarified with the use of the new Communion services. Older people tended to stick rigidly to 1662 and to favour the 8 a.m. celebration, where there was a better chance that the old language would be retained but younger people, led by the younger clergy, all anxious to encourage the participation of the children and youth, came down heavily in favour of the new services. But the question 'Did the new services attract more people to Church?' must remain unanswerable. Numbers were declining anyway but it might, at least, be argued that the modern services helped to arrest the decline. 'A successful revision will almost certainly have to be conservative. Even though that may madden the radical and the revolutionary, religious people are conservative (not just in England), and rightly so. The Christian faith is rooted in history, not tied to every passing craze or fancy.'[13]

Whilst every Churchman thought linguistic style a most important consideration in the proposed new Communion Service, even more importance was attached, particularly by Evangelicals, to the doctrinal elements in the new wordings:

Those Anglicans who believe that there is an objective presence in the elements do so because such a belief has been common in the Christian church for many centuries. They believe that this view is consistent with Scripture and with ancient tradition. They argue that when our Lord said 'This is my body' over the bread at the Last Supper, he is to be taken literally; they also contend that the words in John 6 about eating Christ's flesh and drinking His blood confirm and back up this interpretation which, as has been said, is widely held in the church. Evangelicals, on the other hand, would argue that such an interpretation does violence to Scripture, Our Lord meaning His words in a symbolic and figurative sense, and that this sense is consistent with what Scripture says about justification by faith.[14]

Inevitably, if revision of any kind were to become acceptable to all within a comprehensive Church, it would have to contain a measure of ambiguity and, even, of compromise:

Another regret stems from fear that the elements of bread and wine are described too objectively as being Our Lord's body and blood. This is an understandable fear, and it needs allaying.'that they may be unto us . . . ' is certainly less receptionist than ' . . . that we receiving . . . may be partakers . . . ' Is it, however, so obviously less scriptural? So long as the service comes to a climax with a distribution in which the elements *are* 'unto us his body and blood', the language is surely unexceptional? Our Lord *almost* said 'This is unto you my body'. Insofar as He did not say just that He said something even stronger.[15]

In the revised edition of Alternative Services 1 and 2, the service of Holy Communion was given a probationary period of optional use until the Alternative Service Book's publication in 1980. And so the debate continued, now at parochial level. 'Prayers for the dead' had been softened in evangelical ears by: 'And we commend to thy gracious keeping, O Lord, all thy servants departed this life in thy faith and fear, beseeching thee, according to thy promises, to grant them refreshment, light and peace.' In the Alternative Services Series 3, the prayer for the dead had been replaced by the mere words, 'We commemorate the departed, especially . . . ' When the Alternative Service Book reached its final form, the intercessory prayer became even more acceptable to evangelicals: 'Hear us as we remember those who have died in the faith of Christ . . . ; according to your promises grant us with them a share in your eternal kingdom.'

The other matter which had been the subject of continuous debate was the words of administration of the elements. To give as wide an acceptance as possible and to provide for the many shades of understanding of the Eucharist, within the comprehensiveness of the Anglican fold, three alternative wordings were suggested for the administration: 'The Body of Christ (to which the reply was "Amen")' or 'The Body of Christ preserve your body and soul unto everlasting life', or 'The Body of our Lord Jesus Christ, which was given for you, preserve your body and soul unto everlasting life.'

Evangelicals were forced to admit that, within the wide-ranging doctrine of the Lord's Supper represented in Anglicanism, it was necessary to have these alternatives and to allow for different interpretations. In Series 3, the words of administration were simplified to become 'The Body of Christ keep you in eternal life', thus emphasising the newer understanding of eternal life's 'here and now' but leaving the actual significance of the elements somewhat vague. In the A.S.B. for the distribution of the elements there were alternative words: 'The Body of Christ keep you in eternal life', or 'The Body of Christ'.

Thus, the ambiguity was meant to satisfy the whole spectrum of belief concerning the nature and significance of the bread and wine. However, there was little hope of satisfying all Evangelicals by such a compromise as seen in the following broadside ante-dating the proposed actual liturgy ' "The Body of Christ" – "The Blood of Christ". Little ambiguity there – little consideration for the scruples of Reformed Bible-taught Christians.'[16]

Unquestionably, the new communion services produced a much greater freedom of expression of fellowship and, on the whole, Evangelicals rejoiced in the unfreezing of the people of God in participation of this, the central act of worship of the body of Christians. Nonetheless, unhappiness was still felt by many at the rigidity of Anglican structures over admission to Holy Communion, which was governed by the rite of Confirmation:

The starting point theologically for this is that Christians are in Christ, members of the body of Christ, and share a common oneness by that very fact. It is not a man-made oneness; it is God-given and man cannot destroy it. Baptism, the sacrament of Christian initiation, symbolises this oneness. Now if Christians share the sacrament of initiation, why should they not share the other gospel sacrament of Christian continuation? The sacrament of Holy Communion, like that of Baptism, belongs to God, not to any particular church or group of Christians, so the question is not whether we ought to allow some other Christian to come but whether we have any right to turn him away.[17]

Intercommunion as it was called, was considered a pre-requisite to reunion and, indeed, to any practical unity between Churches at local level. The question of intercommunion between Anglicans and Roman Catholics was, of course, a much more difficult one and, however hopeful some Anglo-Catholics might be of sharing with their Roman brethren, there could be little hope for the Evangelical Anglican of sharing the Lord's Supper in any really meaningful way in an R.C. church. The following refers mainly to holidays abroad:

A Christian who believes in the biblical Lord's Supper cannot just go to mass, because mass is not the Lord's Supper, and in fact is a complete denial of what the Bible tells us about the eucharist. We can, and certainly should, welcome the new atmosphere and willingness to consider change and reform that is now evident throughout much of the Roman Communion . . . But where Rome upholds the sacrifice of the mass against the sacrament of the Lord's Supper, we shall be forced into 'nonconformity' in that country and have to seek a church where the biblical understanding of the eucharist is upheld. To participate in the mass would be to deny the Lord's Supper . . . It should be stressed that such action is determined by theological principle, not by any mere anti-Romanism (an attitude of mind which has no virtues) nor by any Victorian hang-over in the shape of hatred of the very word mass. After all, Lutherans have a service which they call mass, but it is very different from the Roman mass. Theological substance is the key thing, not mere negative attitudes or names.[18]

With the passage of time more and more thought was being given by Anglicans as a whole to the *possibility* of reunion with Rome and this in spite of the collapse of the talks on possible reunion with the Methodist Church. Clear heads and firm resolve were required (and still are) by Evangelicals to stand for the Reformed Faith and to insist on the continued confession of sound doctrine. In all this, they were immeasurably helped by the crystal clear theology and doctrinal understanding of Dr Packer:

For four hundred years following Henry VIII's breach with Rome there was no co-operation between Anglicans and Roman Catholics in any form of joint Christian action. Anglicans had no wish to worship or work with Roman Catholics, for they thought the Roman creed erroneous, the Mass blasphemous (see Articles XXVIII, XXXI), the authoritarianism of pope and priest demoralising, the Roman clergy untrustworthy, and their laity deluded and perhaps disloyal to the crown. Roman Catholics had no wish to worship or work with Anglicans, for they thought the Anglican creed deficient, the Anglican church schismatic and Anglican orders invalid (the latter position was re-affirmed by Leo XIII in 1893, and still stands). Each side sought only the conversion of the other, spurred on in most cases by the belief that the other's position was spiritually dangerous, and likely to lead its adherents to eternal perdition. One of the most striking changes during the past century, however it be estimated, is the extent to which this belief has waned on both sides.[19]

Churchmen as a whole, numbering many Evangelicals among them, welcomed the new Communion Service and saw many advantages:

a It restored the Lord's Supper to the position of being the main service for the people of God.
b It made the preaching of a sermon obligatory.
c It made provision for reading from portions of both the Old and New Testaments.
d It demonstrated the oneness, the gathered-togetherness, of the local church in the one main service.

Interesting and additional light is thrown on the debate by the following comment from an unexpected source:

If the service is to demonstrate the unity of Christians with one another as well as with their Lord it is obviously destructive of this idea to have more than one service. It may be argued as a practical necessity, but we feel that if the service is to carry its full meaning the practical difficulties in the way must be and can be overcome. Secondly, it is also necessary to have the service at the time when it is most convenient for the majority to gather for it, and once this principle is granted there seems to be little future for the early morning administration, which has unconsciously helped to form wrong ideas about the service in people's minds.[20]

Originally, the 'early service' of Communion was introduced in the parochial pattern primarily to enable those in domestic service to receive Communion. Also the element of fasting before the early service was seen as beneficial. Subsequent events have indeed shown a marked falling off in the number of communicants at 8 a.m., attendance at which, in most parishes, is confined to the over sixties. It has been convincingly shown that the service of Family or Parish Communion at a later hour has the greater appeal, except to the traditionalists who, in the main are the older churchgoers.

Additionally, there were possibly other extra benefits, as evangelicals saw then, of this enforced reappraisal of the Holy Communion:

i The Holy Table might be moved away from its semi-mysterious east-end position, inherited and beloved by Tractarians, into a more central position. It was the Tractarians who introduced the eastward position for the celebrant and we may note with interest that by 1953, the westward position was in use, on theological grounds, in such Colleges as Queens, Birmingham, Clare, Cambridge and St Aidan's, Birkenhead. From these it spread to the rest of the church.

ii A whole loaf of bread might be used to demonstrate the oneness of the people of God.

iii Extemporary prayers, in some places led by lay members, were envisaged in the section provided for intercessions.

As Colin Buchanan pointed out, Evangelical Anglicans in the past 'have proved good at protestant apologetics about Holy Communion, but poor in attendance'. They tended to 'stay behind' after morning or evening prayer, with just a few others, for a shortened form of 1662 Holy Communion Service. However, they made an excellent and positive contribution to the debates over the Second Series Communion Service and it is noteworthy that much of the work was undertaken by the Church Society and by Latimer House, Oxford. The latter, founded in 1960, is a centre for study, research and writing, with provision for two residential scholars. Its first chairman was the Rev. John Stott, who was succeeded by the Rev. Dr J. I. Packer. The present warden is the Rev. R. T. Beckwith. The aim of Latimer House is to produce literature applying 'the Gospel to the Church in a constructive, contemporary way'. It describes itself as being 'committed to the ideal of creatively applying Biblical and Reformation theology to the ongoing life of the Church of England and the Anglican Communion'. As a research and resources centre it occupies, for Evangelicals, an influential position in the Anglican Church. However, during the period under review, it did not publish under its own imprint to any noticeable degree.

Not surprisingly, the new service of Holy Communion gave rise once more to the question of doctrinal differences with the Church of Rome and there were hopeful signs that Rome was softening in some of its attitudes. Non-Roman Christians became known as 'separated brethren' as they were being wooed back into the fold, from which they had fled under political pressures invoked, it was asserted, by a selfish English monarch. However, increased emphasis on personal bible study was being enjoined on the Catholic laity whilst on the Protestant side Archbishops Fisher and Ramsey visited the Pope. Dr Packer wisely points out in his memorandum that, in spite of many hopeful signs, Rome still stood fast on transubstantiation, purgatory, tradition as a supplement to Scripture, good works to accompany faith as the means of personal justification, the propitiatory character of the elements in the Mass as a sacrifice at one with Christ's sacrifice on Calvary and the infallibility of the Pope. To these dogmas were added the Immaculate Conception and, in 1950, the Bodily Assumption of Mary. These matters are held by Rome as 'infallible and irreformable'. Dr Packer:

Can changeless Rome, who proclaims herself *semper eadem* – 'always the same' – mend her doctrinal ways? It is hard to see how she would be able to do this but equally hard to see how, if she takes Scripture seriously, she will be able to avoid doing this sooner or later. Evangelicals should be neither starry-eyed optimists nor resolute sceptics at this point. We must watch to see what the God of reformation will do.[21]

Dr Packer mentions four 'Guiding Principles for Local Action':

1 We should not decline all forms of contact with Roman Catholics.
2 We need to be masters of our own position before we talk with Roman Catholics.
3 We need to be clear regarding principles of Christian unity before we join in united action with Roman Catholics.
4 Where Anglican–Roman meetings take place, we should press for joint Bible study as a main activity.[22]

It was salutary that such a leading Evangelical Anglican should sound the note of warning and leave Anglicans in no doubt that the differences of belief, as they stood, were absolutely irreconcilable:

Rome has made her position quite clear, that she is now thinking of reunion; and that by reunion she understands the restoration of the reformed churches to a 'full catholic faith within the fold' within hearing distance of the Voice of the Shepherd. One of the profound misjudgments of the Anglican Church since the nineteenth century has been to cling to the cassocks of Rome, whilst at the same time sitting loose to her far sounder and more creditable tradition, and all too often 'playing it cool' with Free Churchmen.[23]

At that time, Dr Hans Kung, the German radical Roman Catholic professor of theology, was coming into prominence with his critical views which were snapped up by Evangelicals and others, hopeful of any gleams of reformation. 'Let us not underrate the power, still today, of the Word of God written. For the Word of God to prevail would mean a radical reformation of the Roman Catholic Church comparable to and along the same lines as the Reformation of the Church of England in the sixteenth century. With God all things are possible.'[24]

The insistence on dogma and tradition, without proper scriptural foundation, however, induced a widening gulf between Evangelicals and Roman Catholics, which the ecumenical movement as a whole was inclined to gloss over. Emphasis on churchmanship and mission became increasingly ecumenical, the new openness to discuss at local level was more than welcome but evangelical thought was wise in directing the Anglican Church to the essential differences of belief in the means of salvation, which existed between the two Churches. A starry-eyed ecumenicity was sweeping the Christian world; it has its head in the very sand where indeed it was being built:

This then is the situation in which we find ourselves at the present moment. The main issues are clearly enough delineated and there is no excuse for closing our eyes to the facts or looking at them through sentimentally tinted spectacles. But God is Sovereign, and there are truly exciting possibilities when the Holy Spirit of God and the Word of God are at work together in the hearts of men.[25]

With the ecumenical breezes still blowing freely, even in the far corners of localised Roman Catholicism, there was a hope, right through the seventies, that a new formula could be found to bring together the Protestant Churches in some form of union but thoughtful members of every Church were wondering just how a common basis of belief could be achieved beyond the simple statement 'Jesus is Lord'. Dr Packer again:

Ours is an age of doctrinal unsettlement in which Western culture is drifting away from its historic moorings into a secularised pluriformity . . . Formularies are viewed with a jaundiced eye as shoes that pinch the intellectually enterprising and their stock falls. This has happened in the Church of England in a very obvious way . . . The Articles are today widely thought of as a burden rather than a blessing, a dated witness to convictions by which Anglicans no longer feel bound.[26]

Dr Packer mentions the way in which dogmatic theology has been on the wane in favour of a more philosophical approach, with certainty about almost everything being unfashionable. Evangelicals have always stood for the revealed truth of justification by faith as opposed to the twin errors, as they saw them, of justification by good works and sacramental salvation. It behoved them, therefore, to be explicit in doctrinal statements: 'The Reformation confession of Jesus as the one in and through whom sinners are justified by faith alone and saved by sovereign grace was an elucidation and defence of the same apostolic confession, this time against a semi-Pelagian doctrine of salvation by meritorious churchmanship.'[27]

There are those, particularly within the free churches, who regard a doctrinal statement of faith or a Confessional Faith as an intellectual strait-jacket. However, by far the majority of Evangelical Anglicans, realising the dangers of any kind of united church without a creed, would vote for the Confessional basis. 'So we conclude that as creedless Christianity is a contradiction in terms, so is a professed church without a credal commitment; and to resolve the problems of having such commitment by abandoning it would be like amputating one's leg to cure one's bunions.'[28]

Of course there were many who could see no possible good emerging from a scheme for unity, who regarded the ecumenical decades as thoroughly dangerous and moved off into isolationist positions, often very evangelical ones.

How, then, can we engage in what purports to be a co-operative enterprise with those who implicitly or explicitly deny the necessity of the new birth? If a man claims that grace is channelled via the sacrament, he is by implication denying the necessity of the new birth. If a man preaches a message of salvation via good works he is likewise denying the need to be born again. So, too, the ecumenical slogan 'brothers by baptism', which has been popularised by the Roman Catholic Ecumenical Directory not only lays the stress in the wrong place, but assumes that baptism confers the new birth – Simon of Samaria is a standing refutation of such a theory.[29]

Such reasoning is overdone: sadly, the writer (no longer an Anglican) can see no good in co-operation of any kind with other Christians. He makes much and quite rightly of the integrity of the gospel which he sees threatened by the ecumenical movement. He sees compromise in agreeing to work with those with whom he will differ in some vitally important matters of faith and doctrine.

Perhaps the most remarkable book on Christian Ecumenism, written from very different standpoints, was produced by two Catholics and two Evangelicals, all within the Anglican fold.[30] Although *Growing Into Union* was published in 1970 in the wake of the great debate on the 1968 scheme for Anglican–Methodist unity, in some ways it antedated the scheme which did not finally collapse until 1972. Appendixes to the book, published for the sake of the record, were backward looking to 1969 and included statements, by the writers of the book (including the signature of Canon Michael Green in the first instance) which had been laid before the Convocations of York and Canterbury in May and July, 1969.

In *Growing Into Union* the Rev. E. L. Mascall, an academic, and Graham Leonard, then Bishop of Willesden (now Bishop of

London) represented the Catholic viewpoint and the Evangelical one was taken by Canon Colin Buchanan and Dr Jim Packer. They started from a piece of common ground. 'Only a personal God can love to the uttermost; only an omnipotent God can save to the uttermost. Catholic and Evangelical alike have traditionally shown a true instinct in seeing Pelagianism, the doctrine of self salvation through self-sufficient self-reliance, as among the profoundest of heresies.'[31] Their joint authorship proved to be honest, heart searching and fresh in its thinking. 'The Eucharist is placed in the tension typical of Christians themselves – a sign simultaneously of the past work of Christ on Calvary, from which the community takes its origin, and of the present reign and lordship of the risen Christ who in person presides over the community and purifies it in the way of discipleship.'[32]

Before *Growing Into Union* there had been a distinct tendency for Evangelical Anglicans to take a rather superficial, 'low' view of episcopacy whereas the evangelical authors were able to come to some kind of terms with their Anglo-Catholic colleagues who seemed prepared to yield some of the ground traditionally held by High-Churchmen regarding the mystical nature of the laying on of hands, etc:

All this throws light in its turn on the problem of succession. One difficulty in discussing this subject is that we are all haunted by a view of apostolic succession which is mechanical and isolated from the church's total life; yet succession in some form is inseparable from the Church's life; thus, those churches which interpret apostolic succession wholly in terms of preaching and maintaining apostolic truth substitute a succession of doctrine for a succession of bishops.

Succession, which means the deliberate practice of successiveness, is in all spheres a standing visible witness to the fact that Jesus Christ, our living Lord and Head, is the same yesterday, today and for ever, and that consequently his Church, and the commission and authority which ministers receive from him in his church, are the same too.[33]

The thesis of *Growing into Union* was finely argued and was presented in restrained terms, which commended it to a wide spectrum of evangelicals. However, the work produced a strong reaction from the Free Churches, where Evangelicals felt that, following the National Evangelical Anglican Conference at Keele in 1967 (see the next chapter) they were being left out in the cold.

Growing into Union was to lay a new foundation of agreement between Anglo-Catholics and Evangelicals with a view to there being greater hope that any new coming together, similar to the failed Anglican/Methodist scheme, might have a better chance of success. So they dealt with all matters of moment and established much common ground over scripture, the Church, the sacraments, episcopacy and ministry. However, their endeavours were not appreciated by all Evangelicals, some of whom wondered whether Colin Buchanan and Jim Packer were any longer Evangelicals! Unquestionably there was a divide between those who looked back gratefully to Keele and, having come out of their 'ghettos', were eager to go forward from there and those who thought that Evangelicals had taken the wrong turning at Keele. 'The great divide among evangelicals – the question of ecumenical involvement – is increasingly apparent despite valiant attempts by many to hold the two sides together.'[34]

In 1968, the Rev. John Stott attended the meeting of the World Council of Churches in Uppsala, some Evangelicals questioning his wisdom in so doing but he demonstrated, consistently, a broad sympathy in the service of the gospel without ever compromising its message. The reaction demonstrated the continuing tendency of some Evangelicals always to question each other's bona fides.

That same tendency existed between two evangelical theological colleges in the Bristol area – Clifton, where the Rev. Basil Gough presided and Tyndale Hall, where the Rev. J. Stafford Wright was Principal. They appeared to be very withdrawn from each other but a merger of the two had earlier come within a hair's breadth, not in joining the accommodation together but in uniting the library and teaching facilities of the two colleges.

Attempts were made under the shadow of the impending Runcie Report on theological colleges to merge the two in 1968/9. Canon Alan Neech was chairman of the Tyndale board at the time and Canon James O'Byrne, now of Norwich, was Vice-Principal at Clifton, then after Basil Gough's premature death during the conflict in 1969, Principal.

The question of appointing a new Principal for the merged colleges, newly named Trinity College, caused considerable difficulty and some hurt to the individuals concerned. The present Bishop of Chester, Michael Baughen, was originally nominated as Principal and the Rev. Julian Charley his deputy. Some thought that Dr Jim Packer should have been offered the position of Principal but he became Associate Principal of Trinity in 1972, the Rev. Alec Motyer having been appointed Principal in 1971.

A major issue in the troubles was the doctrinal basis of B.C.M.S. which was adopted by Tyndale but which they were unwilling to give up as Clifton was unwilling to adopt it (there was merely a difference of emphasis). As a result in 1970 the bishops temporarily withdrew their recognition of the colleges, as part of the implementation of the Runcie report, which sought to streamline theological education. Initially, the recommendation was that Tyndale Hall should close and Clifton amalgamate with Wycliffe Hall, Oxford. Eventually, the decision was reversed and Trinity College formed in 1971, with the Bishop of Bristol, Oliver Tompkins, not himself an Evangelical, steadying the ship and chairing the new organisation.

One leading Evangelical describes the eventual merger as a triumph for the hard-liners and there is a feeling that the bitterness of the strife broke Basil Gough's heart, for he was always the gentlest of men. In his obituary in *The Times* he was described as having what Cecil Day Lewis, once Poet Laureate, described in someone else as 'the clover-soft authority of the meek'. This whole chapter of church history, whilst eventually witnessing the creation of a first-class new theological college in the evangelical tradition, now with many men and women training for the ministry, reflects little credit to Evangelicals and is best forgotten or perhaps remembered only as the unacceptable face of Evangelicalism.

In the same year, 1971, Maurice Wood went from Oak Hill Theological College to become the outstanding evangelical Bishop of Norwich and he was succeeded as Principal at Oak Hill by Canon David Wheaton, soon after the death there of the vice-Principal, Alan Stibbs, that most perceptive and delightful Biblical scholar.

13
Charismatic Differences

THE 1960s were years of great social change which inevitably influenced the whole Church, not least Evangelicals. There was a kind of freedom in the air and this coincided with a renewal movement in the Church, often labelled 'charismatic' in nature. For example (it seemed amazing at the time) there were raised hands in Pentecostal praise at a full house in no less a place than Guildford Cathedral. Drama and dance routines were becoming part and parcel of the new life of Christian faith and worship. In some ways, these new joyous dimensions of worship resulted from the freedom of the whole trans-denominational charismatic movement, its spontaneity and youthful lack of inhibition. They may well have been the answer to the Alternative Society, the world of the hippies and the commune and the much greater freedom in resolving the problems of human sexuality. Furthermore, the National Festival of Light's protest against the defilement of public life by pornography and the like brought a crowd of 100,000 to its first rally in Trafalgar Square. The battle lines were being openly drawn between positive Christian standards of morality on the one hand and the world's easy going decadence and promiscuity on the other. There had been a sharp decline in public taste, in what was permissible in the theatre, the screen and literature and the Festival of Light raised the standard against such a fall. The crepe-hung sabbatical silences over sex and morality which characterised earlier decades had given way to freedom, openness in such matters and the Christian Church was being called upon to make a response. These new characteristics tended to overflow into the Christian Church where young people were enjoying a frankness and a freedom unknown to their forebears. Even this presented its problems as young people questioned the time-honoured conventions and indeed the morals of the Christian community.

Slowly but surely authority of all kinds was being questioned and discussion of personal problems was taking the place of a monologue laying down of the law. Elders did not always know

164

better! Concurrently, the non-ordained were being given a greater say in the teaching of the Churches, effectively with the spread of house groups, etc. In the field of ordination, a signifi- cant compromise was reached with the introduction of the Auxiliary Pastoral Ministry under which men entered the priest- hood fully but without a stipendiary appointment on attachment to a particular church, while continuing to fulfil a role in a secular occupation. Thus, whilst continuing to be a solicitor, or excep- tionally a dock-worker, during the working week, a man, after a period of part-time training, and occasional residential instruc- tion, would be ordained and become available to assist the incumbent in a particular parish. It would appear that the Church as a whole was reluctant to accept such a 'half-way house' but the necessities of the coming years were going to insist that the work of the paid members of the profession in Church life be supplemented by trained, unpaid men (and women) who could help to keep going the services demanded by scattered com- munities. One of the more successful ventures in this field was known as the Southwark Ordination Scheme, supervised by a staunch and wise Evangelical of great experience, Canon Frank Colquhoun. This course and others embraced the different shades of churchmanship but it would be fair to say that it was more popular with Evangelicals than with High-Churchmen.

At one time, the Church of England had embraced the idea of worker priests, which had been courageously pioneered in France but for a long time there had been a class of ordained per- son, not actually in the parochial ministry, namely the many ordained schoolmasters. The Auxiliary Pastoral Ministry, later to become the Non-Stipendiary Ministry, came into being to sup- plement the chronic shortage of clergy but additionally the ordained auxiliary brings to the ministry the extra richness of his working experience as a Christian and this feature became very attractive to Evangelicals, always believing in a narrowing of the gap between the ordained and others. The Church was bound to be enriched by this development.

Although pioneered by Southwark, both Oak Hill Theological College and the Oxford Diocese ran part-time courses for the Auxiliary Pastoral Ministry, also both Exeter and Truro organised joint Non-Stipendiary Ministry Courses. However, there was a feeling abroad, expressed, for instance, by Crockford Clerical Directory (O.U.P. 1971–2 page ix), that the auxiliary ministry might 'be used as a back door to ordination, a means of avoiding the full rigours of training'. Whether men in the new type of ministry will ever be fully considered for an incumbency has yet to be seen for it would appear that the 'long-stayer' in the ministry is always preferred to the part-timer.

Numerous efforts had been made in recent decades, to change the pattern of services, making them less formal in content and more suitable for the whole family; fresh liturgy in the form of Family Worship and the new Communion Service had become the norm in most churches and many modern English versions of the Bible were everywhere in use. But who was to do the work of the Evangelist, how were the unchurched masses to be brought into church to receive the good things on offer? In 1967, under the auspices of the Evangelical Fellowship of the Anglican Communion, the Rev. John Stott issued a searching book on the subject of Evangelism.[1] The author adopted a logical presentation with the following sequences:

The Glory of God	The Evangelistic Incentive
The Gospel of God	The Evangelistic Message
The Church of God	The Evangelistic Agency
The Spirit of God	The Evangelistic Dynamic

All Souls, Langham Place, itself provided a wealth of experience in Evangelism and the author himself had for many years conducted evangelistic missions in different parts of the world, notably at the universities. He stressed that parochial Evangelism is 'the regular work of a local church':

Again, all so-called 'missions', because sporadic in character and professional in leadership, can actually discourage genuine 'mission', which is the non-stop responsibility of non-professionals.

Of this too Billy Graham is convinced. I heard him say at a conference on evangelism convened by Dr John Mackay at Princeton Theological Seminary in December 1956: 'If all churches were engaged in perennial evangelism, I don't think there would be a need for a person like me'. In saying this, I think he somewhat overstated the case, for Christ does appoint 'evangelists' and there is room for special evangelistic missions.[2]

The work of Evangelism, the Rev. John Stott stressed, is that of every Christian, making up the local Church. Whether through home meetings, guest services or individual friendships, this work is continuous and unfinished.

Certainly not confined to the Church of England, there arose in the sixties another debate which in its earlier manifestations developed much heat – that of the gift of tongues and the 'fulness of the Holy Spirit'. By 1966, the controversy had become quite fierce, in that there were those who contended that 'tongues' were a sign, to be coveted, of the Spirit-filled Christian life whereas others opposed with the view that to speak with tongues was a distraction from main-line truth and an embarrassment to fellow believers. It was, they said, divisive:

Nor do we ever read that Jesus spoke in tongues, although we know that the Spirit was given to Him in all His fulness. Why then should any think or teach that speaking with tongues is an indispensable sign of the possession of the Spirit, and particularly of the experience of His outpouring, when the incarnate Son of God Himself did not speak with tongues.[3]

Referring to the day of Pentecost, the argument continues:

This remarkable phenomenon was, however, only introductory – a meaningful but a passing sign. The three thousand, who were converted on that day were led to saving faith in Christ not by the speaking in tongues but by Peter's sober preaching and exposition of Scripture.[4]

Nevertheless, it must be remembered, reasoned Alan Stibbs, that St Paul has spoken in favour of the gift of tongues in 1 Cor., chapters 12–14, but that he insisted it was only one of the many and varied gifts of the Spirit. Furthermore, he contends 'that God's normal way of speaking to His believing people is not by tongues but by intelligible speech (1 Cor. 14.21f)'.[5]

The origins of the Pentecostal movement are to be found mainly in the Pentecostal Churches, the Assemblies of God and the Elim Church. However, these denominations have not been really accepted by Evangelicalism at its heart, represented by the Keswick Convention. The Assemblies of God regard 'speaking in Tongues' as the only valid expression of the baptism of the Holy Spirit, whereas the Elim Church does not insist on such a manifestation. 'The British Holiness movement, one of the sources of which was the Keswick Convention, either rejected the Pentecostal movement out of hand or ignored it, although much in Pentecostal teaching is a legacy from Anglicanism, through the mediation of Wesley.'[6]

Emphasis was initially placed on speaking with tongues and out of this eventually grew, in the late 1970s, the whole charismatic movement which became thoroughly trans-denominational in scope:

It could almost be claimed that today the Holy Spirit is no longer what He has often been called 'the neglected Person in the Godhead'. Certainly, there is in our generation a welcome renewal of concern about His ministry in the Church and the world. There is also a recrudescence of 'Pentecostalism' in non-Pentecostal churches, which rejoices some and bewilders or even alarms others.[7]

Part of the origin of the Pentecostal or Tongues Movement was to be found in the debate which ensued regarding the manner of the giving of the Holy Spirit – whether only initially at the New Birth or additionally and subsequently in a kind of 'second blessing'. Like so many religious phenomena, speaking with tongues originated in the United States, with the Pentecostalists, but by the 1960s a number of Episcopalian churches there had also experienced the gift. 'In September 1963 some 2,000 Episcopalians were said to be speaking with tongues in Southern California alone.'[8]

However, the movement did not spread so rapidly in England, particularly in the Anglican Church. W. J. Hollenweger describes it rather colourfully in that context as 'a blending of Aristocratic Anglicanism and Welsh Revivalism'.[9] Behind the idea of the former characteristic may well have been the weight given to the Charismatic movement by a curate of All Souls, Langham Place, the Rev. Michael Harper who, in 1958, had gone to work there with special reference to the chaplaincy of West End stores. The Stores Plan had earlier conceived that a curate – initially the Rev. C. J. E. Lefroy, followed by the Rev. Richard Bowdler – should devote one day a week to each of the five big Oxford Street stores, four of which were to make a contribution to his salary. In 1964 'Mr Harper found himself being drawn increasingly into meetings associated with the charismatic movement so that he faced an inevitable conflict with the Stores Chaplaincy and he eventually resigned to form the Fountain Trust.'[10]

Neo-Pentecostalism, as it was somewhat disparagingly called by some, spread in Great Britain, to embrace adherents ranging from Roman Catholicism to the Free Churches but it would not be unfair to say that only a minority of Evangelical Anglicans went so far as to speak with tongues, although, in the seventies, a larger number would call themselves Charismatic in varying degrees and almost all would agree that the worship and life of their churches had been favourably influenced and enriched by the Charismatic movement, producing a warmth, a freedom and a spontaneity in church services and fellowship which was almost wholly beneficial. These were fortunate traits of a movement which began with a certain amount of feeling and controversy; inevitably, polarised positions were adopted. At the one end was the Rev. John Stott, assuming a considered, restrained and kindly approach and, at the other, representative of the Tongues Movement, the Rev. Michael Harper, after he had left the staff of All Souls, Langham Place, to become General Secretary of the Fountain Trust, which positively led the way in advocating the charismatic position, albeit with quiet and gentle advocacy. The Charismatics emphasised those portions of the New Testament where speaking in tongues was commended by St Paul and where it was recorded as an experience of the early church in the Acts:

This revelation of the purpose of God in Scripture should be sought in its *didactic*, rather than its *historical* parts. More precisely, we should look for it in the teaching of Jesus, and in the sermons and writings of the apostles, and not in the purely narrative portions of the Acts. What is described in Scripture as having happened to others is not necessarily intended for us, whereas what is *promised* to us we are to appropriate, and what is *commanded* us we are to obey.[11]

Much of the debate centred on the question of the 'second blessing', to which some Christians were able to advance but, apparently, not all. It would be fair to say that some elements of the Keswick Convention had implied that a second blessing or a filling of the Holy Spirit was necessary to a complete Christian experience. However, it was pointed out that 'Water-baptism is the initiatory Christian rite, because Spirit-baptism is the initiatory Christian experience.'[12]

Not that the non-Charismatics would have denied that a normal Christian life required constant re-filling, as a means of renewal and revival of the individual spirit. The arguments so often turned on whether or not the detailed events of the early Church were to be expected in contemporary Christian experience. 'All the time people have the events of the Day of Pentecost at the back of their minds. They forget that the supernatural signs associated with Pentecost are no more typical of every baptism of the Spirit than those on the Damascus road are of every conversion.'[13] John Stott pointed out that, of all the groups of people in the Acts who received the gift of the Holy Spirit, only three were said to have spoken with tongues.

The danger of the charismatic position was that it tended to stereotype Christian experience, to class as second-rate, by implication, those Christians who did not have the gift of 'tongues' and to divide Churches into the 'real holiness' group and the others:

The idea that the baptism of the Spirit is a post-conversion experience inevitably creates division between Christians, for it unavoidably draws a line between the ordinary Christian and the 'Spirit-baptized' Christian, between the Christian ignorant of the gift of tongues and the Christian who speaks in tongues.

Further:

When gifts in general and tongues in particular are linked inseparably with the baptism of the Holy Spirit, it further follows that the presence or absence of gifts (generally the more dramatic ones are in mind) becomes the yardstick of spirituality.[14]

Most evangelical theologians agreed that the Bible gave no warrant either for the normality of Christian experience in the speaking in tongues or for a post-conversion second giving of the Holy Spirit. 'The distinctive doctrine of Pentecostal churches which is basic to their teachings on glossolalia, namely, that every believer must seek a postconversion spirit-baptism, has no basis in Scripture.'[15] Several writers pointed out the dangers of exalting one spiritual gift above another or above all others and it was recalled that the Corinthian Church, which had experienced the gift of tongues, was deficient in true spiritual life.

An American psychotherapist, John P. Kildahl, conducted interviews with tongue-speaking Christians over a period of ten years and published his findings:

Dr Paul Qualben learned through careful interviewing that more than 85% of the tongue-speakers had experienced a clearly defined anxiety crisis preceding their speaking in tongues. Their anxiety was caused by marital difficulties, financial concerns, ill health, and general depression. Sometimes the crisis was of an ethical or religious nature and involved concern about spiritual values, guilt, and the ultimate meaning and purpose of life.[16]

Reporting on the American scene, Dr Kildahl said that up to one-third of a Church's membership might have left as a result of division on the tongues issue, but in Great Britain, in Anglican churches at least, the battle-lines were not so sharply drawn. Eventually the Charismatics, led by the Rev. Michael Harper, supported by Canon David Watson of St Michael-le-Belfry, York, agreed with the non-Charismatics, led by the Rev. John Stott, and the Church of England Evangelical Council on the basis of seeing good in each other's viewpoints and in 1977 a joint statement was issued by the Fountain Trust, the charismatic movement and C.E.E.C. under the title 'Gospel and Spirit', setting out very fully the result of four separate day conferences over a period of eighteen months at which they explored the difficulties and differences which had arisen between 'charismatic' and 'non-charismatic' leaders of Anglican Evangelicalism, bringing both viewpoints to 'the bar of scripture'. The statement concluded:

The goal of renewal is not merely renewed individuals but a renewed and revived Church, alive with the life of Christ, subject to the word of Christ, filled with the spirit of Christ, fulfilling the ministry of Christ, constrained by the love of Christ, preaching the good news of Christ, and thrilled in its worship by the glory of Christ.

Looking back to the origins of the Holiness Movement, the Second Blessing and the Fulness of the Holy Spirit, one can see that the Keswick Convention always had the doctrine of Sanctification high on its agenda. But also one should not ignore the influence of a relatively small but spiritually elite missionary society, the Ruanda Mission, founded in 1920, where they experienced the freedom, fellowship and liberation of a definite movement of the Holy Spirit in that part of Africa. The influence of 'Ruanda' on Evangelical Anglicans was considerable.

Subsidiary benefits of the charismatic movement were seen as the renewed understanding of ecumenism, based on an evangelical common ground and the rediscovery of the laity as fully operative members of the church. Nonetheless, the movement, overall, revealed a divisive bias in favour of a positive 'second blessing':

The literature published by the Fountain Trust (London) shows that these churches have taken over not only the experience but also the theological interpretation placed upon it by Pentecostals, that is, the two-stage way of salvation and speaking in tongues as a necessary sign of the baptism of the Spirit.[17]

A further criticism of the Movement on several fronts is contained in the following appraisal of the features of Pentecostalism:

the idea that between the Acts of the Apostles and the Azusa street revival in Los Angeles nothing of importance took place in the history of the church apart from sporadic revivals; the pietistic failing of not seeing the world as God's world; the absence of any preaching which gives due place to the prophetic Christian concern for social ethics; the readiness to form schismatic groups.[18]

The sixties also saw the emergence of a movement firmly rooted in the Reformed, Puritan Past, known as the 'Banner of Truth Trust'. In the main, it saw its role as the renewed emphasis on Calvinistic truth and the Sovereignty of God; it re-issued the works of such spiritual heroes of the past as J. C. Ryle, C. H. Spurgeon and Andrew Bonar. Significantly, in 1966, the Trust re-published *The Office and Work of the Holy Spirit* by Professor James Buchanan, first published as long ago as 1843.

The various strands which represented Evangelicalism in the sixties included a strong element of 'hard-line' Calvinism, which was somewhat anti-Keswick and quite ready to oppose other evangelicals thought to be Arminian in outlook. Those in this category were seen as 'Banner' men, they tended to generate a rather unattractive hardness of dogma. In seeking to exalt the Sovereignty of God they tended to minimise what the Sovereignty of God, working through grace, could do with a man. They may have led some to think that the Fall might prevent the redeemed Christian mind from understanding fully divine revelation. In all this, such influential forces as Church Society, Latimer House and the Rev. Jim Packer, took a counterbalancing view.

Summarising the decade with which we have been immediately concerned, Canon Colliss Davies wrote:

The 1960's were on the whole a depressing period for the Church. The publication of *Honest to God*, in which a bishop raised doubts on accepted Christian doctrines, brought relief and intellectual freedom to some, but undermined the faith of others. There was a general failure of nerve on the part of the clergy, a hesitation to preach positively on the old basic doctrines, which were replaced by emphasising the social gospel, stressing the need to help the plight of the hungry and homeless and the Church's duty to turn words of comfort into action.[19]

Without doubt it was a complex decade; large liturgical and doctrinal issues were at stake, through debate and re-assessment. Evangelical Anglicans, generally, were in the thick of the fight but it would be difficult to assess their measure of success or the progress of the Gospel achieved. But through it all, ran charismatic, pentecostal threads, giving colourful patterns. Even Roman Catholicism boasted a significant number of bishops of that persuasion, led by Cardinal Suenens of Belgium and the whole of the Christian Church felt the bracing breath of the Spirit, manifested in joyous worship, liberating expressions of praise and fellowship. After the controversy on 'tongues' was

172

over, Evangelicals as a whole thanked God for the charismatic movement and voted it their best hope for the renewal of the church in an age of coldness and indifference. Many Christian communities were being renewed, often assuming new forms of worship and fellowship.

14
Keele – A Watershed

ONFERENCES have always been part of the evangelical scene and at the annual Keswick Convention, Anglicans have been much in evidence, often playing the leading part. Moreover, the Islington Clerical Conference, previously held in January, has been a most important platform for Evangelical Anglican thought and has attracted clerics from all over the country. Not so well known, perhaps, but very influential, was the Oxford Conference of Evangelical Churchmen arranged for many years by Church Society. More serious study was possible at this residential gathering which, sadly, lapsed in the 1970s, to be succeeded, in a way, by the Protestant Reformation Society's annual get-together and, to some extent, by the annual Senior Evangelical Anglican Clergy conference, held at Swanwick. These were all most important occasions but relatively 'parochial' compared with the National Evangelical Anglican Congress held at Keele University in April 1967, for which plans were being made two years beforehand when the title 'Christ Over All' was projected. (Subsequently, from 1983 the Anglican Evangelical Assembly gained the position of pre-eminence in the calendar and eclipsed Islington.)

The Anglican Church was undergoing a slow change from being 'the Conservative Party at prayer', with its set patterns of liturgy and government, to a much freer set-up with more lay participation and new experimental forms of worship. In all this, Evangelicals were not being left behind, many of them feeling restive in the old structures. Two incumbents, the Rev. Herbert Carson and the Rev. Albert Rainsbury, had resigned over the question, as they saw it, of 'indiscriminate baptism' and eventually it was generally agreed by Evangelicals that baptism of infants should take place in the parish where the family was resident and then ideally in the presence of the regular Sunday morning congregation, thereby emphasising the family aspect of the local church and the fact that the child was not only becoming a responsibility of its members but also being admitted by the

174

church's faith to the covenant mercies of God to His people. The growth of Family Services, with or without Holy Communion, meant that baptisms could be happily incorporated into the new patterns of worship and so there came about a most healthy sense that baptism was much more than a private, social occasion for 3 p.m. on a Sunday afternoon with champagne calming the consciences of non-churchgoing godparents.

Another area in which Anglicans were on the move was in relation to the *force majeure* of dwindling manpower and lack of financial resources. It was felt by many that a number of churches in a given area might be served by a Group Ministry, with a senior clergyman acting as chairman and non-ordained ministers (readers) taking a part. However, the idea was not a popular one; many saw in it a depersonalising of pastoral care and some clergy resented giving up the idea, hallowed by centuries of tradition, that they personally were in charge of a parish, however small. But in country districts, small parishes were being joined together in twos and threes, each group retaining the services of its own parson, although he was forced to drive from one service to another in a tight Sunday morning schedule. In order to keep options for the future open, some small country parishes had to be content with a 'priest-in-charge', implying that he might have his appointment terminated if circumstances changed.

There is no doubt that the rejection of the scheme for unity between Anglicans and Methodists went rumbling on in more thoughtful evangelical circles, where it was wondered whether, after all, a shining Biblical faith would come out of involvement with those who did *not* share that viewpoint. Archbishop Geoffrey Fisher had resigned from his primacy in 1961 (to be succeeded by Dr Michael Ramsey), but it did not prevent him from 'slamming' the unity scheme. In some ways he represented changeless Anglicanism which, however slowly, *was* on the change. 'Unity but not yet' seemed to be the watchword of Anglicanism as a whole but in 1965, an inter-Communion Commission was appointed, there being a strongly-held feeling, supported by Evangelicals, that it was wrong to exclude from the Lord's Supper in Anglican churches bona fide members of other denominations. Quite understandably, it was felt that unless it was agreed that churches should admit to Communion each other's members, there was little chance that the ministers of the Churches concerned would unite. 'Open Communion' became the goal of all Evangelicals and of many beside and was, in fact, achieved under Canon Law B 15 A by which the Anglican Church welcomed to the Lord's Supper, as occasional visitors, those full communicant members of good standing from other Christian Churches.

Lay eldership was another matter where Evangelicals pioneered and in September 1965 the Bishop of Bristol, Dr Oliver Tomkins, appointed six elders in St Luke's Church, Barton Hill, Bristol. The idea was to appeal to a large number of Evangelical Anglican churches where a shared ministry became the order of the day. In other words, the incumbent was thereby indicating that in the ministry of the Word and Sacraments and particularly in the pastoral work of the ministry, the responsibilities were to be shared by him with the senior, duly approved and spiritually qualified members of the congregation.

A new type of young Evangelical Anglican clergyman had appeared on the scene. He was less conscious of his separateness, more relaxed (with or without guitar) and he grappled with the problem of reaching, with the gospel, the youth of the Church who were desperately trying to grapple with the new openness in sexual morality thrown up by the loose ideas of such non-Christians as Dr Alex Comfort. Typical of this generation of Evangelicals were Gavin Reid, David Watson, Michael Green and Richard Bewes. They splendidly communicated the Christian faith to a younger generation which was dubbed as permissive, affluent and rebellious, which indeed it was, as a whole. They were often assisted by Cliff Richard who communicated the faith of a Christian pop star and they were aided by the publication, in 1966, of *Youth Praise* which Michael Baughen edited and launched. *Youth Praise* was republished in an enlarged edition in 1969 and *Psalm Praise* followed in 1973.

Dr Billy Graham arrived in London in May 1966 for a brief Greater London Crusade at Earls Court and the pattern of Harringay was repeated, with large numbers of inquirers being counselled of whom, it was estimated, 50 per cent were already regular attenders at public worship.

The factors of changing structures, the discontent of disunity and the need for reappraisal caused the Keele Conference to be eagerly anticipated. The Conference Prayer, widely published beforehand, ran:

O God of our fathers, our hope in every generation, we commit to you the National Evangelical Anglican Congress. May your Spirit guide both speakers and delegates into an understanding of Your will for today. Prosper their common endeavour, that Your truth may be conserved, Your Church renewed and Your gospel proclaimed. And grant our humble prayer that Christ over all may be acknowledged by all, for the glory of His great Name. Amen.

The origins of Keele are worth recording for posterity. In 1956, the Rev. Raymond Turvey went to St George's, Leeds and began to feel that evangelical clergy in the Northern Province, thin on the ground as they were, had no rallying point, so he arranged a short residential conference at the Ripon Diocesan Retreat House where, on a very memorable occasion, they were ministered to by Alan Stibbs of Oak Hill Theological College. The conference was so successful that when, in subsequent years, numbers attending reached between 100 and 200, a move was made to a larger centre at York. Later speakers included the Bishop of Liverpool, Sir Norman Anderson and Dr Jim Packer. The forum created became important for mutual encouragement and for consideration of trends and pastoral concerns.

The northern evangelical constituency, always feeling themselves to be out on something of a limb, took considerable pride and pleasure in suggesting to their brethren in London that a National Congress should be planned and accordingly a meeting took place between Raymond Turvey, and others from the north, John Stott, Jim Packer and Peter Johnston, vicar of Islington. From this point plans went forward for the historic Congress which became known as 'Keele '67', perhaps the most significant evangelical landmark in twentieth-century Anglicanism. The Congress was to have nine speakers:

Professor Norman Anderson	University of London
Canon James Atkinson	University of Hull
Rev. Michael Green	London College of Divinity
Canon A. T. Houghton	Retired Secretary of B.C.M.S.
Rev. Philip E. Hughes	Columbia Theological Seminary
Canon William Leathem	St John the Baptist, Harborne
Rev. Alex Motyer	St Luke's, Hampstead
Rev. Dr Jim Packer	Warden, Latimer House
Rev. John Stott	All Souls, Langham Place

The subjects covered were to be the Church, its message and mission in the world, its structures, worship and unity. There were 1,000 delegates. It was hoped that the Congress would issue 'no platitudes' (The Rev. John Stott's words) and that it would not be a 're-cap' of *In Understanding be Men*.[1]

A certain amount of pre-Congress anxiety was expressed lest there should be a cleavage between the conservative and radical Evangelicals but the Rev. John Stott hoped that the coming together of so many Evangelicals would 'commend the evangelical faith to the Church as a whole'.

It is fair to say that nothing like this Congress had ever taken place before in evangelical circles. To date, it was the most momentous evangelical happening, on a corporate basis and with so many like-minded Christians in the Anglican Church coming together it was certain that evangelical life and witness would never be the same again. To provide sufficient preparation and a kind of theological backup to the Congress, a paperback was published beforehand (over 2,000 copies sold) with weighty contributions from all nine speakers.[2] Dr Packer himself contributed the initial chapter on 'The Good Confession – our crisis and God's Christ' and he emphasised the need, in a day of ecumenism, for an evangelical thrust in the form of a confessional affirmation of the Christian faith. He stressed the ever-present dangers of pietism to Evangelicals. The Rev. John Stott's chapter dealt with 'Jesus Christ our Teacher and Lord – towards solving the problem of authority'. With typical clarity, he wrote: 'Submission to Scripture, and Scripture only, is the only *Christian* solution to the problem of authority, because it is included in and required by our submission to Christ.'[3] But, lest Evangelicals should think their behaviour and life styles were settled for ever, he added: 'It is the genuine desire of evangelical churchmen to keep reforming themselves according to the Word of God and never to require of ourselves or others what God's Word does not plainly require.'[4]

Undoubtedly, there had been a tendency for Evangelicals to think they 'knew it all', that non-Evangelicals were barely Christian and that they might be contaminated in some way by fellowship with other Christians. The stage was being set for the main outcome of Keele in the hope that Evangelical Anglicans would become very much part of the mainstream of the Church of England.

Under the title – 'Christ's sacrifice and ours – relating Holy Communion to the Cross', Michael Green dealt firmly and courageously with the Eucharist (the Giving of Thanks), as it had come to be known, and the perennial problem of preserving the sacrament from Anglo-Catholic emphasis, etc. Confusion undoubtedly existed in the minds of many Anglicans as to the once-for-all nature of the Cross and the false re-enactment of the sacrifice in the consecration of the elements.

In this sense the Eucharist is the church's responsive sacrifice of thanksgiving to her creating and redeeming Lord. There are then, these senses in which the Holy Communion may rightly be called a sacrifice. And if this were all that was meant, the Evangelical would have no quarrel of principle with the use of the word sacrifice for Holy Communion, though, with his eye on past history, and on the ambiguities of the word *sacrifice*, he would doubtless in any case have serious reservations about calling the Eucharist by this name.[5]

And, with greater succinctness, he added:

It is being widely urged these days that in the Eucharist the Church unites her offerings, imperfect though they be, with the perfect offering of Christ. But that is just what we do not do.

His atoning sacrifice is the root of our salvation; our responsive sacrifice of praise, thanksgiving and self-dedication is the fruit of it. May we never see the day within our Church of England when the two are confused.[6]

There seemed little doubt that Evangelicals would remain absolutely united over the true meaning and purpose of the Eucharist or Holy Communion. However, a re-statement of the evangelical position before Keele was timely. The area where there had been some widening of horizons and fresh thought had been in that of the Church, visible and invisible, ecumenical and comprehensive. The Rev. Philip Hughes dealt in *Guidelines*, with the subject 'The Credibility of the Church – understanding the Church in an ecumenical age'.

The inescapable problem of the visible Church is in the mixed character of its composition, and it is the mixed church which presents a constant threat to its credibility in the world. There are tares mixed with the wheat; the net contains bad fish as well as good; there are hypocrites and impostors alongside true believers.[7]

Canon Leathem sketched out the possibilities of development at the level of the local church and it was in this area that Evangelical Anglicans were to take a positive lead as new patterns of church services and structures began to emerge. He expressed the principle that,

Order is both itself an expression, and a means of the further expression, of the Church's true ministering life. It is, therefore, a conception which must be understood as covering not only the offices of the ordained, but also – and indeed primarily – the functioning of the whole fellowship as it lives, loves and serves under the guidance and constraint of the Word and Spirit.[8]

Many new concepts were being launched. In the field of ministry, there were eldership and ministry teams, local elders and house groups, whilst in the area of church based services, there was parish or family communion, besides family services and an entire re-think on the function and shape of the evening service.

The penultimate chapter of compulsory reading for Keele was by perhaps the most distinguished layman of his day active in Church affairs, Professor Norman Anderson, later to be knighted for his outstanding contribution to debate as lay chairman of General synod. Appropriately, he was a Reader, the only one at the time, on the staff of All Souls, Langham Place. His title was arresting, to say the least – 'Christian Worldliness, the needs and limits of Christian involvement'. He brought up to date evangelical thought on innumerable issues for, sadly, since Shaftesbury and Wilberforce, Evangelicals tended to fight shy of politics, culture, social functions and the like. They were strong on church-building based Christian activity, but very weak in Christian enterprise and influence in the world. Professor Anderson, in 1967, was breaking relatively new ground as he emphasised the loss of social concern in work, leisure and culture. He tackled, in a fearless way, finance and economics, industrial relations, race, social justice, distribution of wealth and family planning. No longer would it be possible for Evangelicals to excuse themselves from these issues on the grounds that instead they were teaching and preaching the Word of God.

Encouraged by the new ground being covered by Evangelicals at Keele, Professor Anderson wrote an interesting book, published the following year. He dealt with such issues as 'Work and Leisure', 'Culture and Learning', 'Politics and the State', 'Social Service and Education in the Welfare State', all areas in which Evangelicals had failed in earlier decades to make a really significant contribution. But the tide had changed and was coming in fast – evangelical involvement was the watchword for the future. 'How can one possibly love one's neighbour as oneself and yet remain passive and silent when that neighbour is treated unjustly in circumstances in which it would be perfectly possible not only to expostulate, but also to take active steps to get unjust laws changed or autocratic action restrained.'[9] Professor Anderson was even more emphatic as he invoked the teaching of the New Testament: 'In a democracy the issue is far less agonising, for the Christian can – and should – play his full part in formulating policy and framing the laws under which he has to live. Any attempt to opt out of this responsibility constitutes a misunderstanding or misapplication of New Testament principles which must be condemned.'[10]

Another field in which some Evangelical Anglicans became active in the 1960s was designated 'Clinical Theology', the Association of that name having been founded in 1962 to bring together psychiatrists and theologians of orthodox schools. The movement is well documented in a work by Dr Frank Lake entitled *Clinical Theology*.[11] After the anti-Christian assertion of Freud, in earlier days, it was refreshing to find that the psychiatric was being welcomed by the theological in seeking to understand man's inner ills. There were many areas of human experience where Christians in general had little or nothing to say but now there was plenty of dialogue and counselling for such conditions as depression and accidie, with schizoid and paranoid personalities being helped towards a more harmonious experience of life. Dr Lake wrote of his publication:

Somewhat like the New Testament letters, this book is the product of an interaction between the writer and the priests and pastors with whom he has worked. I am therefore indebted for its existence in this sense to those who launched me in the work, to the Rev. Canon Max Warren, D.D., and Harold G. Anderson, M.D., M.R.C.P., of the Church Missionary Society, who directed me into psychiatry, and to the four friends who agreed to recommend my original approach to the diocesan bishops, to Dr Donald Coggan, now Archbishop of York, to Bishop H. H. V. de Candole, long associated with the Parish and People movement, to the Rev. Canon Ernest Southcott, Provost of Southwark, and to the Rev. Geoffrey Rogers, then Warden of Lee Abbey, now Canon Missioner in the Diocese of Coventry.[12]

Clinical Theology was another example of evangelical involvement at the point of human need and happened to coincide, chronologically, with the new emphasis on wider influence from Keele. However, it was a movement sponsored by liberal Evangelicals and grave misgivings were expressed by many main-line Evangelical Anglicans that the field being covered was too removed from the paths of the gospel.

Before Keele, Evangelical Anglicans had regarded themselves as 'a race apart', almost as a Church within the Church. Many were now seeing the Anglican fold as inclusive and comprehensive, one in which evangelicals had a most important part to play. Critics of the larger view accused their brethren of 'doctrinal indifferentism' or worse, whereas Evangelical Anglicans have always been strong on doctrine and have been the first to uphold the view that the Church of England, by law established, is the National Church.

Evangelicals at Keele expressed a new commitment to the Church of England. This was fresh light, almost a blinding light to some who were beginning to escape from their hide-outs. Clearly there would be dangers in the new exposures and a great deal of understanding would be required. Referring to a conference arranged by Latimer House, the Rev. Roger Beckwith wrote:

It was explained by Dr Packer at the conference that we were living in a time when all theological convictions were regarded as relative, not absolute: no one was going to force us out deliberately, when what they wanted us to do was to *contribute our insight* – one among many. Reassuring though this was in the circumstances, it may perhaps have misled some evangelicals into accepting other people's valuation of evangelical theology, and inclined them to be content with a tolerated position within a much more broadly comprehensive church.[13]

It ought to be mentioned that N.E.A.C. or *Keele '67*, as it became known, was organised by a Committee, the chairman of which was the Rev. John Stott and the secretary the Rev. Raymond Turvey, vicar of St George's, Leeds, who had been the leading instigator of the Congress. From the start, the Committee had the backing of the Church Pastoral Aid Society, the Church Society, the Church of England Evangelical Council, the Fellowship of Evangelical Churchmen and the Federation of Diocesan Evangelical Unions. A very considerable contribution to the success of N.E.A.C. was made by Michael Saward, then at the Church Information Office, who magnificently supervised the Press.

Unquestionably, the Rev. John Stott gave a very strong lead and at the 1967 Islington Clerical Conference its chairman, Prebendary Peter Johnston, spoke in no uncertain terms:

Evangelicals in the Church of England are changing too. Not in doctrinal conviction (for the truth of the gospel cannot change), but in stature and in posture. It is a tragic thing, however, that Evangelicals have a very poor image in the Church as a whole. We have acquired a reputation for narrow partisanship and obstructionism. We have to acknowledge this, and for the most part we have no one but ourselves to blame. We need to repent and to change. As for partisanship, I for one desire to be rid of all sinful 'party spirit'. *Evangelical* is not a party word, because the gospel as set forth in the New Testament is not, and never can be, a party matter. We who love the adjective *evangelical*, because it declares us to be gospelmen, must take great care, therefore, that what we are seeking to defend and champion is the gospel in its biblical fullness and not some party shibboleth or tradition of doubtful biblical pedigree.[14]

The die had been cast, the leadership had been compelling. The young men rose to the rallying call. From then on, Evangelicals within the Anglican Church could not be ignored as outside the main stream nor could they be written off as unconcerned with real-life issues in the Church and in the world.

Furthermore, due to the work of the Packer generation of Evangelical Anglicans and also to Keele, the Church of England were forced to take Evangelicals seriously – they were now Anglicans who were Evangelical rather than, as previously, Evangelicals who happened to be Anglicans. The difference was most important. Hitherto, Evangelical Anglicans were virtually only found in opposition but thereafter they were found on the various Commissions of the Church, although Canon Colin Buchanan, by his membership of the Liturgical Commission, had 'ante-dated' Keele by three years. And Dr Jim Packer served as a member of the Anglican–Methodist Unity Commission.

A report of the Congress was immediately published.[15] It recorded:

Thus they converged on Keele: some 1,000 delegates, including 110 theological students, together with 30 observers, amongst them Roman Catholic, Greek Orthodox, and Free Church representatives, and members of the Christian press.

After the opening speeches of welcome and introduction the Archbishop of Canterbury, in what the *British Weekly* described as 'a masterly address', concentrated on the congress theme, 'Christ over all', by proclaiming the certainty of the church's faith in the experience of Christ as Redeemer.[16]

Sir Kenneth Grubb, then Chairman of the House of Laity in Church Assembly, who attended the Congress as an ordinary delegate, made the following assessment:

The Congress has done three remarkable things. It has given Evangelicals a justified sense of their standing; it has emphasised their loyalty to the Church; it has demonstrated that they have much to contribute, not only to individual faith, but also to the great spiritual challenge of contemporary society. Can one expect more?[17]

A rather more searching and, in one respect, a challenging appraisal was contributed by Canon D. M. Paton, Secretary of the Missionary and Ecumenical Council of the Church Assembly:

First, the generally positive and open attitude of the Congress confirmed the change of temper among Evangelicals which has been noticeable for some years in the theological writing, ecumenical work, overseas mission and social ethics.

Second, this change is not in the body of evangelical doctrine, but in the way the doctrines are held and in the readiness to tackle new questions. In this respect, Keele seemed not unlike Vatican II!

Thirdly, a question. Have Evangelicals fully grasped that to play a real part in the corporate life of the Church of England involves taking very seriously (positively as well as negatively) the existence and views of those in the Church of England who are not Conservative Evangelicals.[18]

The Congress Statement was introduced by the chairman, John Stott, who pointed out that it was a beginning rather than an end product and that Evangelicals ought to be ready to contribute more fully to the life of the Church of the Nation. 'We certainly hope in future to be more flexible in our evangelical application of principle to policy', he said.

The Statement itself was a well ordered document, readable and succinct. It covered the Church's Message, Mission, Structures, Worship, Unity and World Setting. It did not mince words on the vexed subject of any kind of union with Rome:

We recognise that the Roman Catholic Church holds many fundamental Christian doctrines in common with ourselves. We rejoice also at signs of biblical reformation. While we could not contemplate any form of reunion with Rome as she is, we welcome the new possibilities of dialogue with her on the basis of Scripture.[19]

Free Church reaction to the Congress was unremarkable. No real coverage was given by the *Baptist Times* which, however, took note that, '1,000 delegates attending the first national Anglican Evangelical Congress last week declared that they "stand firm on theological grounds in maintaining the traditional Anglican practice of an 'Open Table' ".' The statement called for reformation of the Church of England, 'the theological chaos' of which caused both 'grief and shame'.

There were no real surprises in the Keele Statement. It expressed, within a small compass, old and new evangelical thought; it restated doctrine and re-cast its contemporary appli-

184

cation. Keele was an evangelical rallying point for Anglicans, a coming together of equal numbers of clergy and laity to feel and to express their fellowship, their unity and their resolve. There had never been anything remotely like it before. But there was one major change of stance: 'Nothing in the Keele Statement has aroused more argument than the passage urging participation in the ecumenical movement. For some it has been a rude shock to discover that a large Congress of Evangelicals has declared itself ready to learn from other Christians.'[20]

From then on, Evangelical Anglicans were somewhat divided in their assessment of Keele. Some, led by the Rev. John Stott and the Rev. Jim Packer, declared that they were more than ready to leave their evangelical 'ghettos' of the past while others, not as yet vociferous and not very numerous, later to be lined up behind the Protestant Reformation Society, felt that the pass had been sold to error at Keele. But the strongest anti-Keele voice, at that stage, came, not from within the Anglican Church, but from Dr Martyn Lloyd-Jones, Minister of the Westminster Congregational Chapel and for many years a force within the whole of Evangelicalism, notably through the Inter-Varsity Fellowship.

Following the Congress at Keele, Evangelicals not only questioned time-honoured formulae but had some very positive things to say about the way ahead. No longer were they able to see the ministry of the local church as the sole prerogative and preserve of the clergy, for at last it had dawned on thoughtful Evangelical Anglicans that the *laos* was the whole people of God and that 'clergy and laity' was a wholly false differentiation. Where a church had grown to very large proportions, as in All Souls, Langham Place, the magnitude of the problem of caring pastorally for all the members was, clearly, beyond the ability of the clergy and so the whole matter of gifts in the body of Christ had to be thought through from Biblical first principles. In February, 1968, the Rev. John Stott gave the Pastoral Theology Lectures in Durham University and the substance of these was published in the following year.[21]

Extreme forms of clericalism dare to reintroduce the notion of privilege into the only human community in which it has been abolished. Where Christ has made out of two one, the clerical mind makes two again, the higher one and the other lower, the one active and the other passive, the one really import-ant because vital to the life of the Church, the other not vital and therefore less important. I do not hesitate to say that to interpret the Church in terms of a privileged clerical caste or hierarchical structure is to destroy the New Testament doctrine of the church.[22]

The author, as he had often done in his preaching and writing, called for a complete reversal of the commonly held belief in the roles of clergy and laity:

There must be many of us in the Church, both clergy and laity, who need to perform a complete mental somersault. It is not the clergyman who is the really important person and the layman a rather inferior brand of church-man, but the other way round. It is the laity who are important, the whole Church serving both God and man, the vanguard of Christ's army as it advances to the conquest of the world, and the clergy are the servicing organisation.[23]

Fellowship or House Groups, established at All Souls Church and most evangelical churches, were beginning to realise the value of the house meeting where Christians could invite their neighbours and friends to informal discussion and biblical study which would lead some unbelievers into real belief, whereas they might find the move into churchgoing a step they felt, at that stage, unable to take. Thus there came into being the lay-led groups, because, clearly, there were insufficient clergy to go round:

Do lay people resent the lay leadership? Far from it! We pastors may cherish the illusion that we are needed and missed, but the groups consider that they get on better without us! In the questionnaire I asked: 'are you in favour of the lay leadership of the groups?' 95 out of 108 who answered were in favour. They gave three main reasons. The first was biblical principle, that lay leaders 'are sharing in the ministry of the church', that 'the gift of spiritual leadership is not conferred by ordination', that such experience 'helps to develop the spiritual abilities of the laity', and that 'this makes us more aware that we are the church'. The second was pastoral necessity, that the clergy do not have the time to exercise all the leadership and must therefore share it. And the third reason was rather embarrassingly personal. Lay leaders, the questionnaire answers inform us, are 'more human and understanding', par-ticularly because they are themselves living and working in lay situations.[24]

Another post-Keele re-examination was carried out in the Rev. Gavin Reid's book on 'the failure of the church to com-municate in the television age'.[25] He was thinking along similar lines to those suggested by the Rector of All Souls, Langham Place: 'Today's type of non-literary man responds well to the informal, relaxed atmosphere of the small group. Many churches are seeing this and capitalising on it through home meetings.'[26]

Whereas, in the earlier part of the century, church members

and, possibly, also, their friends, were prepared to go once or twice a week to attend meetings in their church halls, so often cheerless and Victorian in their furnishings, modern man, it was discovered, was often prepared to give up an evening's television in favour of visiting a neighbour's house for coffee and informal discussion of the Christian faith. Gavin Reid remarked:

The Keele Congress of Anglican Evangelicals had possibly more wisdom than they recognised when they hammered out this section in their congress statement: Our primary concern must be with what God thinks of the Church, not with what men think. Nevertheless, we are concerned that many obstacles to evangelism are created by such things as the archaism of the language, the dress of our clergy, the quality of our publicity and the state of our premises.[27]

The Rev. Gavin Reid forcibly examined the Church's relative failure to communicate the gospel in terms intelligible to contemporary man, to reach the unchurched masses in ways which might yield a better harvest than recent decades had seen:

Thus the answer in the day of mass media is relatively simple; get on T.V. and radio, print tracts and imitation newspapers and literally spray words in all directions. Quite frankly, Christians have been doing this for some time, and it is hard to think that in any Western country today there are people who have not, in this sense, 'come under the sound of the gospel'. Unfortunately, there is very little to show for it.[28]

The book seeks to state the problem rather than to suggest solutions. Its author was in his mid-thirties when he wrote, passionately, of the Church's inability effectively to communicate the Good News but he was wise enough to appreciate the problems of actually 'releasing' congregations into the life of the world.

The Rev. John King was editor of the *Church of England Newspaper* from 1960 until 1968 and he wrote a telling postscript to Keele which he saw as a 'moment of truth' for contemporary Evangelicalism:

Evangelicalism is largely concerned with correctness and concern for correctness makes for timidity. The extensive doctrinal section of the Keele statement (*Keele '67*, published by C.P.A.S.) betrays a nervous preoccupation with precision in doctrine which makes a noticeable contrast with naive paragraphs elsewhere. Plainly much more thinking goes on about doctrinal definitions than about making the Gospel meaningful to the people on the housing estate.[29]

In a chapter entitled 'Did Keele change anything?', the author deals with what was seen by him to be the main outcome of the Congress:

The outstanding effect of Keele was to deal a death-dealing blow to the idea of an Evangelical unity existing as a kind of alternative to the ecumenical movement. This particular will-o'-the-wisp was extinguished once and for all – to the accompaniment of protestations of everlasting friendship to Evangelicals in other churches than the Church of England (the protestations were received with coolness by Free Church Evangelicals).[30]

It must be admitted that, prior to Keele, many Evangelical Anglicans had viewed themselves as a party and, subconsciously perhaps, as the only truly Christian party in the Church. Their elitism was unspoken except on special occasions such as the Islington Clerical Conference. The self-criticism of Keele had evoked an uneasy feeling of their ineffectiveness within the established church, recognising that the voice of Evangelicals had not been listened to in the counsels of Anglicanism. It was hoped that, after Keele, Evangelicals would come in from outside. However, John King was not optimistic: ' "Forward from Keele" remains an empty aspiration. Evangelicalism has a built-in bias towards conservatism and this not only in theology. The bias is evident in the focal points of Evangelical power – the societies; these are for the most part of long standing, which is another way of saying that they are in the hands of old men.'[31]

However, Keele splendidly demonstrated evangelical commitment to the Church of England and, significantly, the phrase *Forward from Keele* was the title of a leaflet issued by the organising committee after the event. It was estimated that 600 parishes used the preliminary study course and that 700 parishes were represented at the Congress. Regional Conferences were suggested by way of follow-up and it was envisaged that these would take place on a Saturday afternoon in forty to fifty centres. Panels of speakers on the relevant subjects were set up and conferences took place in many places during 1967 and 1968. However, so that the impetus of Keele be maintained, the leaflet urged that Parochial Church councils should grapple, at the grass roots, with the live issues generated at Keele.

The Rev. John King in *The Evangelicals* felt that the trouble with Evangelicals was that they were disunited and he forecast a parting of the ways over practical issues, although doctrinal unity was not in question. He found many faults in Evangelicalism and saw it in need of urgent renewal to prevent fossilisation and

Keele, he avers, 'awoke the pilgrims to the new duties required of them in unfamiliar territory and rough weather'.[32] These elements were the climate within the whole Church of England to which Evangelicals were now, it seemed, fully committed: 'Evangelicals now see themselves as members of the continuing historic Church. They are not Evangelicals who happen to be Anglicans. They are fully paid-up members of the historic Church ready to think positively and constructively about their role.'[33]

The author advocates what he describes as 'reformed catholicism' as the route for Evangelicals, both conservative and radical. He contends that Evangelicals must see themselves, not as occupying every pulpit in the land, but as contributing to the totality of the Anglican Church, through the parishes and its power structure:

An Evangelical asks whether a man has faith in Christ, not whether he has been episcopally confirmed. An Evangelical asks (or should ask) what gifts God has given to a variety of people, not what man-made regulations limit the exercise of ministry. An Evangelical believes that Christianity is Christ, that God's mercies are covenanted in Christ, that man's proper response is to be identified in baptism with Christ's death and resurrection and to work out that identification during the remainder of his days.[34]

The decade which followed the National Evangelical Anglican Conference at Keele University in 1967 was one of flux and change, notably in Church structures, both national and local. In addition, strong feelings persisted that unity ought soon to be achieved between the various Protestant churches and that Evangelicals, now that a much greater understanding had been reached by them on their place in the whole of the Anglican Church and, therefore, by implication, within the larger whole of the Reformed Churches, were anxious to play their part.

Church Assembly, officially the National Assembly of the Church of England, had endured as the governing body from 1919 but in 1970 it was superceded by the General Synod:

In the reformed mode of government, the key word is 'participation'. First, there is to be the participation of laity in matters where formerly the clergy alone either made the decision or had the initiative in taking action. The parallel existence of Church Assembly and the clerical Convocations will largely disappear; the authority of both bodies being inherited by the General Synod, in the running of which clergy and laity will occasionally sit separately.[35]

Church Assembly had 750 members and the Synodical Government Measure envisaged a total of 560, about half being lay. The Deanery Synod replaced the Ruridecanal Conference and Diocesan Synod the Diocesan Conference. The greatest change numerically was at diocesan level where the membership was to be between 150 and 270 as opposed to, in some cases, over 1,000 members under the old system: 'The Measure has created the bare bones for government by synod but it is church members who must clothe the skeleton with sinews and flesh and God alone who can breathe life into the legal framework for the running of His church.'[36]

Evangelicals, on the whole, have never been very keen on taking their part in the government of the Church and generally it has been left to a few enthusiasts for liturgical and administrative niceties to battle through the very slow-moving business of the Church at deanery, diocesan or national level. But Evangelicals owe a great deal to men like Colin Buchanan, Michael Saward, Oliver Wright Holmes and Gervase Duffield for holding the evangelical standpoint through long and tedious general debate and much committee work. Their work is too easily forgotten.

15
Evangelical Identity – A Problem

THROUGHOUT THEIR HISTORY, Evangelicals have been proud to own that name but, since Keele, many of them have questioned its meaning and younger Evangelicals, notably those leaving theological college, have wondered whether they would be more acceptable generally if they were known simply as Anglicans, or even, merely as Christians. These views have been held partly in the hope of ending what some see as a divisive party spirit, for so long the bogey of comprehensive Anglicanism, and partly in an endeavour to draw nearer to non-Evangelicals. Evangelicals have held, obviously in opposition to their Anglo-Catholic brethren, that Evangelicalism is the equivalent of historic Anglicanism but, since the Oxford Movement, there had been a tendency for parts of the Church of England to drift from biblical anchorage, moving towards a return to medievalism and, in recent decades, leading evangelical theologians and scholars like Dr Jim Packer, the Rev. John Stott and the Rev. Roger Beckwith, have done a great deal not only to substantiate but also to clarify the Evangelical position within Anglicanism, also to move away from an entrenched position behind a previously held very Protestant Evangelicalism: 'What name we take or others give us is a trifling question in comparison with the great doctrines by which we seek to live, and whether they are true.'[1]

The author, well aware of the prevailing spirit of ecumenism and the desire by some to 'close ranks' for the sake of the gospel and in the face of shrinking churches, took issue with the 'lowest common denominator' type of Protestantism which, in contradistinction to changeless Rome, seemed willing to end up with a watered-down Christian faith rather like the old liberalism, now dead and buried. The danger of this position was that it would not only overlook differences between, say, Anglicanism and Congregationalism, mixed now with Presbyterianism, but also the fundamental differences which existed between any World Council of Churches amalgam and Rome, 'always the same', with her unscriptural doctrines of the Virgin Mary, the Pope and the Mass:

Evangelicals therefore regard as the only possible road to the reunion of churches the road of biblical reformation. In their view the only solid hope for churches which desire to unite is a common willingness to sit down together under the authority of God's Word, in order to be judged and reformed by it.[2]

Admission was made that Evangelicals had in the past some- times made use of selected passages of the Bible to suit their own convenience but it was doubted whether there was now any real substance in such a charge, except perhaps over purely denomi- national issues, within Evangelicalism as a whole:

The evangelical testimony is to the whole of Scripture, as it unfolds what Paul termed 'the whole counsel of God'. Indeed, since one important meaning of the word 'catholic' is 'loyal to the whole truth', one would dare even to say that, properly understood, the Christian faith, the catholic faith, the biblical faith and the evangelical faith are one and the same thing.[3]

The author, not unnaturally, had one eye on the ever recur- ring theme of theologians that the Christian faith must be updated to appear in new, fashionable colours, casting away its ancient garb in favour of some outrageous and extravagant gar- ments called either 'New Directions', 'New Morality', 'New Theology' and even, possibly, 'New Christianity'. As John Stott has consistently counselled, Christians, and evangelicals perhaps in particular, need constantly to submit themselves to the reforming and re-invigorating factor of Scripture and whilst accepting the urgent need to state the Gospel in modern, relevant language, to realise that its truths are as changeless as God Himself:

This, then is the claim which evangelical believers have always made. It is that evangelical Christianity is theological in its character, biblical in its sub- stance, original in its history and fundamental in its emphasis.[4]

Evangelicals have constantly been at loggerheads with fellow Protestants who have contended that reason, as an authority, must be held in balance with Scripture; with Roman Catholics who hold that tradition and the Church are equal factors with Scripture and with their High Church counterparts who have, as Evangelicals see it, departed from Scripture, for instance, in con- tending that the historic episcopacy of the Church of England is vital to reunion with the free churches. Thus, to be an Evangelical is and always has been to submit to the sole and absolute certainty of Scripture, 'God-breathed' but, like the Lord Christ Himself, containing both the human and the divine. Evangelicals, whilst rejecting the 'mechanical' view of the Scriptures, accept them as being substantially as the Spirit of God designed them.

It became obvious, after Keele, that 'the old days of entrenched "Party" isolationism are gone'.[5] However, it became equally true that statements of evangelical doctrinal belief were more than ever necessary. As the leaders of Evangelical Anglicanism took a broader stand than they once did, chiefly in relation to their fellow Anglicans, so it became necessary for them to re-emphasise the absolute fundamentals of Evangelicalism. Dr Packer, for example, came under a good deal of evangelical fire for his part in what some saw to be the dangerous adventure of *Growing into Union* (S.P.C.K., 1970). Through the evangelical authors' outspoken largeheartedness, critics felt that ground was being given up, the position compromised and Protestantism put in jeopardy. However, it had taken forty years of waiting to see the flood tide of evangelical reform, positive action and regeneration, since the landmark of the defeat of the Prayer Book revision which had in many senses been a low-water mark. 'Victory in the Prayer Book debates of 1927–28 was in a deeper sense defeat, for it established an image of evangelicals as blind enemies of all change and made their name mud in the church for many years.'[6]

With as many as one-fifth of the clergy having an evangelical commitment, much ground had been gained in that period. The slightly mannered, rather dictatorial and prim evangelical vicar with his total liturgical allegiance given to the 1662 Book of Common Prayer was, it seemed, fighting a rearguard action but there were also younger men willing to fall in behind the old guard and bemoan the spirit of Keele. The resurgence of the Protestant Reformation Society bore witness to this.

The new men of this new evangelical age were carrying their thoughts and endeavours into every field of Christian activity. Ecumenical involvement was difficult but for men like the Rev. John Stott by no means an insuperable problem. And involvement in worldly affairs, so often eschewed by the inter-war years Evangelicals, forgetting their illustrious socially reforming forbears, was now becoming much more realistic. Neither Sir John Laing, head of the famous building company which bore his name nor Sir Frederick Catherwood, chairman for a time of the National Economic Development Council, was an Anglican but they were strong evangelicals having a considerable influence on the whole of evangelical Christian thought. Sir John Laing, in his ninety-ninth year, died leaving only £371[7] as his net estate and, long before his company became really famous, as early as 1940, he was giving away £20,000 per annum, a considerable sum having gone to the work of the then Inter Varsity Fellowship. Sir Frederick Catherwood, an intellectual with a most distinguished business career, wrote: 'The Christian should have no fear of stepping into the world of affairs. Men of faith have been there before him. Joseph was a ruler of Egypt. Daniel was a ruler both of Babylon and Persia. Moses was one of the greatest law-givers the world has ever known.'[8]

The author hit hard at a Protestant pietism which always regarded the world as a wicked place in which to do business and in which to have social intercourse but that attitude was rapidly passing away with the greater feelings of freedom among Evangelicals and their willingness to get involved in the really difficult areas of life such as big business, politics and finance. Also, Sir Alfred Owen, like Sir John Laing, head of a large family business, was a strong Evangelical Anglican, a Staffordshire County Councillor and Pro-Chancellor of Keele University. He died in 1975, he had been fearless in Christian testimony, with a simple faith and a zest (which eventually killed him) for work of all kinds. In 1959, with Mr John Cordle, he purchased the *Church of England Newspaper*, which after his death became a charitable Trust.

The *Church of England Newspaper* is the weekly journal of Evangelical Anglicans and represents a very substantial commitment in time and effort by many people. It has had a most gifted line of editors, more recently David Coomes, now on the religious broadcasting staff of the B.B.C., who has been succeeded by Anne Tyler who combines a lively journalistic sense with youthful charm and disarming authority. *C.E.N.* publishes the whole spectrum of Anglican news with special reference to the evangelical standpoint and it never fails to arrest by its headlines or interest by its views and news items.

In the academic world, Sir Norman Anderson stood out as an intellectual Evangelical and a most prominent Anglican layman. His influence, notably through I.V.F., was very marked but, of a slightly older generation of laymen, Dr Basil Atkinson, Under-

Evangelical identity – a problem

Librarian in the University of Cambridge, left his stamp on generations of Evangelicals in that university. A slightly eccentric, hotly anti-Roman Catholic bachelor, he virtually followed Charles Simeon and Handley Moule as the 'patron-saint' of the Cambridge Inter-Collegiate Christian Union, at his Sunday tea-parties holding court to successive generations of C.I.C.C.U. members, when he would answer questions of many kinds. He died in 1972.

The common reaction against the rigid, over-authoritative patterns of earlier days had spilled over into evangelical circles and not more so than in the area of ministry and pastoral care. It is difficult to imagine, in the 1970s, a man of Dr Atkinson's style answering, with a consummate authority and didacticism, every question put to him by evangelical students. The age of the panel of experts, of team ministry and equality of status was by the seventies influencing the Church of England. In addition, the Church was involving non-ordained members, so often referred to as 'frozen assets', in the work of the ministry, whereas previously they had only been allowed to look after finance and re-roofing the church. 'The New Testament knows nothing of the one-man-band type of clergyman, so familiar in our church circles. Oversight and teaching are a group responsibility, if we are to follow the New Testament pattern.'[9]

An earlier evangelical line of thought would have been that a Christian could only have an adult teaching and pastoral ministry if he became ordained: 'The situation needs correcting in three ways: (1) The vicar must climb down from his paternalistic perch. (2) He must demonstrate that his ministry is a man-sized, relevant job and not a leisurely hobby. (3) He must give man-sized jobs to man-sized men even if they are outside the church.'[10]

It is not clear how far the writer in this symposium is prepared to go in employing within the Church those who are outside it or, indeed, how this is possible but the thought of involving non-Christians is, at least, challenging. The momentous move of appointing Lay Elders is also dealt with, in a chapter by Roy Henderson. 'It is because I saw many of the ills and problems of the Church of England being due to our acceptance of this unbiblical monarchic pattern of ministry in the local church, that I believed we had to return to the concept of a body of elders, and not continue to have one presbyter in sole charge of a congregation.'[11]

195

Clearly, very many expansive and revolutionary ideas were being accepted in parish life and with the positive blessing of some bishops. It appeared that Evangelicals were taking the lead or, at the least, not nowadays being left behind in current thought and practice.

'A Call to Avoid Unnecessary Polarisation' was issued in an important booklet published at this time.[12] In this, the author, *inter alia*, called for a rapprochement between the newly emerging 'radicals' among Evangelicals and the 'conservatives'. he guys, in the nicest possible way, those who resist change of any kind, even in dress or hair style, and he writes:

A radical, on the other hand, is someone who asks awkward questions of the Establishment. He regards no tradition, no convention and no institution (however ancient) as being sacrosanct. He reverences no sacred cows. On the contrary he is prepared to subject everything inherited from the past to critical scrutiny. And his scrutiny often leads him to want thoroughgoing reform even revolution (though not, if he is a Christian, by violence).

And he points out:

Thus Jesus was a unique combination of the conservative and the radical, conservative towards Scripture and radical in his scrutiny (his *biblical* scrutiny) of everything else.[13]

Certainly, the post-war Church of England had encountered many radical Evangelicals and almost all had had beneficial effect on their times. John Stott also makes a plea for a synthesis between 'Form and Freedom', particularly in worship structures and church allegiance:

The early church sets us a healthy example in this matter. We read that, immediately after the Day of Pentecost, the Spirit-filled believers were 'attending the temple together and breaking bread in their homes' (Acts 2.46). So they did not immediately reject the institutional church. They worked to reform it according to the gospel. And they supplemented the formal prayer services of the temple with their own home meetings.[14]

In the seventies, the collar and tie was replacing the 'dog-collar' whenever possible, even robes and choirs were not all that popular in some evangelical churches. And Evangelical Christians, as a whole, revolted against the Age of Affluence, as they pleaded for simple life styles. The Bishop of Winchester, an Evangelical, created a considerable stir in the Christian conscience with a book on this subject.[15] Simplicity had been carried over into ways of addressing God and 'You' and 'Your' were much more in favour than the 'Thee' and 'Thou' so beloved by the adherents to '1662'.

Evangelical identity – a problem

A most important milestone was reached in 1974 with the holding of a Congress on World Evangelisation at Lausanne. 4,000 participants from 500 countries attended under the chairmanship of Bishop Jack Dain of Sydney. The Congress lasted ten days and drew together evangelical leaders from the whole world, including Billy Graham and John Stott, with Malcolm Muggeridge as a visiting speaker. The Congress marked the end of the dichotomy between Evangelicalism and ecumenism and was another witness to the decline in rigid Fundamentalism and triumphalism. John Stott told the gathering of their social responsibility in Evangelism and that God was calling Evangelicals 'to immerse themselves in the secular world of politics, economics, sociology and race relations.'

Another benefit derived from Lausanne was that Evangelicals learned to agree or disagree over minor matters, as they seemed. That same year, the Senior Evangelical Anglican Conference also witnessed the reaching of a milestone:

The Lausanne Congress revealed so clearly the remarkable gifts that John Stott has in resolving differences and divisions and keeping Christians who differ together. He has done it again at Swanwick and proved to all charismatics that he has, in addition to other gifts, the *charisma* of wise leadership as well as the grace of humility. (*Church of England Newspaper*, 26 July 1974).

In 1975, the World Council of Churches assembled in Nairobi and significantly, in its summer issue, *The Churchman* devoted almost the entire journal to preparing Evangelicals for the experience. Two of the contributors were the then Bishop of Truro, Dr Graham Leonard, and Bishop Stephen Neill, formerly Professor of Religious Studies at the University of Nairobi and an experienced missionary statesman. Not surprisingly, the articles were mainly critical, reflecting the general feeling among Anglicans towards the W.C.C.

Another contributor was the Rev. Andrew Kirk, who at that time taught theology in Buenos Aires, who came to be something of an authority on the new Liberation Theology emanating from Latin America. In 1980, he published *Liberation Theology* (Marshall, Morgan & Scott), in which he wrote:

Liberation Theology is a Latin American phenomenon which, over its comparatively brief history of fifteen years has generally been approved by liberal theologians but has been viewed with suspicion by evangelicals. Paradoxically, just as the liberal theologians are wearying of its jargon and

197

are admitting its deficiencies, there is an attempt to salvage it by evangelicals.[16]

High on the Agenda at Nairobi was the call for social justice, for the uniting quality of the gospel and for the freedom for nations and individuals to be found in Jesus Christ.

In view of the generally acclaimed success of 'Keele '67', it was not in the least surprising that, ten years later, it was succeeded by 'Nottingham '77' or the National Evangelical Congress, held at Nottingham University in April, 1977. In the ten years, there had been considerable growth in evangelical churchmanship and the full impact of Keele had been absorbed, so that it was possible to attract a most representative 2,000 delegates to Nottingham, about equally lay and clerical and representing not only every evangelical parish in the land but also every aspect of Anglican Evangelical life. As before, the other churches sent their representative observers. Already, the prophets of gloom and doom among Evangelicals were wondering if everyone at Nottingham was a 'real' Evangelical for they thought it amazing that so many should come to such a conference. They were almost disappointed! However, the Congress was a great thrill to all the delegates, the spirit of unity was evident and the working sessions were very much 'down to brass tacks'.

The preparatory books for the Congress were masterpieces of presentation and range of content and the Rev. John Stott, general editor of the series, was able to persuade Lady Collins of the publishing house which bears her name, to publish the three paperbacks.[17] This itself was a remarkable indication of how far Evangelical Anglicans had progressed in obtaining recognition and, even, respectability, over the previous decades. No longer need they rely solely on purely evangelical publishers. A much broader canvas was used than for Keele in *Guidelines*. The layout of the series is worth recording.

Volume 1 *The Lord Christ*

Obeying Christ in a Changing World	John Stott
Jesus Christ The Lord	J. I. Packer
Jesus Christ the Only Saviour	Michael Sadgrove and Tom Wright
Understanding God's Word Today	Tony Thiselton
Christian Beginning	George Carey
Christian Maturing	Michael Harper

Volume 2 *The People of God*

The Church as Community	Ian Cundy
The Life of the Local Church	Trevor Lloyd
Mission and Ministry	Michael Green
The Church as Institution	Timothy Dudley-Smith
The Unity of the Church	Colin Buchanan
The Roman Catholic Church	Julian Charley

Volume 3 *The Changing World*

Power in our Democracy	John Gladwin
The Power of the Media	Raymond Johnston
Education and the Law	David Harte
Marriage and the Family	Oliver O'Donovan
The Gospel and Culture	David Bronnert
Global Stewardship	Philip King

The writers in the overall symposium represented, in themselves, the strength of Evangelicalism in theological and parochial life and were divided equally between those in the academic world and those in parochial positions. The small number of non-ordained persons contributing was clearly regrettable as it demonstrated the continuing clergy domination of the evangelical world, or else the poor way in which the clergy had trained and allowed their non-ordained brethren to develop.

Each delegate to the Congress was invited to major on three of the subjects covered by the books and thus to attend three actual lectures given at Nottingham by the writers concerned. Much of the writing was brilliantly illuminating:

The only-begotten Son, who died for us, presents us to His Father as His brothers and sisters; thus we are adopted. But to this privilege unbelievers remain strangers, to their own infinite loss. As contractors-out gain no benefit from a pension scheme, so one who shrugs off the gospel gains nothing from the mediation of Jesus Christ.[18]

Dr Packer's scintillating illustrations of Christian truth are reminiscent of C. S. Lewis, whose startling clarity had illumined the darkness of the days of the Second World War:

Hopelessness is hell – literally . . . As the deep hopelessness of post-Christian western culture tightens its chilly grip on us, we are made to feel this increasingly, and so can better appreciate the infinite value for life today of that exuberant, unstoppable, intoxicating, energising hope of joy with Jesus in the Father's presence for ever, which is so pervasive a mark of New Testament Christianity.[19]

From controversy to co-existence

Just as co-operation with fellow Anglicans had been the 'shocking' theme of Keele, so Hermeneutics became the 'shocker' at Nottingham and the Rev. Tony Thiselton, a lecturer in the department of Biblical studies in the University of Sheffield, produced the shock waves!

A study of the Bible that is totally uncritical, that never aims at distancing but only at fusion, will always see the text through the spectacles of the tradition in which it already moves. A Christian Union Bible Study Group will hear the text only in a 'Christian Union' kind of way. A parish group or house group will hear it only in the way which bounces back to them what they already expect to hear. The kind of Bible study which takes place today in the context of the World Council of Churches is probably more guilty in this respect than that of most evangelical groups.[20]

The writer emphasises the need to understand the language of the Bible in terms of the usage and meaning of words at the time they were given. He also points out the dangers of pressing meanings too far to suit special circumstances. 'Capitalists draw lessons about economics from the parable of the pounds: socialists argue that Jesus was a socialist on the basis of reading a social programme into the phrase "Kingdom of God".'[21]

Questions of Hermeneutics and Biblical interpretation continued well beyond Nottingham and overflow beyond the chronological limit of this survey. In fact, the manner of interpretation gave rise to questions of biblical authority, still unresolved in some evangelical minds:

New Testament churches, it is argued, did not simply hand down fixed doctrines which came to them from the past, but interpreted the Word and deeds of God afresh for themselves. On this basis some have argued that it is less 'biblical' to look back to a fixed body of doctrine than to state anew what God is for the present. This has opened up new questions about biblical authority, and the relation between the Bible and tradition.[22]

By now, of course, Evangelicals had come to accept the multi-racial nature of their congregation influencing, as it must, the style of the fellowship in its worshipping and social settings:

Local people speaking the local language (Cockney? West Indian? English?) and being part of the local culture will bring with them into church, for example, the local taste in music, the local way of doing things together in community. In a multi-cultural area this means reflecting the different national, social, and age group culture, so that there might be, for example, a steel band or guitars as well as the organ, a raucous sing-song as well as the delicacies of choral evensong to celebrate a festival, a late-night beer and crisps party rather than a coffee morning or vicarage tea-party.[23]

Canon Michael Green, Rector of St Aldates, Oxford, and one of the most radically thinking yet scholarly Evangelicals of his generation, contributed forcefully to the debate on 'lay' presidency at the Holy Communion, which had now become a matter for open debate: 'We have reserved absolution and celebration jealously to that elite status of professional priests (as if one strand within the priestly body of Christ were more priestly than another). The contrast with the New Testament could hardly be more complete.'[24]

Furthermore, he grasped the nettle of real unity, rather than a mere spiritual unity, and Anglican oneness, rather than Evangelical unity – the subject of the rather hot debate which flowed from Keele and which was personalised between the seer of All Souls, Langham Place, and the grey eminence of Westminster Congregational Chapel.

. . . in the New Testament Christians belonged together, visibly. This removes from us two common Evangelical expedients: remaining satisfied, like Keswick with merely 'spiritual' unity for a week while going back to denominationalism for the rest of the year; and the way of Dr Martyn Lloyd-Jones and the F.I.E.C. of withdrawal to a 'purer' church – until it, too, is 'purified' by further withdrawals.[25]

Dr Martyn Lloyd-Jones, one of the greatest preachers of his day (he died in 1981), also a 'father-confessor' of the I.V.F., notably in earlier days, commanded wide respect among Evangelicals, including many Anglican clergy. He founded the Westminster Fellowship for ministers and at their meetings there was no agenda but, although seemingly democratic, he spoke *ex-cathedra* on subjects uppermost in his mind. In June 1966 he called for evangelical unity by exhorting all pastors and ministers in the group to secede ultimately from their Churches to form a new evangelical Church. At a Rally of the Evangelical Alliance in the autumn of 1966, the Doctor, as he was affectionately called, issued a public plea for this to happen but he was strongly opposed by the Rev. John Stott. So great was the strength of personality of this evangelical 'guru', the Doctor of Westminster Congregational Chapel, that after October 1966, no minister in a 'mixed' denomination was permitted to remain a member of the Westminster Fellowship unless he seriously considered ultimately joining the proposed new Church. Most members resigned on the strength of the edict but one or two notable exceptions were registered.

Perhaps the weakest Nottingham contributions were in the third volume dealing with the environment of the gospel and the Church, although the six writers had a difficult task in giving a fair picture of the world of 1977. However, the assessment of sexuality in Christian terms by Oliver O'Donovan, then lecturer at Wycliffe Hall, Oxford, left much to be desired. He seemed to be enjoying some kind of backlash from the greater freedom of sexual discussion which had come down on Evangelicals as heavenly dew and it would have been easy to gain the impression that he was putting the clock back and even advocating celibacy. The chapter on 'Culture' hardly dealt with the subject as it is commonly understood and no treatment was given to the relationship between the faith and the arts, notably to music, painting, poetry and drama. In fact, the Rev. David Bronnert, vicar of St John's, Southall, wrote on 'Culture' simply from the standpoint of Christian life and responsibility in a multi-racial district.

John Gladwin, then Director of the Shaftesbury Project, later chairman of the Board of Social Responsibility and previously a tutor at St John's College, Durham, wrote of 'The character and implications of political and institutional power' 'The battle is on in the Christian world against all who seek to remove the Word of God from the living world of politics and economics. It is a battle which the Church cannot afford to avoid. It is here that one of the key areas of mission and obedience is being won or lost.'[26]

It is interesting to note that The Shaftesbury project was established in 1969 'as an initiative by Evangelical Christians to promote a Biblically-based approach to various areas of social concern'. Study Groups exist working on such areas as 'The Inner City', 'Crime, Law and Punishment', 'Nuclear Energy', 'Marriage and the Family'. The Project publishes a quarterly journal *Shaft*, *inter alia* chronicling the work of the groups. Another monthly magazine, *Third Way*, once published, like *Crusade*, by the Thirty Press, appeared in the seventies dealing with the social, economic and political issues under review by 'The Shaftesbury Project'.

All in all, the three Nottingham books, in content, presentation and format were items of which Evangelicals could well be proud. If nothing else, many of the chapters would have rescued, by quotation, many a dreary but very orthodox evangelical sermon from the depths of mediocrity.

The two archbishops, Donald Coggan and Stuart Blanch (both Evangelicals, with two years' experience in their new office), addressed the Congress and the other 'devotional' addresses were given by Alec Motyer and David Watson. Was this the 'high noon' for Anglicans who were still glad to be termed Evangelicals? Of the inspirational nature of the gathering there can be no doubt – 2,000 taking the Lord's Supper together and a high proportion raising their arms in worship left its unmistakable mark – for good with the vast majority but for ill with a few. The press dubbed the Rev. John Stott 'the Pope of Evangelicalism'; at least in a very pervading, very persuasive, charming yet faintly autocratically firm way, he dominated the Congress which was, after all, perhaps just as well, for regrettably he had and still has no obvious successor. Many evangelical bishops do not, as yet, match up to his personal charisma and authority. The details of the Congress were described as follows:

On each of three successive days, one of the books was the theme of the day. After it had been introduced by a dramatic presentation, the Congress divided into six sections gathered round each author. First the author was questioned by an interviewer, and then the section broke into smaller groups, discussed the questions raised by the draft and submitted written suggestions for alteration or addition. The authors then revised their drafts with the help of their interviewer, an independent assessor and later the Statement Steering Committee. The revised drafts were duplicated, offered on the last morning to nine sub-plenaries for further amendment and finally approved.[27]

Inevitably, diversities of viewpoint on certain issues were included in the statement and unfortunately it was only possible for a section of the Congress to discuss each part of the final document:

Mercifully, there were enough disquieting things at Nottingham to deter us from being complacent. The evangelical essentials were largely taken for granted at Nottingham, when it had become urgent for them to be reaffirmed, and concentration was almost wholly on other matters. In relation to the Keele Statement, consequently, the Nottingham Statement has to rank as a sort of appendix – an appendix of doubtful value at many points.[28]

In so far as Keele was the beginning of a new chapter in Evangelical Anglican history, it might be *fair* to call Nottingham an appendix but not in a derogatory way, for the endorsement in 1977 was one of joy, assurance and commitment to the gospel of grace, through faith alone, in Christ alone. Apart from the commotion caused by the Hermeneutics issue the sea was calm at Nottingham.[29] However, the whole question of inspiration was to persist in the counsels of Evangelicalism and to occupy the attention of its leading scholars and advocates for many years to come – possibly, in varying degrees of intensity, in perpetuity.

Surely, Evangelicals ought to have counted their blessings in 1977. With somewhere between one-quarter and one-fifth of all parishes thought to be Evangelical in varying degrees, Evangelicals were numerically strong, with a demonstrable unity at Congresses ten years apart; the Thirty-nine Articles still intact for all intents and purposes, the Book of Common Prayer had not been ousted, the Alternative New Services provided refreshing new patterns as well as modern language and, most significantly, evangelical theological colleges were full. Church members from Free Churches were admitted as visitors to Holy Communion in Anglican places of worship, dangerous ground doctrinally had been trodden by evangelical theologians trying hard to plot the way ahead and everywhere freedom in worship and fellowship was being experienced. The sixth and seventh Declarations of Intent of the Nottingham Congress read:

We reaffirm our commitment to the goal of visible unity in Christ's church: Deeply regretting past attitudes of indifference and ill-will towards Roman Catholics, we renew our commitment to seek with them the truth of God and the unity he wills, in obedience to our common Lord on the basis of Scripture.

Shortly after 'Nottingham '77', an Open Letter was addressed to all archbishops and diocesan bishops of the Anglican Communion on relations between Anglican Churches and the Roman Catholic, Eastern Orthodox, Old Catholic and Ancient Oriental Churches. It was signed by 130 ordained and lay members of the worldwide Anglican Communion. They referred to the agreed statements issued by the Anglican–Roman Catholic International Commission (A.R.C.I.C.) on the subjects of the Eucharist (1971), the ministry (1973) and authority (1977). The statements listed areas where agreement was not yet possible and the Open Letter made reference to the subjects where still more exploration was required and where Anglicans felt that ground might be given up in the cause of unity. These were 'Scripture and Tradition', 'Justification', 'Church and Ministry' and 'The Holy Communion'. Following this Open Letter, three of the signatories expanded their views and underlined still further the need for critical involvement. 'The Church of England is not a multi-faith Church; its Articles commit it to evangelical essentials, and this commitment is regularly the springboard of Evangelical argument.'[30]

Admittedly, such a statement presupposes Evangelicalism containing the heart of historic Anglicanism but nonetheless, Evangelicals sought to give a positive lead. All the old and ever-recurring difficulties are fearlessly dealt with in the booklet, as one would imagine from three such doughty champions of evangelical faith. It concludes:

We must in honesty confess ourselves doubtful, on present knowledge, as to whether any of the non-reformed churches mentioned in the Open Letter holds and teaches justification by faith in the terms (mainstream Reformation terms, we think) in which we have just set it forth . . .

We note that Roman Catholics still slip into the language of self-salvation through meritorious co-operation with grace, and still teach that the Mass is a propitiatory offering which satisfies God for our sins and obtains for us power to repent, and we wonder whether over four centuries the gap on this central issue has narrowed in any significant way at all. But if the discussions to which this chapter is offered as a preamble ever begin, those who signed the Open Letter will certainly make it a priority to try to find out.[31]

It would certainly appear that the 'duel' and dialogue with Rome was the longest running theme in Evangelical Anglican history and perhaps in recent times it has overshadowed the allied theme of that involved with Anglo-Catholic relationships. The new spirit of Keele, reinforced at Nottingham, has caused Evangelicals within the Anglican Church to come out of their long-held hiding places, whether strictly Anglican or inter-denominational, and join in debate and dialogue as never before. This caused hard-liners of the old school, such as Dr David Samuel, to wag their heads and wonder whether men like Dr Jim Packer were really Evangelical.[32] Then others began to ask at Nottingham 'What is an Evangelical?' and so there came into being what was known as 'The Evangelical Identity Problem'.

On fundamentals all evangelicals are at one. Thus, all evangelicalism is based on the doctrines of the Trinity; Christ's deity; the correlation of grace and faith; justification by faith through Christ's substitutionary atonement; Christ's physical resurrection and present reign; new birth and progressive sanctification through the ministry of the indwelling Spirit; the church as the fellowship of all believers; and the certainty of Christ's personal return. Also, all evangelicalism rests, from a formal and methodological standpoint, on the final authority of Holy Scripture.[33]

Dr Packer lists the alternative 'extras', as it were – matters on which evangelicals differ, such as the 'second blessing' of the Spirit, and refers to these as 'secondary and, so to speak, within the family'. But he writes of the dangers of 'scaremongering':

Thus, fear of being scoffed at or swamped, and the defensiveness that is born of the memory of past roastings for our views, can work in us an obstinate, blinkered, suspicious and rigid immobility ('our doctrine, right or wrong; and if Scripture said that Jonah swallowed the whale, I'd believe it!'): and this attitude falls far short of being a responsible stewardship of truth . . . Again, 'domino' theories charting the expected course of apostasy ('let this point go, and all Christianity will fall') spring naturally from the fear-ridden mind.[34]

He goes on to refer to the old 'siege mentality' of 'the fewer we are together the merrier we shall be'. Keele had put an end to all that for thenceforward Evangelicals felt themselves committed to involvement in every aspect of Anglican life. But with customary style, Dr Packer writes of things – symbols of the old Evangelicalism:

The old symbols of evangelical identity – north side; no stole or candles; exclusive use of 1662 worship forms; the eschewing of tobacco, alcohol and the cinema; deep dog-collars, etc. – are now mostly things of the past. The language of Zion, that spiritual Swahili made up from the Authorised Version and the old hymns, which Anglicans and non-Anglican evangelicals once spoke in just about the same way, has given place to several distinct dialects, based apparently in different modern versions of Scripture and agreeing only in addressing God as 'you' rather than 'thou'.[35]

And on Anglican/Roman Catholic dialogue, he reflects:

The Church of England currently makes gestures towards the Roman Catholic Church that are more friendly and forthcoming than ever before, yet evangelicals seem not to worry as their fathers would have worried. The rumbling hiccups and the fumbling pick-ups on doctrinal points which were noticeable at Nottingham confirmed suspicions that, whatever else evangelical clergy had been doing since Keele, they had not been spending their strength drilling folk in basic evangelical principles as their fathers used to do.[36]

It would seem that Dr Packer is enthusiastic concerning evangelical emphasis, between Keele and Nottingham, on the *most* important issues and he hints that doctrinal strengths will become, as ever, vital.

A most notable contribution to the Anglican–Roman Catholic dialogue was organised by Church Society in 1975. It was subtitled *Agreement in the Faith*[37] and was a brave experiment bringing together, as speakers, such well known Evangelicals as the

Ven. George Marchant, the Rev. Julian Charley and the Rev. Roger Beckwith with those of standing in the Roman Catholic Church, viz. the Rev. A. Hastings, the Very Rev. Canon R. Stewart, the Rev. M. Richards, and the Rev. J. Coventry. This 'common search for the truth', as the 'Foreword' points out, would have been unthinkable fifteen years earlier.

Special mention needs to be made at this juncture of the contribution made by Julian Charley, vicar of St Peter's Everton, Liverpool, the only evangelical member of the Anglican–Roman Catholic International Commission (A.R.C.I.C.), 1970–82. His position as one of eighteen theologians, meeting over a period of eleven years, provided him with deep insights into the problems of reunion and his Grove Booklet, *Rome, Canterbury and the Future* (1982) graciously and fairly summarised his views.

As he died in 1975 and was himself a great innovator in the evangelistic presentation of the truth, the name of the Rev. Dick Rees must be mentioned. He was a unique person – a full-time Anglican Evangelist, almost wholly employed in parish missions for twenty years or so but towards the end of his life significantly he was finding that special house meetings were taking the place of purely church-based services given over to Evangelism, where latterly he had used the services of the Prayer Book, e.g. Holy Matrimony, to demonstrate the gospel.

Dick Rees confined himself, in the main, to parish missions but a wider evangelistic ministry was carried out earlier by the Rev. John Stott, then the Rev. Dick Lucas, later Canon David Watson of York and Canon Michael Green of Oxford. Evangelism came very much to the fore in these decades and University Christian Unions often formed the base from which Evangelism was successfully launched by John Stott, Dick Lucas, David Watson and Michael Green.

Meanwhile, the search for visible unity went on with continuing ardour. Not only were exploratory conversations at various levels taking place with Roman Catholics but *Ten Propositions for Unity* were put before the Anglican Church and the Free Churches. There was nothing new in the propositions for they stated what Evangelicals and many others thought to be unexceptional and both Anglo-Catholics and many Free Churchmen still jibbed because of their view of the episcopacy. So far as Evangelical Anglicans were concerned, they were something of a mixed multitude over non-essentials, e.g. ordination of women, which tended to make some of them very hot under the collar at times. Writing of the 'Evangelical Coalition'[38] Gavin Reid, well known for critical appraisal and trenchant comment, divided Evangelicals into four groups:

The Protestant Strand
The Keswick Strand
The Eclectic Strand
The Charismatic Strand

Only the fourth category, in his view, contained anything like a large proportion of the younger Evangelicals. Both the Protestant and Keswick strands would have represented the 'hard-line', separatist elements within Evangelicalism and the Eclectics reflected the wide compass of Evangelicals following the high-tide of Nottingham.

Representative of the Protestant stance and stand was the following comment:

Those who continue in the Church of England holding primly to the supreme authority of scripture and teaching the Biblical doctrines of the fall, redemption, salvation and glory should not be too disturbed by the fact that the time-honoured description 'evangelical' has been emptied of its true meaning. May the little flock and faithful remnant hold fast to the Truth, and when invited to join the mixed multitude of popular fashion say firmly and politely, 'include me out'.[39]

The long running saga of Evangelicalism seeing itself as a 'little flock' and a 'faithful remnant' was to persist and receive new vigour in a reaction to both Keele and Nottingham. The relative decline in power of Church Society (in terms of its National Church League style) had allowed the Protestant Reformation Society and the *English Churchman* to give voice to a renewed emphasis on Evangelical exclusiveness.

In 1972, efforts were made to draw together C.E.E.C. and Church Society and a joint organisation was proposed for 1975. However, alarm bells were sounded in Church Society, the idea was dropped and ever since, in spite of generosity and brave efforts by some, the spiritual rift between Church Society and the evangelical comprehensiveness of C.E.E.C. has grown, although the Society is still fully represented on C.E.E.C. In the fullness of time, *Churchman*, the scholarly and theological journal of the Society became the storm centre, its editorial board changed by the Council, with the result that a new journal *Anvil* was started by those who had been ousted. It was a sad story of little give and take and undoubtedly helped to polarise Church Society's future.

It is not difficult to see that the Evangelical Identity Problem (rather than the 'Crisis' described by some), was generated at Keele, worked out in the following decade and confirmed at Nottingham, whereupon questions were asked all round as to who and what was an Evangelical in Anglican terms. Of course, an Evangelical has several lines of inheritance in his family tree, which makes him, anyway, a fairly composite, if not complex character. He derives from Protestantism, from Puritanism, from Pietism, for a start, but has by now shed most of these characteristics in favour of a more central Christianity, Reformed, Biblical and Anglican at the same time. Furthermore, the anti-cultural, anti-intellectual and anti-social stance between the wars has gone. Yet the quest for true spirituality went on in a holy dissatisfaction, true devotion and commitment being sought through prayer, bible study and worship.

Dr Packer saw the thirty years from the Prayer Book defeat of 1928 as 'bumping along the bottom', but then 'pastoral and theological talent increased in both quantity and quality, largely through the work of the Inter-Varsity Fellowship among students'.[40] But, he explains, the Protestant element in Evangelicalism, fighting Anglo-Catholicism, did not 'grab' these newly-converted Evangelicals. So far as the shift in social habits is concerned, Dr Packer writes:

A generation ago, 'separation from the world' and avoidance of 'worldliness' were (rightly) pressed as central to the Christian calling, and to explain what this meant a standard casuistry of recommended abstinences went the rounds, approximately as follows: Eschew theatre and cinema-going, except to see Shakespeare and the classics; plays and films are trivial, and acting demoralises. Eschew ballroom dancing for it is sexually inflaming (though folk and country dancing, which involves less physical contact, is all right). Avoid reading novels and general literature (except for history and biography) beyond what one's academic and professional tasks require . . . Do not drink alcohol . . . Females should cut-out cosmetics, fancy hair-dos, bright clothes and depilatory treatment, for this shows sinful pride in outward appearance; one index of unearthly inner beauty is dowdy dress and a bun.[41]

Nowadays, Evangelicals have a life-affirming rather than a life-denying attitude in the world and intend to 'subdue and have dominion in the area of created things', whether God-made or man-made.

From controversy to co-existence

In all probability, the heady days between Keele and Nottingham blinded the latter Congress to the need for re-stating evangelical basics on every major occasion but nevertheless it is certain that although Evangelical Anglicans have changed out of all recognition in the last thirty years, that is to say in all outward appearances, they are at heart and in practice men and women of the Bible, of the Evangel and of the Church of England. To use the Latin tag of Reformation days – *sola Scriptura, solo Christo, sola fide, sola gratia, soli Deo gloria* (by Scripture only; by Christ only; by faith only; by grace only; glory to God only). The outward changes should prove helpful in Evangelism and healthy in the Christian life.

Writing after *Nottingham 77*, the Ven. George Marchant[42] traces the rise of Evangelicals back to an 'Academic Revival' due to the work of the I.V.F. after the First World War:

From then on a growing number of increasingly well-equipped people entered the whole field, grappled with the distinctive problems, contributed articles and literature, and became involved as members of the teaching staffs in colleges and in universities. More young people found a renewed confidence in Evangelical churchmanship, where previously only the most doggedly loyal could go along with the unconvincing, negatively dogmatic pietism of the time.[43]

There can be little doubt that this academic revival has been the bedrock on which modern Evangelicalism has been built. Into the new structure came the heart-warming flow of the Billy Graham Crusades, the first break-through of an ecumenical evangelising spirit. Then the furniture was changed; services and structures, charismatic and non-charismatic answered the swinging sixties, with their moral laxity, anti-authoritarian attitudes and affluence:

There was a brave attempt to meet the situation in the field of books and radio; the guitar was quickly baptised to understudy, if not replace, the organ in the parish church, with the 'group' instead of the choir. Evangelicals in the parishes, once they got over the long hair and the 'winkle-pickers', soon responded in these terms, but with it came the subtle temptation that affected a large proportion in society; to live out a practical existentialism, discounting the knowledge of the scholar, the perspective of history, or even more, any traditional outlooks.[44]

All things considered, we see the rich diversity of Evangelical Anglicanism in three main, inter-related forms, right wing, central and left wing or, in even more simplistic, yet overlapping terms, the hard-liner, the conservative and the more liberal, all gladly owning up to the title 'Evangelical'. It has, one supposes, always been that way but although there is a tendency to division within Evangelicalism, the quarrelsomeness of earlier days seems to have vanished and a somewhat uneasy living together has taken its place. We must not gloss over the tensions within the movement – they may even yield a healthy outcome. At least, Evangelicalism has been able more recently to retain its best minds within the spectrum.

Yet, there are still minor differences between the radicals and the conservatives, the Charismatics and the non-Charismatics, the ecumenicals and the separatists, dialogue with the Roman Catholics and an arms-length acknowledgement, Prayer Book and A.S.B., the 'Kingdom' view and the personal gospel stand-point, the doctrinally centred and the experience orientated, the old evangelical hard-line clericalism (Readers barely tolerated) and the utilisation of every member's gifts. It is an interesting mix and, generally speaking, healthy. Instead of a rigid conformity, there is something of a cohesive diversity, even a colourful attractiveness. Under the authority of scripture, united in the gospel of grace, looking to the empty cross, dependent on the work of the Holy Spirit and united within the Church, Evangelicals remain one in Christ Jesus their Lord, their spiritual inheritance already reaching back over six hundred years to John Wycliffe, Morning Star of the Reformation, an inheritance awaiting completion with the Second Advent of the Day Star Himself.

211

Notes

1. Into battle

1 H. P. Liddon, *Life of E. B. Pusey*, vol. I, p. 255, Longmans, London 1894.
2 Georgina Battiscombe, *Shaftesbury*, p. 100, Constable, London 1974.
3 G. R. Balleine, *A History of the Evangelical Party*, p. 314, Vine, London 1951.
4 Elliott, Binns, *The Evangelical Movement in the English Church*, p. 79, Methuen, London 1928.
5 J. Hanford and F. Macdonald, *H. C. G. Moule*, p. 111, Hodder and Stoughton, 1922.
6 Ibid., p. 193.
7 Harrison and Stuart-Clark (eds.), *The New Dragon Book of Verse*, p. 46, O.U.P., 1977.
8 Vivian Ogilvie, *Our Times*, p. 21, Batsford, 1953.
9 Thomas Hardy, *Selected Poems*, p. 65, Macmillan, 1950.
10 Brian Gardner, *Up the line to death*, p. 142, Methuen, 1964.
11 Ibid., p. 10.
12 Ibid., p. 136.
13 E. L. Langston, *Bishop Taylor Smith*, p. 121, Marshall Morgan, 1938.
14 Ibid., p. 124.
15 Roger Lloyd, *The Church of England 1900–1965*, pp. 215–16, S.C.M., London 1966.
16 J. G. Lockhart, *Halifax*, vol. II, p. 247, Geoffrey Bles, London 1936.
17 E. L. Langston, *Bishop Taylor Smith*, p. 131, Marshall Morgan, London 1938.
18 Ibid., p. 135.
19 R. H. Gretton, *A Modern History of the English People*, p. 1032, Secker, 1930.
20 Alan Wilkinson, *The Church of England in the First World War*, p. 104, S.P.C.K., 1978.
21 Ibid., p. 173.
22 Gretton, *A Modern History of the English People*, p. 1033.
23 John Briggs, *St George's Newcastle-under-Lyme, 1828–1978*, p. 47, 1978.
24 Ibid., p. 47.
25 E. Wingfield-Stratford, *The History of British Civilisation*, p. 1262, Routledge, 1930.
26 Ibid., p. 1262.
27 Hanford and Macdonald, *H. C. G. Moule*, p. 222.
28 *The Evangelistic Work of the Church*, pp. 32–3, S.P.C.K., 1918.

29 Lloyd, *The Church of England 1900–1965*, p. 137.
30 Horton Davies, *Worship and Theology in England*, vol. V, p. 175, O.U.P., 1965.
31 Wilkinson, *The Church of England in the First World War*, p. 231.
32 Jon Stallworthy, *Wilfred Owen*, p. 16, Chatto, Oxford 1974.
33 Wilkinson, *The Church of England in the First World War*, p. 116.

2. The defensive years

1 Stephen Neill, *Anglicanism*, p. 400, Pelican, 1958.
2 Roger Lloyd, *The Church of England 1900–1965*, p. 245, S.C.M., 1966.
3 Horton Davies, *Worship and Theology in England*, p. 130, O.U.P., 1965.
4 Ibid., p. 129.
5 Edmund Knox, *The Tractarian Movement*, p. 69, Putnam, London 1933.
6 Ibid., p. 70.
7 Edmund Gosse, *Aspects and Impressions*, quoted in ibid., p. 72.
8 Henry Wace, *Some Questions of the Day*, pp. 227–8, Nisbet, London 1912.
9 T. S. Eliot, *Murder in the Cathedral*, Faber, London 1935.
10 T. S. Eliot, *Collected Poems*, Faber, London 1934.
11 Lloyd, *The Church of England 1900–1965*, p. 241.
12 Gordon Hewitt, *The Problem of Success*, vol. I, p. 462, S.C.M., London 1971.
13 Ibid., p. 463.
14 Ibid., vol. I, p. 471.
15 Ibid., vol. I, pp. 472–3.
16 Neill, *Anglicanism*, p. 400.

3. Through the Waste Land

1 Joynson-Hicks, *The Prayer Book Crisis*, p. 163, Putnam, 1928.
2 Ibid., p. 165.
3 *Parliamentary Debates, 1927*, vol. 211, pp. 2540–1.
4 Ibid., p. 2642.
5 Ibid., p. 2648.
6 David Samuel, *The Evangelical Succession*, p. 92, James Clarke, 1979.
7 Stephen Neill, *Anglicanism*, p. 396, Pelican, 1958.
8 A. J. P. Taylor, *English History 1914–1945*, p. 329, Pelican, London 1965.
9 Roger Lloyd, *The Church of England 1900–1965*, p. 280, S.C.M., London 1966.
10 Horton Davies, *Worship and Theology in England*, p. 306, O.U.P., Oxford 1965.
11 Joynson-Hicks, *The Prayer Book Crisis*, p. 152, Putnam, 1928.
12 Ibid., p. 156.
13 E. A. Knox, *The Tractarian Movement*, p. 379, Putnam, 1933.
14 G. R. Balleine, *A History of the Evangelical Party*, p. 264, Vine, 1951.

Notes to pages 40–68

4. Continuing nadir

1 Hensley Henson, *The Church of England*, p. 123, C.U.P., 1939.
2 Randle Manwaring, *The Heart of this People*, pp. 55–6, Quaintance, 1954.
3 Horton Davies, *Worship and Theology in England*, pp. 121–2, O.U.P., 1965.
4 Elliott Binns, *The Evangelical Movement in the English Church*, p. 98, Methuen, 1928.
5 Ibid., p. 159.
6 E. A. Knox, *The Tractarian Movement*, pp. 370–1, Putnam, 1933.
7 Ibid., p. 371.
8 Roger Lloyd, *The Church of England 1900–1965*, p. 243, S.C.M., 1966.
9 Ibid., p. 280.
10 A. G. Hebert (ed.), *The Parish Communion*, S.P.C.K., 1937.
11 Lloyd, *The Church of England 1900–1965*, p. 287.
12 Ibid., p. 340.
13 David Thomson, *England in the Twentieth Century*, p. 181, Pelican, 1965.
14 Stephen Neill, *Anglicanism*, p. 400, Pelican, 1958.
15 Davies, *Worship and Theology in England*, p. 177.
16 W. H. Auden, *Thank You Fog*, p. 39, Faber, 1974.
17 Davies, *Worship and Theology in England*, p. 186.
18 Ibid., pp. 209–10.
19 Timothy Dudley-Smith, 'Yesterday and To-morrow', *The Churchman*, p. 205, 1979.

5. The turning tide

1 F. W. Dillistone, *Into All the World*, pp. 18–19, Hodder and Stoughton, 1980.
2 Ibid., p. 221.
3 C. S. Lewis, *Surprised by Joy*, p. 212, Geoffrey Bles, 1955.
4 Ibid., p. 223.
5 Douglas Gilbert and Clyde Kilby, *C. S. Lewis: Images of His World*, p. 72, Hodder and Stoughton, 1973.
6 Selwyn Gummer, *The Chavasse Twins*, pp. 125–6, Hodder, 1963.
7 Ibid., p. 129.
8 Ibid., p. 142.
9 Roger Lloyd, *The Church of England 1900–1965*, p. 457, S.C.M., 1966.
10 Horton Davies, *Worship and Theology in England*, p. 174, O.U.P., 1965.
11 D. R. Davies, *On to Orthodoxy*, p. 103, Hodder and Stoughton, 1939.
12 Ibid., p. 143.
13 Ibid., p. 41.
14 Davies, *Worship and Theology in England*, p. 253.
15 Stephen Neill, *Anglicanism*, p. 386, Pelican, 1958.
16 H. A. Evan Hopkins, *The Miracle of Britain's Survival*, p. 4, C.S.S.M., 1944.
17 Ibid., p. 8.

18 Ibid., p. 9.
19 A. J. P. Taylor, *English History, 1914–1945*, p. 689, Pelican, 1965.
20 Gummer, *The Chavasse Twins*, p. 160.
21 Ibid., p. 161.
22 Ibid., p. 164.
23 Ibid., p. 164.
24 Ibid., p. 206.

6. Towards the conversion of many

1 D. R. Davies, *Secular Illusion or Christian Realism*, p. 94, Religious Book Club, London 1943.
2 T. C. Hammond, *Reasoning Faith*, p. 80, I.V.F., 1943.
3 Karl Barth, *Against the Stream*, S.C.M., 1954.
4 Selwyn Gummer, *The Chavasse Twins*, p. 183, Hodder and Stoughton, 1963.
5 *Lambeth Conference 1948*, p. 17.
6 Roger Lloyd, *The Church of England 1900–1965*, p. 517, S.C.M., 1966.
7 Ibid., p. 521.
8 Lloyd, *The Church of England 1900–1965*, p. 482.
9 Stephen Neill, *Anglicanism*, p. 387, Pelican, 1958.
10 C. E. M. Joad, *The Recovery of Belief*, p. 82, Faber and Faber, 1952.
11 Ibid., p. 238.
12 Selwyn Gummer, *The Chavasse Twins*, p. 189.

7. Flood-tide of Evangelism

1 Marcus L. Loane, *Archbishop Mowll*, p. 12, Hodder and Stoughton, 1960.
2 Ibid., p. 175.
3 Ibid., p. 205.
4 Cyril Garbett, *The Church of England Today*, p. 67, Hodder and Stoughton, 1953.
5 (Author unknown) *Introduction to Billy Graham. The Work of an Evangelist*, World Evangelical Alliance, 1953.
6 Ibid., p. 5.
7 John Pollock, *Billy Graham. Evangelist to the World*, p. 315, Harper and Row, 1979.
8 Ibid., p. 315.
9 Marshall Frady, *Billy Graham*, pp. 320–1, Hodder and Stoughton, 1977.
10 Frank Colquhoun, *Harringay Story*, pp. 232–3, Hodder and Stoughton, 1955.
11 Ibid., p. 193.
12 Ibid., p. 194.
13 Ibid., p. 177.
14 Ibid., p. 104.
15 John Pollock, *Billy Graham*, p. 167.
16 Ibid., pp. 164–5.

17 Ibid., p. 170.
18 Ibid., p. 202.
19 Selwyn Gummer, *The Chavasse Twins*, p. 207, Hodder and Stoughton, 1963.
20 Ibid., p. 208.
21 John Pollock, *Billy Graham*, p. 209.

8. Anatomy of Evangelicalism

1 'The Church on the B.B.C.'s doorstep', *Radio Times*, p. 80, 29 March 1980.
2 Raymond Luker, *All Souls, A History*, p. 65, All Souls Church, 1979.
3 'The Church on the B.B.C.'s doorstep', p. 89.
4 Ibid., p. 89.
5 Stephen Neill, *Anglicanism*, p. 402, Pelican, 1958.
6 Roger Lloyd, *The Church of England 1900–1965*, p. 608, S.C.M., London 1966.
7 A. F. Lace, *A Goodly Heritage*, p. 23, Monkton Combe School, 1968.
8 Noel Annan, *Roxburgh of Stowe*, pp. 79–80, Longmans, 1965.
9 Ibid., p. 181.

9. The Fundamentalist issue

1 Lord Home, *The Way the Wind Blows*, p. 77, Collins, 1976.
2 J. E. Fison, *The Blessing of the Holy Spirit*, p. 20, Longmans, 1955.
3 James Barr, *Fundamentalism*, p. 5, S.C.M., 1977.
4 Fison, *The Blessing of the Holy Spirit*, p. 6.
5 Barr, *Fundamentalism*, p. 120, S.C.M., 1977.
6 Ibid., p. 120.
7 Ibid., p. 120.
8 Ibid., p. 121.
9 David Edwards, *Church Times*, 15 July 1977.
10 John Goldingay, *The Churchman*, vol. 91, p. 307, 1977.
11 Fison, *The Blessing of the Holy Spirit*, p. 57.
12 *Church of England Newspaper*, 21 June 1957.
13 Max Warren, *Crowded Canvas*, p. 139, Hodder and Stoughton, 1974.
14 Ibid., p. 213.
15 Ibid., p. 214.
16 Gabriel Hebert, *Fundamentalism and the Church of God*, S.C.M., 1957.
17 Ibid., pp. 100–1.
18 Dr Tim Dowley and others (eds.), *The History of Christianity*, pp. 596–7, Lion Publishing, 1977.
19 F. W. Dillistone, *Into all the World*, p. 58, Hodder and Stoughton, 1980.
20 J. I. Packer, *Fundamentalism and the Word of God*, p. 141, I.V.F., 1958.

10. The hard facts of Evangelicals and unity

1 Nick Earle, *What's Wrong with the Church*, Penguin, 1961.
2 Ibid., p. 124.

3 Ibid., p. 128.
4 Ibid., p. 140.
5 R. F. Hettlinger, *Anglicanism and Reunion*, p. 28, Wycliffe College, Toronto 1952.
6 Ibid., p. 39.
7 Geoffrey Lampe, 'Episcopacy and Reunion', *The Churchman*, 1961, p. 13.
8 Cyril Bowles, 'The Church of England, the Free Churches and Episcopacy', *The Churchman*, 1963, p. 234.

11. The Honest to God debate

1 Roger Lloyd, *The Church of England 1900–1965*, p. 603, S.C.M., 1966.
2 Paul Tillich, *The Shaking of the Foundations*, Pelican, 1962.
3 John A. T. Robinson, *Honest to God*, p. 43, S.C.M., 1963.
4 *Church Times*, 22 March 1963.
5 Mervyn Stockwood, *Chanctonbury Ring*, p. 146, Sheldon and Hodder, 1982.
6 J. I. Packer, *Keep Yourselves from Idols*, p. 4, Church Book Room Press, 1963.
7 Ibid., p. 5.
8 Robinson, *Honest to God*, p. 106.
9 O. Fielding Clarke, *For Christ's Sake*, p. 14, Religious Education Press, 1963.
10 Ibid., p. 86.
11 Ibid., p. 101.
12 A. M.Stibbs, *Sacrament, Sacrifice and Eucharist*, p. 11, Tyndale Press, 1961.
13 Ibid., p. 69.
14 Ibid., p. 71.
15 Stockwood, *Chanctonbury Ring*, p. 154.

12. Liturgical debates

1 John Simpson, 'The New Alternative Services' in *The Churchman*, p. 27, 1966.
2 J. I. Packer, *The Thirty-nine Articles*, p. 7, Church Pastoral Aid Society, 1961.
3 Colin Buchanan, 'The New Communion Service', in *The Churchman*, 1966, p. 118.
4 Ibid., p. 121.
5 *Church Assembly Reports of Proceedings*, vol. XLVII, p. 546, 1967.
6 Buchanan, 'The New Communion Service', p. 122.
7 *Church Assembly Reports of Proceedings*, vol. XLVI, p. 739, 1966.
8 Horton Davis, *Worship and Theology in England*, p. 345, O.U.P., London 1965.
9 Roger Lloyd, *The Church of England 1900–1965*, p. 613, S.C.M., 1966.

10 R. T. Beckwith, *Prayer Book Revision and Anglican Unity*, p. 4, Church Book Room Press, 1967.
11 G. E. Duffield, *Revision and the Layman*, p. 9, Church Book Room Press, 1966.
12 Ibid., p. 11.
13 Ibid., p. 12.
14 D. D. Billings, *Services on Trial*, p. 16, Church Book Room Press, 1966.
15 C. O. Buchanan, *A Guide to Second Series Holy Communion*, p. 30, C.B.R.P., 1966.
16 D. R. Hill in *English Churchman*, p. 5, 31 December 1965.
17 G. E. Duffield, *A Guide to Intercommunion Today*, p. 5. Church Book Room Press, London 1970.
18 Ibid., p. 10.
19 J. I. Packer, *Relations between English Churchmen and Roman Catholics*, p. 1, Church Society, 1966.
20 *English Churchman*, 19 May 1969.
21 Packer, *Relations between English Churchmen and Roman Catholics*, p. 4.
22 Ibid., p. 5.
23 Canon J. Atkinson and Rev. P. E. Hughes, *Anglicanism and the Roman Church*, p. 15, Church Society, 1964.
24 Ibid., p. 20.
25 Ibid., p. 30.
26 Dr J. I. Packer, *Towards a Confession for Tomorrow's Church*, p. 4, Church Book Room Press, 1975.
27 Ibid., p. 6.
28 Ibid., pp. 9–10.
29 Herbert Carson, *United We fall*, p. 12, Carey Publications, 1975.
30 C. O. Buchanan, E. L. Mascall, J. I. Packer and G. D. Leonard, *Growing into Union*, S.P.C.K., 1970.
31 Ibid., p. 41.
32 Ibid., p. 59.
33 Ibid., pp. 77–8.
34 Canon R. C. Craston, *The Church of England Newspaper*, 21 February 1969.

13. Charismatic differences

1 John Stott, *Our Guilty Silence*, Hodder and Stoughton, London 1967.
2 Ibid., p. 61.
3 Alan Stibbs, 'Putting the Gift of Tongues in its Place', p. 295, *The Churchman*, 1966.
4 Ibid., p. 297.
5 Ibid., p. 298.
6 W. J. Hollenweger, *The Pentecostals*, p. 185, S.C.M., 1972.
7 J. R. W. Stott, *The Baptism and Fullness of the Holy Spirit*, p. 5, I.V.F., 1964.
8 A. A. Hoekema, *What About Tongue Speaking*, p. 31, Paternoster, 1966.

9 Hollenweger, *The Pentecostals*, p. 176.
10 Raymond Luker, *All Souls. A History*, pp. 63–5, All Souls Church, 1979.
11 John R. W. Stott, *The Baptism and Fulness of the Holy Spirit*, p. 6.
12 Ibid., p. 19.
13 Ibid., p. 24.
14 Donald Bridge and David Phypers, *Spiritual Gifts and the Church*, p. 132, I.V.P., 1973.
15 A. A. Hoekema, *What About Tongue Speaking*, p. 113, Paternoster, 1966.
16 John P. Kildahl, *The Psychology of Speaking in Tongues*, Hodder and Stoughton, 1972.
17 W. J. Hollenweger, *The Pentecostals*, p. 186.
18 Ibid., p. 186.
19 G. R. Balleine and G. C. B. Davies, *A Popular History of the Church of England*, p. 200, Vine Books, 1976.

14. Keele – a watershed

1 Published by the I.V.F. in 1936. Above views expressed in the *Church of England Newspaper*, April 1967.
2 Ed. Dr J. I. Packer, *Guidelines*, Church Pastoral Aid Society, 1967.
3 Ibid., p. 63.
4 Ibid., p. 66.
5 Ibid., p. 109.
6 Ibid., pp. 110, 117.
7 Ibid., p. 164.
8 Ibid., p. 191.
9 J. N. D. Anderson, *Into the World*, p. 45, Falcon, 1968.
10 Ibid., p. 41.
11 Dr Frank Lake, *Clinical Theology*, Darton, Longman and Todd, 1966.
12 Ibid., preface, p. i.
13 Ed. D. N. Samuel, *The Evangelical Succession*, p. 102, James Clarke, 1979.
14 Ibid., pp. 105–6.
15 Ed. Philip Crowe, *Keele '67*, Falcon Books, 1967.
16 Ibid., p. 9.
17 Ibid., p. 15.
18 Ibid., p. 16.
19 Ibid., p. 18.
20 *Church of England Newspaper*, 30 June 1967.
21 John R. W. Stott, *One People*, Falcon, 1969.
22 Ibid., pp. 19–20.
23 Ibid., p. 46.
24 Ibid., pp. 90–1.
25 Gavin Reid, *The Gagging of God*, Hodder and Stoughton, 1969.
26 Ibid., p. 34.
27 Ibid., p. 57 quoting para. 60 of the Keele Statement in *Keele '67*, Falcon, 1967.

28 Ibid., p. 107.
29 John C. King, *The Evangelicals*, p. 89, Hodder and Stoughton, 1969.
30 Ibid., p. 120.
31 Ibid., p. 124.
32 Ibid., p. 145.
33 Ibid., pp. 145–6.
34 Ibid., p. 155.
35 B. J. Stanley, *A Guide to Synodical Government*, p. 4, Church Book Room Press, 1969.
36 Ibid., p. 13.

15. Evangelical identity – a problem

1 John R. W. Stott, *Christ the Controversialist*, p. 8, Tyndale Press, 1970.
2 Ibid., p. 32.
3 Ibid., p. 33.
4 Ibid., p. 46.
5 Dr J. I. Packer, *The Evangelical Identity Problem*, p. 12, Latimer House, 1978.
6 Ibid., p. 24.
7 Roy Coad, *Laing*, p. 215, Hodder and Stoughton, 1979.
8 H. F. R. Catherwood, *The Christian Citizen*, p. 19, Hodder and Stoughton, 1969.
9 Ed. Clive Porthouse, *Ministry in the Seventies*, p. 19, Falcon, 1970.
10 Colin Reed, ibid., p. 67.
11 Ibid., p. 98.
12 John R. W. Stott, *Balanced Christianity*, Hodder and Stoughton, 1975.
13 Ibid., pp. 28, 29.
14 Ibid., p. 40.
15 John Taylor, *Enough is Enough*, S.C.M., 1975.
16 *The Harvester*, Oct. 1980, p. 291.
17 *Obeying Christ in a Changing World*, 3 vols., Fontana, 1977.
18 J. I. Packer, 'Jesus Christ the Lord', in *The Lord Christ*, p. 42.
19 Ibid., p. 43.
20 Tony Thiselton, 'Understanding God's Word Today' in *The Lord Christ*, p. 104.
21 Ibid., p. 113.
22 Dr Tim Dowley and others (eds.), *The History of Christianity*, p. 606, Lion Publishing, 1977.
23 B. T. Lloyd, 'The Life of the Local Church' in *The People of God*, p. 53.
24 E. M. B. Green, 'Mission and Ministry' in *The People of God*, p. 71.
25 Ibid., p. 91.
26 John Gladwin, 'Power in our Democracy' in *The Changing World*, p. 38.
27 J. R. W. Stott (ed.), *The Nottingham Statement*, p. 3, 1977.
28 D. N. Samuel (ed.), *The Evangelical Succession*, p. 108, James Clarke, 1979.
29 For a factual report on Nottingham 1977 see John Capon, *Evangelicals Tomorrow*, Collins, 1977.

30 R. T. Beckwith, G. E. Duffield, J. I. Packer, *Across the Divide*, p. 31, Lyttleton Press, 1977.
31 Ibid., p. 63.
32 See J. I. Packer, *The Evangelical Anglican Identity Problem*, chap. 1, Latimer House, 1978.
33 Ibid., p. 6.
34 Ibid., p. 10.
35 Ibid., p. 12.
36 Ibid., p. 13.
37 *The Oxford Conference*, Church Book Room Press, London 1975.
38 *Church of England Newspaper*, 26 March 1976.
39 *English Churchman*, 26 August–2 September 1977.
40 J. I. Packer, *The Evangelical Identity Problem*, p. 25, Latimer House, 1978.
41 Ibid., p. 28.
42 *The Churchman*, p. 114, vol. 91, no. 2, 1977.
43 Ibid., p. 115.
44 Ibid., p. 117.

Index

Index

Brethren), 5, 21, 45, 96, 105, 126, 151

Christian Introduction to Apologetics, 75

Christian Unions, 49, 54, 103, 129, 200, 207

Church Assembly, 18, 33, 63, 145, 148, 149, 150, 183, 184, 189, 190

Church Association, 3, 6, 94

Church Family Newspaper, 22

Church House, Westminster, 87–8

Churchill, Winston, 10, 67–8, 89

Church Information Office, 182

Churchman, 148, 197

Church Missionary Society, 24–8, 88, 116, 118, 181

Church of England Evangelical Council, 110, 170–1, 182, 208

Church of England, membership, 82

Church of England Newspaper, 22, 93, 104, 121, 187, 194

Church of England Trust, 106

Church of South India, 124

Church Pastoral-Aid Society, 6, 101, 108, 182, 187

Church Society, 3, 6, 22, 58, 94, 101, 108, 110, 157, 174, 182, 206, 208

Church Times, 8, 22, 63, 135, 136

Church Union, 8

Church Youth Fellowship Association, 109

Clarke, Rev. O. Fielding, 140

Clayesmore School, Iwerne Minster, 57

Clayton, 'Tubby', 9

Clergy, numbers of, 81

Clifton Theological College, 54, 59, 162, 163

Clinical Theology, 181

Coggan, Donald, Archbishop of Canterbury, 103, 136, 181, 203

Colquhoun, Canon Frank, 88, 94, 165

Commission on Evangelism, 63, 69

Committee for the Maintenance of Truth and Faith, 34

Communism, 80

Confessional Faith, 159–60

Congregationalists, 124, 128, 191

Congress on World Evangelisation, 197

Conn, J. S., *Menace of the New Psychology*, 54

Conversations between the Church of

England and the Methodist Church, 124

Cranmer, 31–2, 71, 142, 144, 147, 149, 151

Cranmer Hall (St John's College, Durham), 100

Crusade, 94, 119, 202

Crusaders Union, x, 45, 49, 57, 59–60, 109, 129

Daily Service, 97

dance and drama, 147, 164

Darwinism, 5, 12, 17, 41, 53

Davidson, Randall, Archbishop of Canterbury, 12, 18, 30–1, 34, 40–1

Davies, D. R., 64, 70, 73, 76

Davies, Horton, 14, 42, 51, 53

Dudley-Smith, Timothy, Bishop of Thetford, 94, 199

Duffield, Gervase E., 148, 152, 190

Earle, Rev. Nick, 128–9

Eclectics, 110–11, 208

Ecumenical Conference (Amsterdam), 67

Ecumenism, 159–60, 171

Edwards, Rev. David, 135

Elim Church, 167

Eliot, T. S., 23, 65, 74, 79

English Churchman, 208

Evangelical Alliance, 94, 201

Evangelical Doctrine of Holy Communion, 72

Evangelical Fellowship of the Anglican Communion, 166

Evangelical Fellowship for Theological Literature, 118, 122, 123

Evangelical Group in General Synod, 110

Evangelicals, 188

Evangelism, 166, 207

Explorers, 109

Faith and Order, 66

Family Communion, 47, 150, 156

Family services, 166, 175

Fellowship of Diocesan Evangelical Unions, 110, 182

First Prayer Book of Edward VI, 32

223

Index

Fisher, Geoffrey, Archbishop of Canterbury, 81, 91, 92, 123, 157, 175
Fison, J. E., 113–14
For Christ's Sake, 140
Forward from Keele, 188
Fountain Trust, 168–71
Free-churches, 35, 36, 39, 55, 70, 72, 96, 115, 126, 131–3, 148, 152, 158, 159, 161, 168, 183, 188, 192, 204, 207
Freud, Sigmund, 53, 181
Fulness of Christ, 123
Fundamentalism and the Word of God, 121
Fundamentalists, 51, 74, 75, 90, 91, 93, 94, 112–14, 119

Garbett, Cyril, Archbishop of York, 87, 92
General Synod, 35, 103, 105, 146, 189
Gospel and Spirit, 171
Gough, Rev. Basil, 59, 162–3
Gough, Hugh, Bishop of Barking, 88, 90, 93, 95
Graham, Dr Billy, x, 84, 87–95, 103, 112, 121, 130, 166, 176, 197, 210
Graham, Mrs Ruth, 84, 91, 94
Greater London Crusade, 88–95, 176
Green, Canon Bryan, 60, 135
Green, Canon Michael, 58, 97, 122, 160, 176, 178, 198, 201, 207
Group Ministry, 175
Growing Into Union, 160–1, 193
Grubb, Norman, 44
Guidelines, 179, 198

Habgood, John, Archbishop of York, 58
Halifax, Lord, 8–9, 30, 35
Hammond, Canon T. C., 50, 74
Hard Facts of Unity, 128–9
Harper, Rev. Michael, 168–70, 198
Harringay, 88–91, 112, 130, 176
Harte, David, 199
Hebert, Gabriel, 47, 119–22
Hermeneutics, 200, 203
Higher Criticism, 13, 38, 113
History of Fundamentalism, 118
Hitler, Adolf, 19, 49, 52, 62, 68, 73, 74, 134
Honest to God, 134–42, 172
Houghton, Canon A. T., 28, 39, 177

Houghton, Frank, Bishop, 39–40
House Groups, 180, 186
House of Commons, 33–5
House of Lords, 21, 32
humanism, 17, 37, 42, 52, 73, 82, 139, 140, 144
Huxley, Julian, 138

infant baptism, 126
Inskip, Thomas, 18, 32–3, 35, 37, 39 (*see* Caldecote, Lord)
Inter-Varsity Fellowship (Universities and Colleges Christian Fellowship), x, xi, 44–5, 50–1, 74, 114, 119–22, 129, 185, 194, 201, 209–10
Islington Conference, 93, 174, 177, 188

Joad, C. E. M., 52–3, 81–3
Johnson, Dr Douglas, 50–1
Johnston, Preb. Peter, 177–82
Joynson-Hicks, Sir William, 30–3, 35, 37, 39, 43 (*see* Brentford, Lord)
Jung, Carl, 53

Keele '67, 187
Keele, National Evangelical Anglican Congress (1967), xi, 115, 117, 161–2, 174–89, 191, 193, 198, 201, 203, 205, 206, 208–10
Keep Yourselves from Idols, 138
Keswick Convention, 6, 36, 80, 123, 128, 129, 167, 169, 171, 174, 201, 208
Kildahl, John P., 170
King, Rev. John, 187–8
Kirk, Rev. Andrew, 197
Knox, Edmund A., Bishop of Manchester, xi, 10, 20–1, 22, 35, 37, 39, 41, 46, 84, 85, 86, 118
Kung, Dr Hans, 158

Laing, Sir John, 50, 193–4
Lake, Dr Frank, 181
Lambeth Conference, 41, 78, 80, 141
Lang, Cosmo, Archbishop of Canterbury, 41–2
Latimer House, Oxford, 148, 157, 172, 182
Lawrence, John, 128–30
lay elders, 81, 176, 180, 195
League of Nations, 17, 73, 80
Lee Abbey, 110, 181

224

Index

Index

Index